$urplus

SUNY series, Insinuations: Philosophy, Psychoanalysis, Literature
Charles Shepherdson, editor

$urplus

Spinoza, Lacan

A. Kiarina Kordela

State University of New York Press

Published by
State University of New York Press, Albany

Printed in the United States of America

For information, contact State University of New York Press, Albany, NY
www.sunypress.edu

Production by Kelli Williams
Marketing by Michael Campochiaro

Library of Congress Cataloging-in-Publication Data

Kordela, A. Kiarina, 1963–
Surplus : Spinoza, Lacan / A. Kiarina Kordela.
p. cm. — (SUNY series, insinuations, philosophy, psychoanalysis, literature)
Includes bibliographical references and index.
ISBN-13: 978-0-7914-7019-0 (hardcover : alk. paper)
ISBN-13: 978-0-7914-7020-6 (pbk.: alk. paper)
1. Philosophy, Modern. 2. Spinoza, Benedictus de, 1632–1677. 3. Causation. I. Title.

B791.K67 2007
190—dc22 2006013423

10 9 8 7 6 5 4 3 2 1

Truth is the standard both of itself and of the false.

—Spinoza, *Ethics*

If beyond appearance there is nothing in itself, there is the gaze.

—Lacan, *The Four Fundamental Concepts of Psychoanalysis*

Contents

Acknowledgments

This book is written by me only insofar as I am the collective effect of several texts, people, and experiences. Some of these texts are referenced, but acknowledged should be also those that are not, as well as those of my teachers who have never written for the purpose of publication.

Practicing Spinozian monism, I would like to acknowledge indiscriminately the impact, pleasant or unpleasant, on my life and consequently work and career, of the following people: Chiarina Altomare-Sohou, Labros Antonatos, Aristeidis Baltas, Willi Benning, Cesare Casarino, Joan Copjec, Jonathan Culler, Karl Dahlquist, Ben Davis, Ellis Dye, Kiva Garen, Sabine Hake, Gitta Hammarberg, Peter Uwe Hohendahl, Aaron Hubbard, Steve Jaksa, Kojin Karatani, Eleni Katsiboki, Katerina and Chrysa Kyriazidou, Tasos Kolelis, Haris Kontopanagos, Konstantinos Kordellas, Maria Kordela, Penelope Kordella, Maria Koutsilieri, Stella Krouska, Fofo Kypreou, Dominick LaCapra, Peter Machamer, Biddy Martin, David Martyn, Miltos Menexelis, Jonathan Monroe, John Mowitt, Clark Muenzer, Tim Murray, Viki Nassouli, Kostas Pagondiotis, Jochen Schulte-Sasse, Linda Schulte-Sasse, Nikos Skouteropoulos, Demetres and Panos Souleles, Geoff Waite, and Leonidas Zampas, as well as all others of my teachers/colleagues at the Universities of Pittsburgh and Cornell, and colleagues/teachers at Macalester College.

In the second part of the present book, I include some of the ideas proposed at the seminar on Experimental Critical Theory (SECT), organized by the Humanities Research Institute, at the University of California, Irvine (August 16–27, 2004). I take the opportunity to thank the participant-instructors, Alain Badiou, Joan Copjec, Mladen Dolar, Eric Santner, Slavoj Žižek, and Alenka Zupančič, for their engaging presentations and discussions, and lots of fun. My thanks go also to the organizers of the seminar, Kenneth Reinhard and Anna Kornbluh, for inviting me to present my work, and once again Kenneth Reinhard and Julia Lupton-Reinhard for their generous and hearty hospitality, and, of course, lots of fun. I also want to thank the Wallace Research Grant, for financially enabling me to participate. When citing the participants' ideas, I mention the name of the specific interlocutor with no other reference, and I apologize if they have already published these thoughts, without me being aware of it. Needless to say, since these 'citations' are only my paraphrases, it is they to whom I attribute them who have the last word as to what they actually said.

I also want to thank Alain Badiou for giving me permission to cite from Alberto Toscano's translation of his unpublished manuscript *Logics of Worlds*, as well as Peter Hallward for illuminating discussions during the aforementioned seminar and his help with practical matters.

My penultimate thanks go to the students of Macalester whose enthusiasm keeps rekindling mine.

As for the material existence and form of the present book, the remaining reservoir of my gratitude goes to the editor of the series, Charles Shepherdson, the Interim Director of SUNY Press, James Peltz, the two anonymous and insightful reviewers of the manuscript, and Anne Marie Wirth-Cauchon for preparing the index.

And beyond all this, still there remains a surplus. This surplus gratitude needs at this point to be donated, in a discriminating way, to, once again, Cesare, Linda, and Jochen.

Introduction

The Context

> Sublimation is nonetheless satisfaction of the drive, without repression. In other words—for the moment, I am not fucking you, I am talking to you. Well! I can have exactly the same satisfaction as if I were fucking. That's what it means. Indeed it raises the question of whether in fact I am not fucking at this moment.
>
> —Lacan, *The Four Fundamental Concepts of Psychoanalysis*

Postmodern "Neo-Spinozism"

In the in-between that separates Baruch (Benedict de) Spinoza from Jacques Lacan figure eminently—as far as the present work is concerned, and the acknowledged impact of Hegel and Freud notwithstanding—Immanuel Kant and Karl Marx. Here is an initial brief explanation why these names represent the cardinal philosophical quartet of the present work.

Spinoza is the first philosopher to grasp the structure of secular causality, as immanent or differential causality, as we know it since its popularization by linguistics. Here the cause is itself an effect of its own effects. What enabled Spinoza to see this structure was the fact that, as we shall see, he conceived of nature, insofar as it is inhabited by human beings, as a system of signifiers. Far from being autonomous physical things with inherent qualities, signifiers are differential values. And differential values, by structural necessity, constitute a system of disequilibrium, that is, a system that always produces a surplus.

Kant's major discovery lies in the insight that no system can form itself as a totality unless it poses an exception to itself.

Marx's one major innovation is the realization that the structure of capital, too, is a manifestation of the structure of secular causality on the level of economy. What enabled Marx to see this was the fact that he conceived of nature as a system of commodities, that is, again, differential values. His other major innovation lies in overtaking set theory and its paradoxes by understanding that the exception required for any system to totalize itself is simultaneously both its exception and one of its members.

Lacan added, or rather gave name to what the above theories tacitly entailed: enjoyment and the gaze.

The appearance of the name of Lacan as the continuation of a line of thought that begins with Spinoza may strike many a reader as unexpected. The twentieth-century figure most sympathetic to psychoanalysis that one would canonically expect to see in this parataxis would arguably be Louis Althusser. And perhaps, assuming that the combination of Marx and Spinoza would not in itself estrange them, many would tend to see the continuation of the Spinozian-Marxian line of thought not in any theory supportive of psychoanalysis, let alone psychoanalysis itself. Rather, the more intuitive development of the syndesmosis of Spinoza and Marx would for many be found in any of the twentieth-century Marxist representatives of so-called "Neo-Spinozism," notably, Gilles Deleuze, Félix Guattari, Antonio Negri, Michael Hardt, and a long series of other commentators such as Brian Massumi, Tom Conley, and Ian Buchanan, to mention only a few.[1]

Yet, the present work argues that the Spinozian-Marxian line of thought finds its proper contemporary articulation in Lacanian psychoanalysis. Leaving for now this argument aside, let us turn to two main current lines of thought emerging as the result of Spinoza's impact on contemporary theory.

On the one hand, there is the so-called "Neo-Spinozist" line, which having long completed its critique of psychoanalysis, celebrates molecular and rhizomatic forms of identity, organization, and action. Although they themselves do no more than replicate the very structures of global capitalism, these same forms are presumed to be also subversive or revolutionary, to open lines of flight, or, in the more recent parlance of Hardt and Negri's *Empire*, to express the power of the multitude (i.e., all of us). Drawing on a certain twist of Spinozian monism, this line operates according to the logic that, since there is only one substance, or, since there is no exteriority to substance, the same substance must be that which sustains the existing politico-economical system *and* that which undermines it. Thus, this line (inadvertently?) finds itself replicating the logic of the classical Hegelian-Marxist determinism, which presumed that the capitalist system is, by structural necessity, destined to bring about its own collapse. From both logics—assuming that they are indeed two distinct logics—follows that replicating and reinforcing the structures of capital, far from supporting it, amounts to accelerating the advent of its end as an exploitative, oppressing system.

Thus, far from involving any opposition to any oppressive power or even a course of action remotely deviating from the practices fostered by capitalism, the empowerment of the multitude, Hardt and Negri tell us, simply requires the recognition of the power that the multitude has always already had without knowing it. More specifically, Hardt and Negri invite the multitude to cease deeming as its exploitation the fact that in postmodern, informatized capitalism, "the proletariat [i.e., the multitude] produces in all its generality everywhere all day" so that there is no way to differentiate "work time from leisure time," and to see instead in this perpetual labor its own triumph over the Empire (403).[2] The same applies, according to Hardt and Negri, to other major phenomena characterizing postmodern capitalism, such as the ceaseless "mass migrations" of the "multitude," "necessary for production," or the "hybridization of human and machine." Far from being imposed and governed by an oppressive Empire, these movements *are*, Hardt and Negri maintain, the very manifestation of "the spontaneity of the multitude's movements," which is our present reality, a liberated and liberating Empire (398, 400, and 405). If nothing else, Hardt and Negri's argument offers a veritable twist of the performative function of language and of the gaze, whereby the guiding motto becomes that everything lies in the eye of the beholder.[3] "You want to be free?—Then , stop seeing your condition as one imposed on you, and see it instead as your own spontaneous movement!" Isn't this logic, one might wonder, the standard logic of hegemonic politics, as we know it all too well from our everyday life?[4] Insofar as hegemony is based on noncoercive coercion, its primary task lies in presenting impositions as states desired and instigated by the 'free agency' of the subjects on which they are imposed. Why would those presently in politico-economic power and in sane mind object to Sylvère Lotringer's conclusion that if, as

Hardt and Negri argue, "the functioning of imperial power is ineluctably linked to its demise," then, "why call for a counter-power . . . ?" (Hardt and Negri, 361; Lotringer, 16). If they had the brains, those in power themselves would write books like the *Empire*.

Indeed, Hardt and Negri do not even intend to call for a counter-power. On the contrary, they simply conclude by exhorting the multitude to demand the legislative legitimization of certain late-capitalist phenomena, necessary for the latter's functioning in our present day. Their political manifesto is reducible to three major demands: "The Right to Global Citizenship," so that illegal immigrant labor is officially recognized as legal; "The Right to a Social Wage," so that everybody contributing to production, including its aspects of reproduction and unproduction, be equally paid; and "The Right to Reappropriation," so that the multitude have control over the means of production (the technology of information)—though one might wonder, how can the multitude have control over something that is anyway already "increasingly integrated into the minds and bodies of the multitude"? (396, 401, 403, and 407). More importantly, one might also wonder in what, then, does the revolutionary "telos of the multitude" differ from the *telos* of capital itself? (407). Or, conversely, wouldn't the Empire's legislation itself be more than happy to grant these "rights," had it caught up with the pace of global, informatized capital—legislation being always slower in its development than economic and other automatic structures themselves? Capital itself demands the abolition of national boundaries, involves a system of production in which what traditionally was considered reproduction or unproduction is equally a part of production itself (both leisure and unemployment being necessary for the sustenance of capitalism), and is already increasingly entrusting the means of production to the multitude, since the latter is itself constituted by them, reproducing them in body and mind.

For some inexplicable reason, Hardt and Negri nevertheless call their manifesto "*communist*" (413). Unless, of course, they had in mind what Paolo Virno calls "the communism of capital" in Post-Fordism, for indeed, as Lotringer sarcastically puts it, "there is much communism in capital *as capital is capable of* too: abolition of work, dissolution of the state, etc." (17). But, Lotringer continues in a more sobering tone, this is only a "virtual communism," with a "generalized intellect and no material equality" in "any shape or form," so that we have to wonder: "How 'communistic' can that be?" (17).

To stress the point, for Hardt and Negri, these three rights, far from being the path toward the system's collapse or future transformation, themselves constitute the transformation of the present Empire into the ideal state in which the multitude's power will have found its true expression. There is no reference to any further transformation required for their ideal state of communism. In short, there is no distinction in Hardt and Negri's "Neo-Spinozist" monism between the full realization of the force of capital and the full realization of the multitude's power.

Of course, the above questions and criticism are irrelevant and certainly ineffective if one is convinced of the truth of the aforementioned Hegelian-Marxist logic: "but precisely therein lies the point: to undermine a system, find its *telos*, and then accelerate its full actualization, for this way you accelerate its collapse!"

At any rate, on the other hand, we evidence the criticism offered by an alternative line of thought, represented by proponents of psychoanalysis, who, in the face of arguments such as the above, infer, as Slavoj Žižek does, that "it seems as if today we live in an age of a new Spinozism: the ideology of late capitalism is, at least in some of its fundamental features, 'Spinozist' " (1993, 218).

Though I would be justifiably classified under the proponents of psychoanalysis, this book is not a critique of "Neo-Spinozism"—or, more accurately, it is this but only insofar as it critiques the assumption shared by both sides of the debate that Spinoza and the "Neo-Spinozism" in question are one and the same.[5]

Scientific "Neo-Spinozism" and Hegel

A central tenet in "Neo-Spinozism" is the assumption that absolute, transparent, "scientific" knowledge without imaginary or fictional (and, hence, ideological) distortions is possible. And this, it must be from the outset admitted, is an opinion that Spinoza himself held.

Distorted knowledge, Spinoza argued, is due to the humans' arbitrary attribution of will, and hence *telos*, to God and nature. In Spinoza's own words:

> Nature has no end set before it, and . . . all final causes are nothing but human fictions. . . . For if God acts for the sake of an end, he necessarily wants something which he lacks. . . . [T]he Followers of this doctrine . . . have

> wanted to show off their cleverness in assigning the end of things. . . . For example, if a stone has fallen from a roof onto someone's head and killed him, they will show . . . that the stone fell in order to kill the man. For if it did not fall to that end, God willing it, how could so many circumstances have concurred by chance . . . ? . . . And so they will not stop asking for the causes of causes until you take refuge in the will of God, i.e., the sanctuary of ignorance.

All this, Spinoza continues, amounts "to subject[ing] God to fate," and "nothing more absurd can be maintained about God, whom we have shown to be the first and only free cause, both of the essence of all things, and of their existence" (1985, 442–43 and 439; *Ethics*, part I, prop. 36, appendix, and prop. 33, schol. 2).

Given that in God and nature there is neither will nor end, Spinoza's project of a scientific ethics could be understood as an attempt to 'enlighten' humans with regard to this absolute absence of a final cause and to accept the purposeless or meaningless character of life. From the moment one ascribes a "final cause"—which by definition gives a specific meaning to life—to anything occurring in life, one is already in the field of "fictions." Conversely, however, what Spinoza effectively proves here, and is the first philosopher to argue against his own intentions, is that *the only possible truth about the cause, end, or meaning of life is, therefore, fictional*—which is one of the fundamental psychoanalytic premises.

Another equally fundamental psychoanalytic premise is *never to take the analysand's stated intentions at face value.* As Žižek himself admonishes us echoing Lacan's words:

> "There is no metalanguage" insofar as the speaking subject is always already spoken, i.e., insofar as he cannot master the effects of what he is saying: he always says more than he "intended to say," and this surplus of what is effectively said over the intended meaning puts into words the repressed content—in it, "the repressed returns." What are symptoms *qua* "returns of the repressed" if not such slips of the tongue by means of which . . . the big Other returns to the subject his own message in its true form? If instead of saying "Thereby I proclaim the session open," I say "Thereby I proclaim the session closed," do I not get, in the most literal sense, my own message back in its true, inverted form? (1992, 14)

Psychoanalysis is by definition concerned with precisely this "surplus of what is effectively said," not the intended message, but the message "in its true, inverted form"—even as, as we shall see in the second part of the present work, this "inverted form" is not to be understood always as literally as in Žižek's example. It is because Lacan read Spinoza psychoanalytically that he understood that "it is as establishing itself in, and even by, a certain lie, that we see set up the dimension of truth," that "the lie is itself posited in this dimension of truth," and that the function of fiction as truth in human life became one of his central foci (Lacan 1981, 138). For Lacan, the truth in Spinoza's rejection of any final cause as fiction is that truth can emerge only through fiction. If taking at face value Spinoza's "intended meaning" is part of the methodology Deleuze describes as "taking an author from behind," then we must infer that, unlike Deleuze's and Žižek's interest in "taking" other philosophers "from behind," Lacan must have been more interested in taking them in all possible ways (Deleuze 1995a, 6). And "it would" perhaps "be [as] good if Deleuze were to display some readiness to follow this approach"—namely, the advice to "trust the author you are studying . . . proceed by feeling your way . . . silence the voices of objection within you . . . let him speak for himself, analyze the frequency of his words, the style of his own obsessions"—"also in his reading of Hegel," as if Žižek and others were to display the same readiness with Spinoza (Žižek 2004, 47; citing Deleuze as transcribed and translated in Colombat 1999, 204).

As for psychoanalysis, Spinoza is partly a symptom, in the sense that, as we shall see, parts of his theory are proven by other parts to be false. Which is why psychoanalysis treats Spinoza in the way succinctly expressed by Jacques-Alain Miller's statement:

> Comparison is a mode of inadequate knowledge, said Spinoza; it links lacking nothing to that which is; a blind man is not less than a man who sees, because a privation is not of being, it is imaginary. It is the best doctrine in the world. However, what is imaginary does not have fewer real effects. (2001, 13)

By contrast, Spinoza himself (i.e., his enunciation and intention) remained blind to the truth of his symptom and thus persisted on the distinction between moral (fictional) and scientific (true) causes. As an example of this distinction, Spinoza refers to the primal fall and Adam's understanding of God's commandment: "You may freely eat of every tree of the garden; but of the tree of the knowledge of good and evil you shall not eat, for in the day that you eat of it you shall die" (Genesis 2:15). As Deleuze, who obviously accepts Spinoza's distinction between scientific and moral truths, puts it in his paraphrase of Spinoza's argument: "[B]ecause Adam is ignorant of causes, he thinks that God morally forbids him something, whereas God only reveals the natural consequence of ingesting the fruit" (1988, 22). This distinction, however, remains untenable as far as Adam's subsequent action is concerned. For, God's explanation why Adam should not eat of the tree of knowledge is simply that "in the day that you eat of it you shall die." Nothing in this statement indicates whether Adam should prefer to live rather than die, and this preference in itself presupposes an end (to live) as better than another end (to die). For the decision to eat or not from the tree, even if one hears the commandment not as a moral but as a scientific truth, presupposes a choice of a *telos*—a knowledge of what is good for oneself—which, in turn, as Spinoza rightly argues, presupposes a fiction. But without such a fiction, one cannot decide whether to eat or not to eat the fruit. We could in fact say that Miller's conclusion that the "imaginary does *not* have *fewer* real effects" is an understatement. Insofar as it is not the scientific knowledge but fiction that determines the course of the subject's action, fiction has rather *more* real effects than scientific knowledge.

A proper development of Spinozian thought, which was profoundly concerned with the question of fiction and elaborated in detail and with astuteness its function in both religion and politics, presupposes the recognition of fiction as a cognitive factor. This attitude, and not Spinoza's conscious pre-Enlightenment faith in enlightenment, can allow for a revision of Spinoza that is marked by a fidelity to his thought, which is appropriate for our times.

Prescientific and presecular thought was predicated on the fiction of the soul as, in Lacan's words, "the entelechy of [the] body," the "activity" or "ενεργεια" "a body is made for," and by means of which each body "is supposed to know what is good for it," so that, as Aristotle assumed, "everyone must pursue his good" (1998, 88). This soul or a priori knowledge of one's own good "is what the break (*faille*) induced by scientific discourse obliges us to do without," since, with the advent of science, "we don't need to assume the stone knows where it must land" in "order to explain the effects of gravitation" (88). While science is content with presenting laws such as that of gravitation as the explanation of the world, and dismisses the "soul" and its cognates as mere confusion, "analysis allows for this" nevertheless indispensable "confusion" to be taken into account "by restoring the *final cause*, by making us say that, as concerns everything at least related to the speaking beings, reality is like that—in other words, phantasmatic" (88; emphasis mine). For no scientific truth, whether this is God's commandment or the law of gravity, can ever allow the subject to take a course of action.

Adam's problem is not that he is moralizing but that he needs a cause for action. Without this fictional "soul," "good," or *telos*, Adam encounters the same lack that, as Lacan argues, is always "encountered by the subject in the Other, in the very intimation that the Other makes to him by his discourse. . . . *He is saying this to me, but what does he want?*"(1981, 214). If metalanguage is impossible it is because in itself it is an antinomy, a set of two mutually contradicting meanings (e.g., "to eat or not to eat the fruit"). Only a (fictional) interpretation of the *telos* or intention of the Other's discourse renders it meaningful. If God spoke, we would have no idea what It means to say.

Žižek rightly comments that this "attitude of the Spinozist 'wisdom,' " uncritically adopted by several "Neo-Spinozists," "is . . . defined by the reduction of deontology to ontology, of injunction to rational knowledge, and, in terms of speech-acts-theory, of performative to constative" (1993, 217). Every ostensibly purely rational or scientific, constative statement always entails a certain fictional teleology that performatively poses its system of values and dictates a course of action. In Lacanian terms, it entails the paternal metaphor, the "Master Signifier," which, as Žižek writes, "brings about the closure of an ideological field by way of designating the Supreme Good (God, Truth, Nation, etc.)," and without which Adam could never decide what to do (217).[6] And this criticism of this type of "Spinozian 'wisdom' " would equally apply to the positivist critiques of psychoanalysis, which the present work addresses below.

But, whereas Žižek argues against Spinoza, Lacanian psychoanalysis draws the logical consequences of Spinoza's theory itself (i.e., his statements, rather than simply his enunciation). Even as Spinoza wanted to maintain the distinction between scientific and moral truth, *his own theory contradicts him*, for it was the one to posit the primary psychoanalytic principle, namely, that "truth is the standard both of itself and of the false" (Spinoza 1985, 479; *Ethics*, part II, prop. 43, school). We could therefore define the difference between, on the one hand, both the current "Neo-Spinozism" and its critique of the Žižekian type, and, on the other hand, Lacanian Spinozism, as one between a school that takes Spinoza's intentions (his enunciation) at face value, and a school that traces the dimension of truth (statement) in which the lie (enunciation) is posited, respectively.

If Spinoza takes it for granted that God's "scientific truth" suffices for Adam to know that he should not eat the fruit, this is due to the fact that, as Alain Badiou puts it, the " 'perseverance of being' " is for "Spinoza" the "ordinary behaviour of the human animal . . . which is nothing other than the pursuit of interest, or the conservation of the self" (2001, 46). Yet, as Badiou continues, "the test of truth"—that truth through which "the composition of a subject of truth" is possible, and which is presupposed for an ethical subject, a subject who knows what is good or not beyond the question of the mere "conservation of the self"—"does not fall under this law" (46). Spinozian being, Badiou argues, is always "self-interested," which is why this dimension of "truth" and "good" and "evil" beyond the "conservation of the self" or the pleasure principle is missing in Spinoza's theoretical edifice.

If the self-interested "conservation of the self" falls under the law of the pleasure principle, its *beyond*, as we know, obeys the laws of the death drive. Žižek seconds Badiou's thesis on Spinoza by writing:

> What is unthinkable for [Spinoza] is what Freud terms "death drive": the idea that *conatus* is based on a fundamental act of self-sabotaging. Spinoza, with his assertion of *conatus*, of every entity's striving to persist and strengthen its being, and, in this way, striving for happiness, remains within the Aristotelian frame of what good life is. What is outside his scope is what Kant refers to as the "categorical imperative," an unconditional thrust that parasitizes upon a human subject without any regard for its well-being, "beyond the pleasure principle." (2004, 34)

What both Badiou and Žižek overlook is the basic principle of Spinozian monism, namely, that, as we shall see in more detail below, human beings and everything that exists embodies the attributes of the one substance (God) in the same degree of perfection as it. If God or Nature "has no end set before it, and . . . all final causes are nothing but human fictions," if, in other words, one of the attributes of God is this radical absence of will or entelechy, shouldn't, according to Spinoza's system itself, all beings, too, be marked not only by the tendency to increase their power and fulfill their self-interests but also the impulse to undermine this tendency? (Spinoza 1985, 442: *Ethics*, part I, prop. 36, appendix). This "self-sabotaging" impulse is precisely the death drive.[7] And it is in fact only the introduction of a fiction (an end) that allows the one (the pleasure principle or the death drive) to outweigh the other.

The constitution of "truth" transcends "scientific" (read: self-interested) truth by precisely presupposing a "fiction," something "false," which, nevertheless, is not an exception to "truth" but its own precondition, just as the death drive, in Deleuze's words, is "not the exception[] to the [pleasure] principle but . . . its '*foundation*' " (Deleuze 1994, 113). As far as the subject of the signifier is concerned, survival or self-preservation cannot be taken as the a priori tendency or principle—suicide or risking one's life would then be impossible. The human being, that is, the being of the signifier, is the sole living being that is not equipped with instincts, so that even when the subject struggles to survive, this is possible only because of the "foundation" of the death drive that allows the subject to construct a fiction that motivates it to survive. And one of the earliest and most succinct ways of articulating the relation between pleasure principle and death drive is Spinoza's ternary conception of truth, as the standard both of itself and of the false.

A brief parenthesis seems due at this point. I am not arguing against Žižek's or Badiou's criticism of the "Neo-Spinozists," which I think applies for the most part to most of them, even as I see several points in their arguments, particularly in Deleuze's, for which I have a great respect, and so admittedly do these critics, too. My critique of the "Neo-Spinozists" can be subsumed under the statement that they tend to read Spinoza taking at face value his isolated enunciations and not reading the text in itself as a network of statements that, if you rely simply on the level of enunciation, blatantly contradict one another. You cannot do this, in fact, with any great or minute thinker, let alone with a great thinker who also happens to think according to the principle that truth is the standard both of itself and of the false. Lacan's work is another such obvious example that comes to mind. And my criticism of "Neo-Spinozists" is identical with my criticism of Badiou's and Žižek's readings of Spinoza, insofar as both rely on this "Neo-Spinozist" reading of Spinoza. I do not doubt that the reading I propose as the proper reading of Spinoza is a demanding task, one requiring indeed a great psychoanalyst, which is why, as the present work argues, it is Lacan who succeeded in doing it. It takes one to know one. With Lacan, Spinoza becomes, as Althusser said about Hegel, "(unknowingly) an admirable 'theoretician' of ideology [precisely] insofar as he is a 'theoretician' of Universal Recognition who unfortunately ends up in the ideology of Absolute Knowledge" (1971, 181, n. 22). End of parenthesis.

Another point of contention in scholarship is "what, quite wrongly, has been thought of in Spinoza as pantheism," which, as Lacan remarks, "is simply the reduction of the field of God to the universality of the signifier" (1981, 275). Žižek constructs his polemic against Spinoza basically by taking as his point of departure this statement and strangely seeing in Lacan's affirmation of "this Spinozist 'universality of the signifier' " a general critical distance on the part of Lacan from Spinoza. According to Žižek, Lacan would object to Spinoza that he accomplished "a leveling of the signifying chain" that "gets rid of the gap that separates S2, the chain of knowledge, from S1, the signifier of injunction, of prohibition, of *NO!*," so that "the Spinozist substance designates universal knowledge as having no need for support in a Master-Signifier" (Žižek 1993, 216–17). And Spinoza's confidence in absolute or scientific knowledge would indicate, therefore, that his "pantheism" falls short of the postulate of its prefix and applies to everything *except science*.

Indeed, for Lacan the universality of the signifier (S2) is generally possible only under an exception (S1), the injunction of "the moral law." It is therefore reasonable to say that Lacan relies, in Žižek's words, on the Kantian "primacy of practical over theoretical reason," particularly as Lacan explicitly states in this context that "experience shows us that Kant is more true" than Spinoza, whose "position is not tenable for us" (Lacan 1981, 275; Žižek 1993, 217).

To what "experience" exactly is Lacan referring, and who is this "us" for whom the Spinozian "position" is not "tenable"? I do not mean this question as a particularist interrogation as to what is the *individual* "experience" or the *particular* "us" in Lacan's statement. Rather, I am concerned with the kind of collective "experience" and of the universal "us" that Lacan might have had in mind. Lacan offers himself the answer: "the history we have experienced," this "re-enacting [of] the most monstrous and supposedly superceded forms of the holocaust . . . the drama of Nazism" (1981, 275). So, first parameter, Lacan is here specifically concerned with identifying the logic through which historical monstrosities, such as the above, are possible. Lacan is of the opinion that:

> No meaning given to history, based on Hegeliano-Marxist premises, is capable of accounting for this resurgence—which only goes to show us that the offering to obscure gods of an object of sacrifice is something to which few subjects can resist succumbing, as if under some monstrous spell. (1981, 275)

And what exactly is the Spinozian "position" that also cannot explain the historical possibility of the Holocaust and is, therefore not "tenable" in this context of interrogation? Lacan again gives us the answer: "[Spinoza's] *Amor intellectualis Dei* [intellectual love for God]" (275). For, in arguing "that, in the object of our desires, we try to find evidence for the presence of the desire of this Other that I call here *the dark God*," Lacan posits Spinoza as an exception:

> It is the eternal meaning of the sacrifice, to which no one can resist, unless animated by that faith, so difficult to sustain, which, perhaps, one man alone has been able to formulate in a plausible way—namely, Spinoza, with his *Amor intellectualis Dei.* (275).

Unlike the Kantian-Sadean love for a "*dark God*," which entails all possible monstrosities as offerings to him, Spinoza's intellectual love for God cannot account for such monstrosities, for it "produces a serene, exceptional detachment from human desire"—what Kant would call one's detachment from one's "pathological interests." For, although, as "Spinoza says—*desire is the essence of man*," he, nevertheless, "institutes this desire in the radical dependence of the universality of the divine attributes, which is possible only through the function of the signifier," so that "he obtains that unique position by which the philosopher—and it is no accident that it is a Jew detached from his tradition who embodies it—may be confused with a transcendent love" (Lacan 1981, 275). More capable of explaining such monstrosities is, rather, Kant, whose "specification of the moral law . . . looked at more closely, is simply desire in its pure state, that very desire that culminates in the sacrifice, strictly speaking, of everything that is the object of love in one's human tenderness" (275). In fact, not even Kant's position suffices, for desire culminates, "I would say," Lacan continues, "not only in the rejection of the pathological object, but also in its sacrifice and murder," and "that's why I wrote *Kant avec Sade*" (275–76). So, second parameter, far from taking any overall critical distance from Spinoza, Lacan argues that the Kantian categorical imperative with its "rejection of the pathological object," combined with and expanded through sadism, offers us a much more appropriate explanation of motivation in a history capable of producing monstrosities than Spinoza's *amor intellectualis Dei*.[8]

This is certainly true, as is further reconfirmed by the fact that when Lacan is concerned with ethics, rather than that which turns the moral law into a monstrous, superegoic, sadistic injunction, he again passes through Kant and Sade, to arrive, once again, at Spinoza's *amor intellectualis Dei* and its "universality of the signifier." Here, in the realm of ethics, Lacan takes universality in precisely that aspect criticized above by Žižek, that is, as not being based on the exception of the moral injunction, the Master-Signifier, and as being therefore capable of lying beyond good and evil. For Lacan's ethical desire and act presuppose a *retreat from the discourse*—the chain of knowledge (S_2), which is always integrated through a moral injunction (S_1)—into the field of the *universality of the pure signifier*, the *language*, reduced to its function of *naming*. To refer to *Antigone*, Sophocles' tragedy, through whose analysis Lacan attempted to articulate his ethics, "Polynices" is the name of Antigone's brother, and remains his name regardless of whether the person who bears it is deemed to be good or evil. From the perspective of this language, once a body bears a name, funeral rites cannot be refused to it, regardless of its historical past, such as Polynices' treason and fratricide. In Lacan's words: "One cannot finish off someone who is a man as if he were a dog. One cannot be finished with his remains simply by forgetting that the register of being of someone who was identified by name has to be preserved by funeral rites," the latter being not a cultural (and hence historical or discursive) product but that which posits culture as such in the first place (1992, 279). For, in contrast to all other beings and their organizations, all human societies have always had funeral rites.[9] By contrast, "outside of language," in the realm of discourse (S_2), Polynices cannot be detached from his past acts, for there, "the being of him who has lived cannot be detached from all he bears with him in the nature of good and evil, of destiny, of consequences for others, or of feelings for himself" (279). The "unique value involved" in Antigone's ethical contumacy, Lacan concludes, "is essentially that of language," that is, "that purity, that separation of being from the characteristics of the historical drama he [Polynices] has lived through, [which] is precisely the limit or the *ex nihilo* to which Antigone," who intractably persists, not on Polynices' exculpation but, on his burial, "is attached" (279).[10]

Žižek is right to object to the "new Spinozism" that its nonideological or "scientific" "wisdom" is a naïve "reduction of deontology to ontology"; Spinozian metaphysics is of value only insofar as one understands, against Spinoza's intentions, the function of fiction in history (discourse) following from the Spinozian conception of truth as the standard of both itself and fiction. On the other hand, however, the value of Spinoza's "universality of the divine attributes"—the "universality of the signifier" without a Master-Signifier grounding it—lies in remaining for Lacan the "unique" way of "resist[ing] succumbing" to the "sacrifice . . . to which few subjects can resist," and of, consequently, being capable of acting instead ethically (Lacan 1981, 279). Given that, as Lacan argues, "the status of the unconscious is ethical, and not ontic," the ethical "universality of the divine attributes" determines the core of the subject, in the exact opposite sense than that meant by "scientific Neo-Spinozism," namely, in the sense that, to redistribute Žižek's terms, so-called *ontology* is, for psychoanalysis, fundamentally a *deontology* (Lacan 1981, 34). And a proper *deontology* has to address both levels: that of the ethical act in the absence of any Master-Signifier, and that of the action rendered possible by the fiction introduced by any given Master-Signifier.

Within Lacanian thought, Spinoza is operative on both levels. On the plane of ethics, Spinoza's "universality of the signifier" as a non-anthropomorphic system with no Master-Signifier or will constitutes the cornerstone of Lacan's concept of language and the rest of his ethical edifice. On the other hand, Spinoza's intrinsic intertwining of truth and fiction forms for Lacan the matrix for understanding history, discourse, and human action as being motivated by the two major fictions that concerned Spinoza: the fiction, into whose pitfall fell both Spinoza and Kant, that egotistic self-preservation is a "scientific," non-ideological truth; and the fiction of (God's or Nature's) will, according to which human suffering must be just, and hence humans themselves are guilty of and responsible for it—an insight out of which, as we shall see, Lacan developed his concept of *jouissance* (enjoyment).

Therefore, the relation "between Spinoza and Kant," as far as Lacan is concerned, is not one of "opposition," with the Spinozian universe being, in Žižek's words, "a self-sufficient mechanism," in which "we are relieved of all responsibility for it," and the Kantian universe one in which the subject is "ultimately responsible for everything" (1993, 217). As for Hegel, I will also disagree with Žižek and propose instead that he is not the scapegoat on which the otherwise discerning Lacan persists, from the first to the eleventh seminar and beyond, on projecting 'Spinoza's errors.' It is not "wisdom" as the "Spinozean contemplation of the universe *sub specie aeternitatis*" that Lacan truly means and rejects, even as "in his first two seminars, he wrongly attributes it to the Hegelian 'absolute knowledge' " (Žižek 1993, 217). For if in his second seminar Lacan had in mind Spinoza's contemplation *sub specie aeternitatis* without knowing it, the following dialogue between him and Hyppolite would not have been possible. At a certain point, Hyppolite suggests that it is possible that the "function of non-knowledge," namely, Freud's "reconquest of . . . the unconscious," and Hegel's "absolute knowledge" might not be as apart as Lacan argues, insofar as "*absolute knowledge*" is that which "*consciousness misses*," according to the logic: "*[C]onsciousness being in the field, doesn't see the field. Seeing the field, that's it, absolute knowledge*." Lacan replies that this cannot be the case because "in Hegel this absolute knowledge is embodied in a discourse," that is, not in a purely differential language with no *telos*, but in history, including the "end of history," as Hegel's Spirit indicates. Thereupon, Hyppolite seconds Lacan's response with a reaffirming: "*Certainly*" (1991a, 70–71). While for Hegel history knows its *telos*, even as individual subjects cannot discern it, for Spinoza history has no *telos* (just like God has no will), and it is only through the subjects' fictions that history appears as having a *telos*.

If God in Spinoza is, in Žižek's words, "this figure [which] simply gives body to the void of [people's] ignorance," this is so *not* because God is "a transcendent sovereign imposing his aims on the world," which remain unfathomable to humans, but because the Spinozian *God has no "aims" in the first place* (1993, 217). If humans are ignorant of aims it is because God *is* ignorant of aims—this ignorance being the sole possible "absolute wisdom," of which, we must add, humans are, nevertheless, doomed to fall short precisely insofar as they *must* imagine aims in order to be capable of action. But by adding this, we add nothing to the Spinozian statement which already knows that an aim is the standard both of itself (fiction) and the false (truth). The louder Spinoza's enunciation declares the fictitious character of will and aims, the more powerful the reconfirmation of their necessity becomes in his statements. Taking into account both Spinoza's enunciation and statement, *"aims" are real*, in the Lacanian sense, that is, *both impossible and necessary*.

What differentiates Hegel from Spinoza is not a distinction in the conception of "aim" or the "end of history" in terms of either immanent or transitive (linear) causality. Hegel can be read in either way. As Hyppolite says, one could argue either that there is, "in the *Phenomenology* [*of Spirit*], *a series of stages which are prior to absolute knowledge, [and only] then a final stage which Napoleon, anyone, etc. reaches, and which one would call absolute knowledge*," or, following "*Heidegger's . . . tendentious*," yet "*tenable*" "*interpretation*," that "*absolute knowledge . . . [is] immanent at every state of the* Phenomenology," as Žižek also has argued. In either case, Hegelian "absolute knowledge" pertains to history, a concept a priori predicated on the function of "mastery," as Lacan remarks (Lacan 1991a, 71). Mastery remains the absolute, unchallengeable anchor of history in Hegel. To be sure, the master may delude himself that he is a master, but, for Hegel, this only means that "mastery is entirely on the slave's side," that the *true* master is the slave (Lacan 1991a, 72). Mastery may as well lie on the side of any "*world-historical individual*," such as Napoleon, as on that of the proletariat (Hegel 1988a, 32). But in either case, mastery's absolute knowledge is purely necessary, not also impossible. The end of history, whether after "*a series of stages*" or "*immanent at every state*," is inherent in it; it is objectified, if not ontologized, rather than requiring the mediation of the fictitious for its emergence.

Lacan, who maintains that the Other is inconsistent, that "there is no Other of the Other," that the Other in itself has no will or aim, cannot possibly concur with Hegel's conception of either history or absolute knowledge (Lacan 1998, 81). Rather, he adopts the Spinozian conception of history as aimless, and supplements it, according to the Spinozian conception of truth, with a willful and intentional gaze (and, hence, aim), which, however, is "a gaze imagined by me in the field of the Other" (Lacan 1981, 84).

This position is directly correlative to another central Lacanian thesis, which is instrumental in differentiating psychoanalysis from deconstruction and all postmodern thought, namely, that "*God is unconscious*"(Lacan 1981, 59). This thesis derives directly from Spinoza's assertion that "a thing which has been determined to produce an effect has necessarily been determined in this way by God; and one which has not been determined by God cannot determine itself to produce an effect" (1985, 431; *Ethics*, part I, prop. 26). Even though the Other (God or history) has no will, the effects a thing can produce, and hence the actions a subject can undertake, are determined by this Other. But no action is possible without a will. Which is why the Other (God or history) is the immanent, not the transitive cause of all things, that is, the Other will always already have had a will once the thing will have produced an effect. The Other's will is the cause and effect of the thing's effects, just as the unconscious is the cause and effect of any conscious utterance and action. If aims or will inhered in the Other itself (God or history), then they would determine the effects of the thing in a transitive way, whereby the statement "*God is unconscious*" would lapse into essentialism, if not fundamentalism.

Because Hegel autonomizes the Other's will by severing it from the constitution of the subject, his edifice remains for Lacan unsatisfactory. "Hegel," Lacan states in his second seminar, "is at the limit of anthropology," which is concerned only with that aspect of the dialectic in which "each human being is in the being of the other," so that " there is a "reciprocal alienation" (1991a, 72). Within this dialectic, the division between masters and slaves is predicated on the possession or not of "completed discourse, the embodiment of absolute knowledge [which] is the instrument of power, the scepter and the property of those who know," since, of course, "nothing implies that everyone partakes in it" (71–72). Thus:

> [W]hen the scientists . . . succeed in bringing human discourse to a close, they are in possession of it, and those who don't have it have nothing left but to turn to jazz, to dance, to entertain themselves, the good fellows, the nice guys, the libidinal types. . . . Now, this reciprocal alienation, it must last until the end. Think how little effect the elaborated discourse will have on those who are busy with jazz at the corner *café*. And how much the masters will be aching to go and join them. While conversely the others will consider themselves wretched, nobodies, and will think—*how happy the master is in enjoying being master?*—whereas, of course, he will be completely frustrated. That is where, I think, in the last instance, Hegel leads us to. (1991a, 72)[11]

Hegel's limit is anthropological because he remains trapped within the intersubjective or "reciprocal alienation" between a master and a slave who always crave to be in one another's position. "The originality," Lacan continues, "of what Freud contributes in relation to Hegel" lies in the fact that he "got out of" the limits of this dialectic, because "Freud isn't a humanist," and, so, he was able to make "the discovery . . . that man isn't entirely in man" (1991a, 71–72). Freud began "to think of the body as a machine" and as "energy," and "the meaning of this energy myth . . . [is] the manifestation of a certain beyond of the [Hegelian] inter-human reference, which is in all strictness the symbolic beyond," the "network of signifiers," insofar as the latter is a machinic "*automaton*" programmed to perform the single operation of "repetition" (1991a, 73–76; 1981, 52 and 48). While Hegel's dialectic remains constrained within the imaginary relationship structuring intersubjectivity, Freud is concerned with the machine beyond it which eventually leads him to the "elaboration of the beyond of the pleasure principle and of the death drive," with its "need for repetition" (76 and 90; translation modified). What needs to be repeated or "reproduce[d]"? (89). The "discourse," the Other, that is "bequeathed to me," insofar as it is inconsistent, marred by "mistakes," "in complete disagreement with itself" and not "coherent and justified" (89 and 71). For, on the one hand, the Other constantly tells me to do things, and on the other, it has no will that could justify the suggested course of action. I have to repeat the discourse until it emerges, as an effect of this repetition, as willing something, until it remembers, as it were, its will. For "*Wiederholen* (repeating) . . . is related to *Erinnerung* (remembering)," and it is for this reason that "repetition" is a "function" that reveals "the relation between thought and the real," the impossible and necessary will of the Other (1981, 49). It is on this level of the dialectic, beyond the anthropological or humanist reference, between the subject and the "third term," the Other, that "the true axis of the realisation of the human being is to be found" (1991a, 76).

As is known, it took Freud twenty years, from the *Traumdeutung* (1900; *The Interpretation of Dreams*) to *Jenseits des Lustprinzips* (1920; *Beyond the Pleasure Principle*), to formulate the concepts of the death drive and repetition compulsion. It also took Lacan basically fifteen years, from the second seminar (1954-1955) to the seventeenth (1969–1970), to formulate systematically "le chemin vers la mort [the path toward death]" as "ce qui s'appelle la jouissance [that which is called enjoyment]," a concept to which we shall return (1991, 17–18). It is no accident that to name this function Lacan selected the Hegelian master's enjoyment (*Genuß*), as opposed to the slave's pleasure and desire (*Lust* and *Begierde*) (Hegel 1988, 133). But, beyond the sexual and the exploitative connotations introduced through the French translation of the term (*jouissance*), Lacan revised thoroughly the Hegelian concept by reading, as we shall see, Hegel via Marx, in an original configuration, in which the two are juxtaposed as divergent philosophical systems.[12]

In the 1960s, in "Kant avec Sade," Lacan argued that, appearances to the contrary, the sadist—as the subject capable of also performing the monstrosities that mark our history—is not the master but "no more than the instrument of *jouissance*," the object of the Other's enjoyment (1989, 63).[13] What sadism, therefore, shows us is that the so-called dialectic between master and slave, in which the slave turns out to be the true master, is a mirage. In sadism, the positions of the master (Other) and the slave (subject), far from being magically convertible, remain rigid, with the Other always in mastery. Monstrosities do not occur out of the subjects' will to power, but out of their will to offer themselves to the Other as its object of enjoyment, which they do by projecting a will to it.

In conclusion, as the above retrospection of Lacanian thought indicates, both Spinoza and Hegel play equally undeniable, albeit divergent, roles in psychoanalytic theory. There is no point in pitting the one against the other, if the aim underlying this gesture is to show that Lacan draws only on one of them, while the other got it all wrong. The sole result of such a gesture is to reinforce the license with which the rejected party is appropriated by other modes of thought, which often misrepresent it. More than the harm often inflicted on Spinoza's thought by various "Neo-Spinozists" is the damage that psychoanalysis itself can cause by rejecting Spinoza as indistinguishable from these "Neo-Spinozists."

Consensual, Evolutionist "Modern Spinozism"

There is yet another line of thought claiming Spinoza, positivist in its character, albeit in different ways than the "scientific" line. Jonathan I. Israel's rapidly promoted account of secular history, entitled *Radical Enlightenment: Philosophy and the Making of Modernity 1650–1750*, is a recent example. Israel views Enlightenment and modernity as "a revolutionary set of ideas which helped lay the foundations of the modern world on the basis of equality, democracy, secular values, and universality" (Israel, back cover). The decisive premise of Israel's account lies in taking the constituent terms of this "basis" at face value, as forming, if not necessarily fully realized states, at least the solely realizable destiny of the Enlightenment. There is no reason to invoke the Holocaust, for a look at our present historical experience of corporate global capital suffices to contradict blatantly such an understanding of the project of the Enlightenment. So, by analogy to what today is called "vulgar Marxism," we could call this line of positivism "vulgar Enlightenment."

No doubt, it initially appears to come as a welcome, refreshing breath to see today a historical work argue—against the canonical representation of Spinoza since "the nineteenth century" as a figure that "was rarely understood and had very little influence"—that "no one else during the century 1650–1750 remotely rivaled Spinoza's notoriety as the chief challenger of" nothing less than

> the fundamentals of revealed religion, received ideas, tradition, morality, and what was everywhere regarded, in absolutist and non-absolutist states alike, as divinely constituted political authority. (Israel, 159)

Even more, Spinoza was, in a uniquely "radical sense"—far surpassing "Hobbes," whom many "writers," particularly "in Britain . . . deemed . . . more widely pervasive than Spinoza as a promoter of freethinking, irreligion, and incredulity"—the "source and inspiration for a systematic redefinition of man, cosmology, politics, social hierarchy, sexuality, and ethics," and gave rise to the emergence of a whole series of "radical philosophers," without whom the French Revolution would have been impossible, such as "La Mettrie and Diderot." Even "Rousseau" did not escape Spinoza's influence, although he was a "Janus-headed mixing of elements from both the radical and the mainstream Enlightenment" (Israel, 159 and 720). In short, Israel's book advances the claim that Spinoza was the inspiration of what then were perceived as the most "radical" aspects of the Enlightenment, as both a philosophical and a political movement. Thus, Spinoza becomes both the initiator and part of what we today know as the canon of the Enlightenment.

To establish Spinoza's link with the canon of the Enlightenment, Israel argues that "in Spinoza . . . the only possible criterion for judging 'good' and 'bad' once Revelation and ecclesiastical authority are discarded" becomes "the common good defined as what best serves the interests of a society as a whole" (Israel, 720). Israel is concerned neither with the well-known fact that the "common good" for a "society as a whole" is a highly problematic and massively criticized concept nor with the fact that for Spinoza the "good," albeit indeed defined as the "useful," also remains problematic.

Spinoza defines "good" as "what we certainly know to be useful to us," while "evil" is "what we certainly know prevents us from being masters of some good" (1985, 546; *Ethics*, part IV, def. 1, 2). Yet, the "good," as understood by Spinoza, for whom "the mass of mankind remains always at about the same pitch of misery," cannot be aligned with the "good" as understood in utilitarianism, pragmatism, hedonism, or any naïvely devised progressivist assumption of individual or common good (1951, 5; *A Theologico-Political Treatise*). For, given that "God *or* Nature . . . exists for the sake of no end, he also acts for the sake of no end," so that "what is called a final cause is nothing but a human appetite insofar as it is considered as a principle, *or* primary cause, of some thing" (1985, 544; *Ethics*, part IV, pref.). But even this "appetite" turns out not to be the real first or "primary cause," capable of explaining how come that "thing" came to existence, for this cause "is really an efficient cause, which is considered as a first cause, because men are commonly ignorant of the causes of their appetites." In other words, the presumed first cause, "appetite," is caused by something else, of which men are ignorant, being "conscious of their actions and appetites, but not aware of the causes by which they are determined to want something" (1985, 544; *Ethics*, part IV, pref.). The "causes" of "appetite" themselves may, therefore, be as far from what commonsensically appears to be one's good as is, for instance, the psychoanalytic concept of the death drive.

This is a possibility that, while evidently open in Spinoza's thought, is not taken into account in Israel's alignment of Spinoza with a progressivist, humanist tradition, to which nothing could be more alien than Spinoza's thesis that "men are more led by blind desire, than by reason," and that this state cannot change. For, as Spinoza continues to say, "the natural power or right of human beings"—where "by natural right I understand the very laws or rules of nature, in accordance with which everything takes place"—"should be limited, not by reason, but by every appetite, whereby they are determined to action, or seek their own preservation." Now, "I, for my part, admit, that those desires, which arise not from reason, are not so much actions as passive affections of man," but, insofar as "we are treating here of the universal power or right of nature, we cannot here recognize any distinction between desires, which are engendered in us by reason, and those which are engendered by other causes; since the latter, as much as the former, are effects of nature" (1951, 292; *A Political Treatise*, ch. II, parag. 5). What is the value of the statement, concluding Israel's epic work, "Spinoza, Diderot, Rousseau: all three ground their conception of individual liberty in man's obligation to subject himself to the sovereignty of the common good," when any nonrevelatory, human account of the "good" remains in Spinoza an arbitrary fiction motivated not by reason but by some "blind desire" of obscure "causes"?

As for Rousseau specifically, as Israel himself writes, one of his "most basic . . . points of his diversion from the Spinozist tradition" lies in the fact that, "by propounding a doctrine of two substances in man, Rousseau" can argue "that one of the substances in man is indissoluble and immortal, namely the soul," from which he is then "able to argue for a form of reward and punishment in the hereafter and the absolute quality of good and evil" (Israel, 719). What is the point of momentarily differentiating Spinoza, the most ardent critic of the division between body and soul and the immortality of the latter, from Rousseau, if at the end one is to lump them indiscriminately together as the 'fathers' of a modern liberalism grounded on social consensus and the "universal good"? To speak of "good" within Spinozian monism, one must take into account the function of the false or fiction in the constitution of truth—something that is equally illegitimate both in Israel's own epistemology and methodology and in his account of the tradition of the Enlightenment.

Another major theme in Israel's argumentation is that Spinoza is the forefather of the "principle of evolution" insofar as he inspired the eighteenth-century "modern Spinozists' " to conclude "qu'il n'y a que de la matière, et qu'elle suffit pour tout expliquer [that there is nothing but matter, and that it suffices to explain everything]" (Israel, 713; citing "Article 'Spinoziste,' " Diderot et al. *Encyclopédie*, XV, 474; translation mine). First, let us note that this "modern Spinozist" conclusion in itself could not lie any farther from Spinoza, for whom there is only one substance which, as we shall see in more detail, is *not* matter, but difference, whether you call it signifier or value. To be sure, Spinoza is an absolute materialist, leaving no possibility for the existence of anything remotely spiritualistic, but *materialism itself is not a naïve system of thought that assumes that there is only matter*. Is only matter what's going on in my mind right now, or, for that matter, in the market when I consume?

Second, even if there were only matter, how do we arrive from there at the "principle of evolution"? It is indeed legitimate to argue that a materialism that derives animated life, including the speaking subject, from matter itself presupposes Spinoza's metaphysics, in which not only motion is inherent in matter but matter is God. It would be, however, a leap, to argue, as Israel does, that "the probing towards the concept of evolution from inert matter, and of *higher from lower forms of life*, was derived . . . *directly* from the doctrine that motion is inherent in matter, a concept generally regarded with horror and universally acknowledged in the Enlightenment Europe as quintessentially Spinozist" (160; emphasis mine). For evolutionist thought is predicated not only on the materialist assumption that life comes from "inert matter" but also on the idealist assumption—which tears evolutionism and materialism miles apart—that "higher . . . forms of life" derive "from lower," that is, that there are hierarchical stages of life, whereby each stage tends toward the most perfect stage. This notion is radically alien to Spinoza for whom "perfection and imperfection . . . are only modes of thinking" (i.e., imaginary), and "reality and perfection" are "the same thing," so that "by perfection in general I shall . . . understand reality, i.e., the essence of each thing insofar as it exists and produces an effect, having no regard to its duration" (1985, 545; *Ethics*, part IV, pref.). It is true, as Israel writes, that, "as its foremost champion, Diderot, stressed," "the concept of evolution . . . was derived" from what had "bec[o]me the very trademark of the *Spinozistes*," this, however, being only, as Israel himself admits, the "claim that Nature is self-moving, and creates itself"—not that it also divides life into subordinate groups, depending on the extent of their development toward some ideal of perfection (160).

Israel's derivation of evolutionism from Spinoza is as lacunar as his subsequent conclusion that "[t]hus the origins of the evolutionary thesis seemingly reinforce Einstein's proposition that the modern scientist who rejects divine Providence and a God that governs the destinies of man, while accepting 'the orderly harmony of what exists,' the intelligibility of an imminent [sic?] universe based on principles of mathematical rationality, in effect believes 'in Spinoza's God' " (Israel, 160; citing Clark 502–503). What is the connection because of which, once we "reject[] divine Providence and a God that governs the destinies of man" and instead "accept[] 'the orderly harmony of what exists' " and "the intelligibility of . . . [the] universe based on principles of mathematical rationality," we find ourselves so smoothly, if not necessarily, within the realm of the "evolutionary thesis"? The only way to render this syllogism coherent is to presume that hierarchies and their entailed discriminations are part of " 'the orderly harmony of what exists.' "

To praise Spinoza as the most influential philosophical force of secular modernity on the ground of arguments such as the above only makes one wonder whether it would have been better to have left him in his quasi-anonymity.

Unlike Israel's premises regarding historical causality, the present work does not attempt to ground the importance of Spinoza on the possibility that a "single seventeenth-century author . . . an aloof, solitary figure raised among a despised religious minority who lacked formal academic training and status, can have fundamentally and decisively shaped a tradition of radical thinking which eventually spanned the whole continent, exerted an immense influence over successive generations, and shook western civilization to its foundations" (Israel, 159). Nor does it want to support the "universal conviction during the revolutionary age, beginning in the early 1780s, that it was 'philosophy' which had demolished the *ancient régime* . . . and that it had accomplished this feat long before the first shots were fired at the Bastille," with Spinoza figuring "as the chief author" within this (pre)revolutionary philosophy (Israel, 715). The present work does not aspire to compete with either Hegel or Hollywood.

Rather, following the Spinozian model of causality as immanent, the present work considers historical events in secular capitalist modernity as not running behind external causes on a serial line of distinct causes and effects. Neither has modernity been made the way it has because of the "single seventeenth-century author" we call Spinoza, or any other individual, for that matter, nor did the French, or any other, Revolution occur because of "philosophy," regardless of the causes to which the characters involved might attribute their "appetites" or "desires." Spinoza, philosophy, the French Revolution, and everything in secular modernity, far from being causes and effects of one another, are all effects of the "natural right of [the] universal nature" of this modernity, and its "laws or rules." It is the "universal nature" of modernity to consist of one substance that "is in itself and is conceived through itself," and which determines the modes of "everything [that] takes place" to be the same as its own attributes (Spinoza 1951, 292; *A Political Treatise*, ch. II, parag. 4; 1985, 408; *Ethics*, part I, def. 3). And, nevertheless, these laws and attributes are not the aim of history, and only a fiction can turn them into precisely that.[14]

After the Context

Unlike this introduction, which contextualizes the present work in terms of the current theoretical (and, consequently, political) debates around Spinoza and "Neo-Spinozism," the first part of the present work could be described as a brief intellectual history, focusing on the development of the concept and function of causality in secular thought, up until the psychoanalytic introduction of the concept of enjoyment. A central thesis in this part concerns the aforementioned Spinozian and Marxian subjection of the world to value, and hence the homology between economic and semantic systems of exchange in secular capitalist modernity. The second part addresses the distinction between the Kantian and the Marxian conceptualizations of the preconditions allowing a system (economic or semantic) to form a totality, as well as on the surplus, as it manifests itself in the field of semantic exchange, that is, as gaze. Both subjects are examined in their relevance to a psychoanalytic theory of ethics.

Part I

Secular Causality and Its Enjoyment

The book-keepers of compulsive actions are everywhere: they have not let Grillparzer, Lenau or Kleist escape them, and as for Goethe's sorcerer's apprentice, they only disagree as to whether it is masturbation or bed wetting that is being sublimated. If I tell them they can kiss my ass, I must have an anal predilection. . . . Appearances are against me. It would be wasted effort to try and prove that libido isn't involved—they have caught me!

—K. Kraus, "Unbefugte Psychologie"

And so they will not stop asking for the causes of causes until you take refuge in the will of God, i.e., the sanctuary of ignorance.

—Spinoza, *Ethics*

The effects are successful only in the absence of cause.

—Lacan, *The Four Fundamental Concepts of Psychoanalysis*

From the First Cause to Transference

Knowledge, Aristotle argued both in *Physics* and in *Metaphysics*, is knowledge of causes, that is, understanding why something changes (or does not). Aristotelian knowledge is complete when the following four cardinal causes have been identified: (1) the material cause, the substrate or substance of which an object is made, such as the stones that make up a house; (2) the formal cause, the shape or form of the substance, such as the specific design of the stone house; (3) the final cause, the use, purpose, or end for the sake of which something was made, such as habitation in the case of a house; and (4) the efficient cause, the primary instigator of the process of change, such as the agent who commissioned the construction of the house (see Aristotle 1970, 28–31 and 37–39; bk. II, chapters 3 and 7, 194b16–196a30 and 198a14–198b10).[1]

Scholasticism adopted this Aristotelian model to its own purposes, namely, to prove that the cause for the existence of all things lies in the creating will of God. God is both the first or efficient cause and the final cause, because of, and for the sake of which, all material and formal causes exist. Scholasticism did not challenge the number of causes. In his *Summa Theologiae,* Thomas Aquinas, one of the major revisionists of Aristotle, maintained that all physical beings are subject to four kinds of change or motion (*motus*), fashioned after the model of the Aristotelian four cardinal causes. But, going beyond Aristotle, he also argued that the process in which A moves B, B moves C, and so on, cannot go on to infinity, for such an infinity would not explain anything. There must, therefore, be a different kind of "mover," a first mover not moved by another, and hence not a member of the chain of movers and not of the same nature as all movable, bodily things. This mover is what Christianity calls God.[2] This theory of God as the primal mover or first cause beyond and above all other causes was more or less the explanatory model dominating not only medieval theophilosophy but also the first attempt to secularize thought and to ground truth on human reason itself: the Cartesian *cogito*.

In 1637, René Descartes' (1596–1650) *Meditations* introduced the notorious *cogito* as the inaugural moment of the philosophical discourse of secular modernity and subjectivity. However, as is amply known, this is marked by a double logical failure. On the one hand, by deducing from the "I think" the "I am," Descartes commits a logical leap from thought to existence. On the other, as we shall see in more detail below, Descartes fails to ground truth on human reason itself, first because he is eventually forced to invoke God as the guarantor of truth, and, second, because the necessity of God's existence is itself proven through a circular logic. Descartes' *cogito* can therefore be said to be a seminal moment (patriarchal connotations included) in the history of thought only insofar as it *demanded* that reason ground logically its own truths, rather than accepting them as revelatory—but *not* because it did indeed ground them.

If the Cartesian *cogito* can justly be regarded as a hallmark in the history of thought it is actually because of the simultaneous critique *and* legitimization of its logical inconsistencies or circularity, offered in 1663 by Baruch Spinoza (1632–1677). It is in this sense that Spinoza, as Hegel put it, is "a direct successor to this philosopher [Descartes] . . . and one who carried on the Cartesian principle to its furthest logical consequences" (1974, 257; part III, sec. 2, chap. 1, sec. A. 2.).[3] Spinoza revealed the leap from thought to existence in Descartes' *cogito* by declaring that the *"I think, therefore I am,"* far from being a "syllogism," is "a single proposition which is equivalent to this, *"I am thinking [ego sum cogitans]"* (1985, 234; *The Principles of Philosophy Demonstrated in the Geometric Manner,* part I, "Prolegomenon," I/144). In other words, the purported syllogism is a tautology, for whether we say "I think" or "I am," the "I" that is reconfirmed in either case is not the existential but the thinking "I," the "I" of the "I am thinking," and not of the 'I am." Similarly, regarding Descartes' proof of God's existence, Spinoza showed, in Karatani's succinct formulation, that:

> The attempt to prove the existence of God by starting from the *cogito* . . . is itself a *para doxa*—nothing more than circular reasoning. It is what Kierkegaard would call a "leap". . . . I doubt because I am imperfect and finite—which itself is the evidence (proof) that a perfect and infinite other (God) exists. (1995, 150)

Although Spinoza's critique appears to repudiate irredeemably Descartes as a malady within an otherwise healthy body of reason, Spinoza's own conclusion from Descartes' 'error' was that the entire tradition of knowledge, with its understanding of causality, was itself debilitated. In the itinerary that separates Aristotle from Descartes, knowledge had been set up in such a way that sooner or later it had always to invoke a "first mover" whose existence cannot be derived from the logic of causality from which all other causes derive. The compulsory invocation of a "first mover" was beneficiary to theocracy, whose agenda was precisely the perpetual reconfirmation of God as the first and final cause of everything. But the secular agenda set as its cognitive task to ground truth by means of reason, whereupon the inevitability with which knowledge kept returning to God revealed a structural flaw inherent in secular reason itself. It is not Descartes who committed a contingent, and hence avoidable error; it is secular reason that committed a structurally necessary error. Spinoza saw in Descartes not an aberration from secular reason, but its symptom—that is, the pathological moment that reveals the structure of the 'normal' state of things.

The real break, which Descartes failed to procure, came, therefore, with Spinoza's revolutionary reconceptualization of causality, which intrepidly legitimized Descartes' tautological or circular logic as the sole possible cognitive mode of secular thought.

Accepting the Aristotelian position that there is substance (material cause) and properties or predicates of this substance (formal cause), Spinoza argued, against Aristotle and his aftermath, that these properties are not accidental but necessary or essential properties of substance. Substance, therefore, is nothing other than its properties, or, the material and the formal causes are one and the same. For if a property of a substance were contingent, then its cause could only be the action of another substance on the first, which would have this property either as necessary or as accidental, and if the latter were the case, one would have to find a third substance having this property, and so on, until we finally find a substance in which the said property is necessary, and only then could we explain it through its necessary connection with this ultimate substance. This means that a property cannot be explained but as necessary to a substance, or, conversely, that a substance is the cause of its own properties. Hence, as far as the causality of properties (and hence knowledge) is concerned, there are not two or more substances, the one transitively effecting the other, but only one substance, which is immanent to its properties, and with which any given property has a necessary connection. Similarly, Spinoza concludes, both in *The Principles of Philosophy Demonstrated in the Geometric Manner* (1663) and in the *Ethics* (1677), to explain or know a substance is to reveal it as the cause of its properties, that is, as *causa sui* (self-caused). This, in turn, entails that there is only one substance, which is the cause of itself by dint of the mere fact that it is the substance that it is, and, further that there can be only one ultimate cause, and hence only one ultimate explanation.

The ultimate consequence of the concept of *causa sui* is that God *is* the created world—"Deus, seu Natura . . . una, eademque est ["God, *or* Nature . . . are one and the same"]"—and not some creator or first cause preceding its effect, the created world (1990, 436; 1985, 544; *Ethics*, part IV, preface). Hence, all causes, material, formal, and final, are efficient, this being God or Nature. God or Nature is a substance that is its properties, and which exists by existing and for the sole sake of its own existence.[4] By thus obliterating the dualism between God and the effects of divinity—a central distinction constitutive of Judaism and Christianity alike—Spinoza safeguarded for himself the double position of both a heretic Jew and an anathema to the Christian church.

As far as knowledge is concerned, no stone could be left unturned after Spinoza's radical revision of its core concept, causality. For centuries, knowledge had been performing the same movement in which distinct causes and effects follow one another in a linear or transitive chain that is necessarily doomed to an "infinite regress" of causes, unless it invokes a "first cause" of another kind (Spinoza 1985, 321; *Principles of Philosophy Demonstrated in the Geometric Manner*, appendix, part II, chap. 3). Far from explaining anything about the world, knowledge invariably proved that something entirely different than the world (God) necessarily exists. By equating God and nature, cause and effect, Spinoza introduced the pathbreaking idea that "God is the immanent, not the transitive, cause of all things" (Spinoza 1985, 428; *Ethics*, part I, prop. 18). This is a conclusion that means no less than that which is assumed to be the first cause is in truth an "immanent" cause, a cause that is itself the effect of its own effects and does not exist but in its own effects.

In a subversive turnaround, if God is the immanent cause of the thinking I, that is, if God *is* the thinking I, then, suddenly God *is*, just or precisely because "I think." What is more, I also am, but only insofar as I think, and, conversely, I think only insofar as I am. For, as Spinoza writes, there is a "union of Mind and Body," so that "*the object of the idea constituting the human Mind is the Body, or a certain mode of Extension which actually exists, and nothing else*" (1985, 457–58; *Ethics*, part II, prop. 13 and schol.) Although Descartes' *cogito ergo sum* derives existence from thought, at the end of the day it posits each as independent—which is why the soul can continue its immortal existence after the death of the body. By contrast, Spinoza's *ego sum cogitans* precludes the possibility of either without the other, which is why it also repudiates the immortality of the soul. The discrepancy in their conclusions is predicated on a crucial epistemological difference. The Cartesian *cogito* is possible through an invalid, presumably transitive deduction, which can pass for valid only by repressing its logical "leap." The Spinozian *cogitans*, by contrast, derives its possibility from immanent causality, that is, from a reason that is conscious of the circularity between causes and effects.

Inversely put, Spinoza showed that, paradoxically, secular reason can extricate itself from the circular reasoning of the Cartesian type only by acknowledging its circularity—in this case, the fact that the presumed ground of its truth (God) is arbitrarily posited by itself.

With Spinoza, the distinction between truth and falsity is displaced onto the distinction between (presumably) deductive or transitive and circular or immanent modes of cognition, that is, between a thought that can sustain itself only by remaining blind to the logical leaps that it necessarily commits, and a thought that takes into account its own arbitrariness as a constitutive part of itself. Secular thought is one that accepts that "truth is the standard both of itself and of the false" (Spinoza 1985, 479; *Ethics*, part II, prop. 43, schol.).

Thus, with Spinoza, the seed is sown for a third, radically new explanatory model besides positivistic deduction and religious belief. Given that in this type of knowledge, causes do not exist but in their effects, an object (cause) does not exist but in the knowledge thereof (effect). In other words, this cognitive model acknowledges that an effect and its cause, and, hence, that it itself (cognition) and its own cognitive object, stand in a transferential relation—in the psychoanalytic sense of the word. Just as in the analytic situation, or, for that matter, any situation in which a person "speaks to another in an authentic and full manner," there is "transference . . . something which . . . changes the nature of the two beings present," so, too, in secular (immanent or tranferential) knowledge, the nature of both knowledge and the object being known changes (Lacan 1988a, 109).

Indeed, psychoanalysis is an attempt to produce a systematic body of knowledge grounded on the Spinozian principle of immanent, rather than transitive, causality. Its central concept itself—the unconscious—is defined as a structure that, as Louis Althusser and Étienne Balibar put it, "is immanent in its effects in the Spinozist sense of the term, that the *whole existence of the structure consists of its effects*, in short that the structure . . . is nothing outside its effects" (193).

Causes or Reasons?

Just as scientific knowledge and religious belief have been in rather unfriendly, if not inimical, terms with one another, positivist or experimental and transferential knowledge are also antagonistic. While the latter challenges scientific knowledge by arguing that there is (unacknowledged) transference also between positivistic science and the objects under its scrutiny, positivism denies the status of a science to psychoanalysis precisely because of its explicit acknowledgment of transference as its fundamental methodology.[5] Psychoanalysis' own pride is the very reason for its broad infamy.

Eminent among the earlier critics of psychoanalysis figures Freud's compatriot Ludwig Wittgenstein (1889–1951), who argued that epistemologically legitimate causality presupposes a "cause," something that "is found by experiment" (1979, 40).[6] While the validation of a "scientific cause" transcends the will or agreement of the experimenting subject, psychoanalysis offers epistemologically illegitimate "reasons," for a "reason entails as an essential part one's agreement with it" (40). Given that "the success of the analysis is supposed to be shown by the person's agreement," and that "there is nothing corresponding to this in physics," psychoanalysis, Wittgenstein concludes, is possible because of "a muddle . . . between a cause and a reason" (39). What is more, far from being restricted to psychoanalysis, this "muddle," as Jacques Bouveresse observes, "is in a way, from Wittgenstein's perspective, the philosophical confusion par excellence" (27).

Marring all philosophy, this "confusion," Wittgenstein argues further, consists in mistaking for "scientific" an "aesthetic investigation," which, unlike science, establishes an analogy between the object to be analyzed and the linguistic field (1979, 39). As an example P. M. S. Hacker mentions the fact that "we can significantly say of architectural features: 'This is rhetorical (or, bombastic).' " Such "an analogy like the linguistic one used in architecture does not generate hypotheses that can be tested in experiments, nor does it produce a theory that can be used to predict events," and neither is it " the result of new information, nor does it lead to new empirical discoveries" (Hacker 486; as cited in Bouveresse 31). And the "psychoanalytic way of finding," for example, "why a person laughs is analogous to [such] an aesthetic investigation" (Wittgenstein 1979, 39).

Nevertheless, both Hacker and Bouveresse admit that a linguistic analogy, its professed cognitive sterility notwithstanding, "yields new forms of comparison, *changing our understanding* of buildings and *affecting the way we look at things*" (Hacker 486; as cited in Bouveresse 32; emphasis mine). If this is the case, isn't then an "aesthetic investigation" a system of knowledge rather more powerful than a positivist science, since it effects reality on the most decisive level, the level of "understanding" and of "the way we look at things"? Whether the ignition of a bomb will result in its explosion is arguably experimentally testable. But whether a person will decide to ignite the bomb—which is the nub of the matter—is not. For this decision depends precisely on "linguistic" and "aesthetic" factors. While science can merely *predict* events, it is only "linguistics" and "aesthetics" that, with the exception of certain natural events, can *cause* them to happen. If knowledge is *knowledge of the causes of change*, and insofar as the change in question involves human agency, then only a *linguistico-aesthetic investigation* is, properly speaking, *knowledge*.

Hacker's reference to a "linguistic analogy" could not be more accurate. Knowledge of causes in the human domain operates according to the logic of linguistics. First, because, as Spinoza's pantheism entails, the whole world, including nature, is for the human subject a linguistic field, that is, a signifying system. Second, because linguistics treats the elements of a signifying system as relating to one another differentially, that is, in the mode of immanent causality. That the human subject "is the effect of the signifier" means precisely that human—psychoanalytic, philosophical, historical, cultural, social, political, etc.—knowledge is epistemologically and methodologically linguistic (Lacan 1981, 207). By "linguistic" is here of course meant not the field canonically defined as "linguistics," but any transferential knowledge, as defined above.

The critics of psychoanalysis discern in its logic the loop of immanent causality but invariably fail to recognize that it is required for the examination of something that it itself operates according to this causality. What we actually witness in these critiques is a "muddle" between a 'critique' and an accurate 'description' of a methodology. Bouveresse's 'critique,' for instance, is a perspicacious description of a fundamental insight organizing transferential methodology: "The cure for neurotic behavior is achieved by producing the conditions that make admission possible; and this allows us to identify the impossibility of that admission as having been the cause of the patient's suffering all along" (33). Indeed this is so, for "repression [cause] and the return of the repressed [effect] are one and the same thing, the front and back of a single process," in which the "symptom [effect] acts as a language that enables repression [cause] to be expressed" in the first place—in short, "repression . . . is structured" not like a physical but "like a linguistic phenomenon" (Lacan 1993, 60 and 62). Far from needing to be reminded of its "circular," immanent logic, as if it were its *faux pas* or unconscious lapsus, psychoanalysis (like properly secular philosophy and any proper analysis of the subject, culture, and society) consciously bases itself on it.

Given this linguistic structure of repression, the repressed (cause) is a signifier, which, as such, is differential, that is, "[il] ne peut être considéré comme ayant une portée univoque [it cannot be considered as having a univocal impact]," for "les éléments signifiants doivent d'abord être définis par leur articulation avec les autres éléments signifiants [signifying elements must first be defined through their articulation with the other signifying elements]"—*all* of them, including, not least, the elements signifying the return of the repressed, that is, the symptom (effect) (Lacan 1994, 289; translation mine).[7] A signifying element cannot be the cause of the symptom unless it becomes such in its relation or articulation with it, or, to put it more strongly, unless the symptom itself deems it to be its cause.

The arbitrariness of the admission of the cause is no different than the one involved in the possibility that a person might laugh under the same conditions that might make another person cry. This phenomenon cannot be explained without taking into account as one of the initial givens that one cause may have different effects. For *what is effected* (i.e., the person who laughs or cries) itself determines the cause (i.e., the conditions conducive to laughter or crying). Unlike transitive causality and positivism, immanent causality and transferential knowledge take arbitrariness as one of their initial givens. For the arbitrary effect is *not* an accident additional to the necessity of substance, but is itself necessity. That God is the immanent cause of everything in the world means that laughter, crying, symptoms, and all occurring "modes of the divine nature have also followed from it necessarily, and not contingently. . . . For if they have not been determined by God, then . . . it is impossible, not contingent, that they should determine themselves" (Spinoza 1985, 433–34; *Ethics*, part 1, prop. 29, dem.).

There is also another "muddle" persisting in the positivist critiques of psychoanalysis, specifically, the one between the properly secular (Spinozian or pantheistic) conceptualization of nature qua culture and the Cartesian nature, which must at all costs remain separate from the soul or thought.[8] Such critiques are an expression of what Žižek describes as "the traditional philosophical attitude which compels us to maintain an insurmountable distance between 'nature' and the symbolic universe, prohibiting any 'incestuous' contact between the two domains" (1996, 283). Strictly speaking, this "attitude" is prephilosophical, since philosophy proper begins with the Spinozian moment that takes into account its own logical leaps, or, as Hegel put it, albeit for the wrong reasons, since philosophical "thought . . . begin[s] by placing itself at the standpoint of Spinozism; to be a follower of Spinoza is the essential commencement of philosophy" (1974, 257). This is why Bouveresse is correct in identifying in Wittgenstein's critique of psychoanalysis essentially a critique of all philosophy.

Not only psychoanalysis and philosophy, but *any* field of knowledge whose object is the speaking subject is by its object determined to employ the methodology of transferential knowledge and to develop an epistemology in terms of immanent causality—and it does so whether it knows it or not. One may want to call an immanent cause a "reason," if this is merely a matter of nomenclature, but if by that one means that it pertains to the realm designated by Wittgenstein's notorious finale of his *Tractatus*, then one effectively argues that one should remain silent about everything that happens in the world of speaking subjects.[9]

Science of Differential Substance

It may appear that the above conclusion assumes that nothing in the domain of the speaking subject is effected by anything other than the signifier, such as economy, or something that would be the object of physics, the positivist science par excellence according to these critics. Far from this, the underlying assumption is that the objects of these fields are at least partly also signifiers (i.e., differential), and that accordingly, if Wittgenstein's advice applies to psychoanalysis and philosophy, science should also remain silent.

As is known, quantum physics does not have much to do with positivism, exhibiting, as Slavoj Žižek argues, even "parallels [with] . . . Lacanian psychoanalysis" (1996, 282). This is due to the "homologies between the quantum universe and the symbolic order," that is, the order of the signifier, given the "purely 'differential' definition of the particle, which directly recalls the classic Saussurean definition of the signifier (a particle is nothing but the bundle of its interactions with other particles)" (282–83). In the fields of both particles and signifiers, as Ferdinand de Saussure (1857–1913) himself would put it, "there are only differences *without positive terms*," with "both the signified and the signifier," or particles and waves, being "purely differential," for "in any semiological system," just as in any system of particles, "whatever distinguishes one sign [or particle] from the others constitutes it" (Saussure, 120–21).[10]

Because the field of particles is a kind of a "semiological system," in quantum physics, unlike in mechanics, as Werner Karl Heisenberg (1901–1976) has argued, there are only programs, no exact predictions (see Heisenberg 1957 and 1963). Quantum indeterminacy refers to what Žižek wittingly calls an "ontological 'cheating,' " insofar as it describes the phenomenon in which "an electron can create," *ex nihilo*, as it were, "a proton and thereby violate the principle of constant energy," under the precondition that "it reabsorbs it quickly enough" so that its "environs" do not have the time to " 'take[] note' of the discrepancy" (1996, 279). As John Gribbon puts it in his popular *In Search of Schroedinger's Cat*, this extra energy can be there "before realizing its mistake," but upon "acknowledging its own unreality," it "turn[s] around to go back from where it came," that is, in Žižek's paraphrase, "into the abyss of Nothingness" (Žižek 1996, 279; Gribbon, 201). The said indeterminacy is real only when both conditions are fulfilled: (1) that the "environs," the "modality and direction of our search participate in the creation of the object for which we are searching"—the point that Žižek stresses; and (2) that, insofar as "events . . . go on 'in the twinkling of uncertainty while the universe 'isn't looking,' " it remains indeterminate *whether or not* the electron will create a proton while we are 'not looking' (280–81). For, otherwise, we would speak of exact prediction, since we would know that whenever we are 'not looking' this is what the electron invariably does.

The same is true of the example from the field of the signifier with which Žižek compares the above example of quantum indeterminacy. It is one of Žižek's favorite jokes, the one

> about the conscript who tries to evade military service by pretending to be mad: he compulsively checks all the pieces of paper he can lay his hands on, constantly repeating: "That is not it!" The psychiatrist, finally convinced of his insanity, gives him a written warrant releasing him from military service; the conscript casts a look at it and says cheerfully: "That *is* it!" (1996, 281)

"What we have here," Žižek comments, "is a paradigmatic case of the symbolic process which creates its cause, the object that sets it in motion" (281). In truth, however, far from being "a paradigmatic case" of the performative function of language, through which the latter "creates its cause, the object" that motivates it (the warrant releasing the conscript), this joke, alas, describes a highly exceptional or aberrant case, which is why it can function as a joke in the first place. Its humor derives from precisely its total elimination of the signifier's indeterminacy. In actual life, most objects (not the least release warrants), as many conscripts who have attempted to evade military service by pretending to be mad know very well, are not produced with such unexpectedly unmediated determinism. If we are taken by surprise and laugh it is because the joke treats the relation between signifier and object not with the uncertainty marking real life but with the same confidence with which behaviorism shackles together stimulus and response.

As late as 1945, Bertrand Russell was arguing that Spinoza's metaphysics is "incompatible with modern logic and the scientific method," for "the concept of substance, upon which Spinoza relies, is one which neither science nor philosophy can nowadays accept" (560; as sited in Woods, chap. 5). Such a statement is possible only from a perspective that restricts scientificity within the confines of mechanistic physics and generally empiricism. The truth, however, about both science and Spinoza is rather the opposite. As Alan Woods aptly puts it, "by not restricting himself to the narrow confines of empirical philosophy," Spinoza "was able to transcend the limits of the mechanistic science of the day" (chap. 5).[11] By defining substance as the cause of itself, and by equating substance with God and nature, Spinoza effectively argues that the subject is the cause of itself. This conception of causality has been transcending "the limits of . . . mechanistic science" since the seventeenth century.

The claim of self-causation may at first sight appear to contradict the obvious and undeniable observation that there is a rich variety of external factors effecting the subject. But, just as in quantum physics the existence of a particle presupposes that it 'knows' whether another slit is aware of it, in human life, too, the existence of an external factor presupposes that it 'knows' whether the subject itself is aware of it. To say that the subject is the cause of itself amounts to the assertion that *everything* can be the cause of the subject, under the precondition that the subject 'agrees' that this is its cause. As the increasing proliferation of causes amply testifies, it takes a gaze that sees something as a cause for a cause to exist. There was a time when not even history, society, and culture were considered to be the causes of the subject—let alone those more recent and still embryonic finds, such as the discourses on sexuality, insanity, race, or biopolitics. *Self-causation is not the opposite of historical determinism but its proper understanding.*

Similarly, self-causation could not lie any farther from either the relativism of 'everything goes' or the idealism of the 'free subject,' assumed to be capable of becoming whatever it wills. As in the quantum universe, in Spinoza's nature qua signifier there is only one substance: a *differential substance.* Subject or object A is one mode in which the differential substance manifests itself *while and because* this same substance manifests itself in all other actual (i.e., also potential) modes (all other subjects or objects) under whose gaze A perceives itself as being seen. To speak of differential substance effectively means to speak of value, rather than a fixed matter that is defined by inherent characteristics such as its mass and quality.[12] And values, whether semantic (signifier) or economic (capital), do not obey the laws of transitive causality, for, as Karl Marx (1818–1883) put it:

> [Value] differentiates itself as original value from itself as surplus-value, just as God the Father differentiates himself from himself as God the Son, although both are of the same age and form, in fact one single person; for only by the surplus-value of £10 does the £100 originally advanced become capital, and as soon as this has happened, as soon as the son has been created, and, through the son, the father, their difference vanishes again, and both become one, £110. (1990, 256)

In the realm of value, "causation," as Geoff Waite remarks, " is not . . . a *temporal* relation but rather a *logical* one," in which all "terms" are "*reciprocal*" and "simultaneous," and which therefore, is the kingdom of immanent causality and its laws (25). Or, as Kenneth Burke puts it:

> Though there is a sense in which a Father precedes a Son, there is also a sense in which the two states are "simultaneous"—for parents can be parents only insofar as they have offspring, and in this sense the offspring "makes" the parent. That is, logically, father and Son are *reciprocal* terms, each of which implies the other. (32)

To put it on the plane of history, the two centuries that separate Spinoza from Marx do not make the former's work the cause of the latter's. Nor is Lacan's work their and Freud's (1856–1939) effect or the cause of the work of those thinkers enumerated in chronological detail in an earlier endnote here. For far from constituting a series of causes and effects, the one diachronically causing the other, all these figures derive their possibility equally from the emergence of value, the differential substance of secular, capitalist modernity. It is this that for the first time in history renders the existence of transferential systems of knowledge possible, just as it renders possible their critique.

The intrinsic characteristic of differential substance is the one identified by Saussure as marking value. In his words, "[A]ll values are apparently governed by the same paradoxical principle." They "are always composed: (1) of a *dissimilar* thing [signified, the concept of an object to which it points as its referent] that can be *exchanged* for the thing of which the value is to be determined"—just as the value of a dollar is composed of itself, a thing that is dissimilar to the amount of gasoline (use-value) for which it can be exchanged and whose value is to be determined through the dollar. And "(2)," they are composed "of *similar* things [the value of other signs] that can be *compared* with the thing of which the value is to be determined"—just as are quarters, dimes, pennies, other amounts of dollars, and all other currencies (exchange-values) with which the one dollar can be compared (Saussure, 115; see Marx 1990, 125–63). In other words, differential substance is something that in itself cannot be positively given to experience but rather manifests itself empirically as two different things: on the one hand, as exchange-value or signifier, and, on the other, as specific commodities, the "object[s] of utility" ("use-value") or objects, as the referents of the signified (Marx 1990, 152). Capital and objects of utility, and signs with their referential objects are the two modes of the empirical manifestation of differential substance on the economic and semantic levels, respectively.

The homology between economic and semantic value as two of the domains of differential substance precludes the classical Marxist assumption that the "base" (economy) determines the "superstructure" (sign, hence, culture), as well as its idealist bourgeois inverse. Both are directly caused or determined to exist in this way by the differential substance whose modes they are. And insofar as substance (God) is the immanent cause of its effects, it itself is the effect of its own modes.

Two important, perhaps counterintuitive conclusions follow here. First, the above argument does not entail an ontologization of capitalism. Capital is *not* substance; *nor* is the secular sign substance. Unlike capital and sign which are empirically given, substance is a differential nonentity, something whose ontological status is negative. It is this differential that determines capital and sign to exist as they do, but it is simultaneously capital and sign that determine their own cause (differential substance) to determine them in this way. The empirical effects its own transcendental preconditions, just as the inverse is true. Immanent causality*de-ontologizes ontology*, insofar as the latter is no longer an immutable entity but a historical effect, albeit not realized within historical reality. With immanent causality, Being in itself, the universal beyond historical relativism, is real, but, as Joan Copjec puts it in the context of Lacan, "the real displaces transcendence," insofar as it is itself the unrealized effect of the historical (2002, 5).[13] Like theocratic feudalism, with its "ternary" sign (Word) and fixed, nondifferential substance, capitalism too, with its "binary" sign and differential substance, is yet another historical episode.

The important thing that the present ontology allows us to understand, however, is that capitalism is *not an autonomous*, purely economic phenomenon that could dissipate while the structures of the sign and of the cause of both sign and capital (differential substance) remain intact. That the virtual is actual means that reality could change only under one of the following two conditions. Either differential substance can manifest empirically in economic and semantic exchange in further modes beyond those so far known as capitalism and secular sign, or differential substance should be replaced by another substance of radically other attributes, which would manifest in other modes, for the modes could be other than what they are only if the substance that determines them were other than what it is.

Second, as a consequence, and since knowledge is knowledge of causes, neither capital nor the sign can be known if examined in isolation, as separate fields, since they are both caused by one and the same substance. The analysis of capitalist economy, therefore, must be included among the sciences whose object is a mode of the differential substance, such as the analysis of all fields that involve the examination of language.[14] For otherwise knowledge ignores a whole array of effects of the cause it examines, as well as a whole array of causes that effect this cause.

Secular Ontology: Differential (Non-)Substance and the End of (Anti-)Platonism

This is the moment to spell out the difference between, on the one hand, both Spinoza's and Marx's monism and, on the other, what both "Neo-Spinozists" and their critics mis-conceive as monism. As we shall presently see, Spinozian and Marxian monism constitutes a radical break with all Platonic thought (whether straightforward or its anti-Platonic reaction), whereas "Neo-Spinozism" (including its critique), not unlike bourgeois idealism, continues to be a rendition of Platonism, or, what amounts to the same, a form of anti-Platonism. The latter point becomes clear through Badiou's assessment of Deleuze's work as Platonic/anti-Platonic, that is, as an overturning of Plato that nevertheless sustains the Platonist premises.[15]

Let us begin with a thesis that could be unanimously agreed upon by all four, Plato, Deleuze, Badiou, and the author of the present work, even if not necessarily as meaning the same thing for all four: there is "one Being and only for all forms and all times," or, as in the more aptly modified translation cited in Badiou's book on Deleuze: there is "one Being and only one for all forms and all times" (Deleuze 1990, 180; Badiou 2000, 119). In what can this eternal univocity of Being consist, when, as the present work maintains, Being is a substance that is both transcendent and the effect of historical reality? In that it is precisely *that which each historical state produces as its own transcendent surplus*. Everything else of Being is multiple. This is the thesis of the present work on Being, but not one shared by the other thinkers in question.

According to this thesis, the surplus of theocratic feudalism was Being that was God, insofar as everything that existed was His manifestation, or, in the Platonic idiom, His simulacrum. In secular capitalist modernity, Being, as follows from Spinoza's immanent causality, is the first cause, insofar as it is lacking.[16] Or, what amounts to the same, Being, as follows from Marx's analysis of capital, is surplus, insofar as it is not given to experience. The surplus in question is conceived as surplus-value in economy, and, as surplus-enjoyment on the level of the signifier and the subject. Neither is empirically manifest as such. Surplus-enjoyment is the first cause, which is nothing other than the gaze, "not as such but in so far as it is lacking," and it is always lacking since "the gaze I encounter . . . is not a seen gaze, but a gaze imagined by me in the field of the Other" (Lacan 1981, 103 and 84).[17] Similarly, surplus-value is also not given to experience, insofar as, in Marx's words:

> Certainly M [money] becomes M + ΔM, £100 becomes £110. But, considered qualitatively, £100 is the same as £110, namely money . . . the value of the £110 has the same need for valorization [*Verwertung*] as the value of £100, for they are both limited expressions of exchange-value. . . . At the end of the process, we do not receive on the one hand the original £100, and on the other the surplus-value of £10. What emerges is rather a value of £110, which is in exactly the same form, appropriate for commencing the valorization process, as the original £100. At the end of the movement, money emerges once again as its starting point. (1990, 252–53)

In the realm of experience, we cannot ever have a surplus-value in our hand; what we hold is exchange-value. Surplus-value is a concept, an idea with no empirical referent, which we infer from the purely quantitative difference between the originally advanced and the resulting amounts of exchange-value. Nevertheless, it is the cause both of capital and of all things. For, on the one hand, surplus-value is the cause of "the transformation of money into capital," and, on the other, although "the circulation of money as capital is an end in itself," nevertheless "capital cannot . . . arise from circulation, and it is equally impossible to arise apart from circulation," so, "it must have its origin both in circulation and not in circulation," in the realms of both capital and of non-capital, that is, use-value or objects of utility, material things (Marx 1990, 245, 253, and 268). Conversely, therefore, if there were no exchange between exchange-values and things, there would be no surplus-value either. Hence, the latter is both the cause and the effect of everything that exists—which is why beyond being a concept, it is also the *one* substance.

In truth, only surplus-value is differential substance in the proper sense of the word, that is, a purely differential (non-)substance, a form rather than a substance in the traditional sense of the word, which applies even to exchange-value, insofar as it is always embodied in some form of material currency. For in any system of value, or, as Saussure put it, "in any semiological system, whatever distinguishes one sign from the others constitutes it. Difference makes . . . value . . . *language is a form not a substance*," in which "there are only differences *without positive terms*" (120–22). This is the accurate definition of value as a purely differential relation, which is never given to experience as such. For empirically, we can only deal with either exchange-value or words, both of which have material existence as coins, paper money, letters, sound, etc. Strictly speaking, they are differential substance, whereas *Being is a differential (non-)substance.* Therein lies the difference between modes and attributes.

According to the Spinozian-Marxian-Lacanian line of thought, Being in itself is transcendent to all that is given to experience, both exchange-value or signs and use-value or things, while it is their cause and (unrealized) effect. The attributes of (non-)substance determine the modes of substance to be as they are, just as they are determined by the modes to determine them in this way, since the modes presuppose them. Surplus or Being is the immanent cause of all that exists.

In this ontology, *both exchange-value or signs and use-value or things are simulacra* of the transcendent differential (non-)substance. *Being is neither things or beings nor words or ideas, while both equivocally attest to the historically univocal power of Being*, for they are the two empirical modes through which Being, *as the historical effect of secular capitalist modernity*, points to itself. *This Being, in turn, attests to the transhistorical univocity of Being, as the transcendence effected by the very historical experience it causes.*

This having been said, in his defense of Platonism against Deleuze's professed anti-Platonism, Badiou writes something that, like Deleuze's afore-cited passage on Being, initially may appear to be at least partly akin to the present ontological thesis:

> Certainly, it is true that sense [in Plato] is distributed according to the One and that beings are of the order of the simulacra. . . . But it in no way follows from this, as Deleuze assumes is the case with Plato, that the simulacra or beings are necessarily depreciated or considered as non-beings. On the contrary, it is necessary to affirm the rights of simulacra as *so many equivocal cases of univocity* that joyously attest to the univocal power of Being. (2000, 26)

I have no problem concurring with Badiou on this point and granting that the "hierarchy" that "Deleuze suspects Plato of" is not necessarily there, even if Badiou seems to contradict himself when he writes in the same paragraph:

> One does far more justice to the real One by thinking the egalitarian coexistence of simulacra in a positive way than by opposing simulacra to the real that they lack, in the way Plato opposes the sensible and the intelligible. (2000, 27)

In any case, and without making clear whether the following passage applies to Plato or Deleuze or both, Badiou goes on to state something that again appears to be in partial agreement with the ontology presented here:

> For, in fact, this real [One] lies nowhere else than *in that which founds the nature of the simulacrum as simulacrum*: the purely formal or modal character of the difference that constitutes it, from the viewpoint of the univocal real of Being that supports this difference within itself and distributes to it a single sense. (2000, 27)

I can more easily see Deleuze rather than Plato in this statement, but, in the last analysis, it turns out that, as far as Badiou is concerned, it does not matter whether these are paraphrases of Plato's or Deleuze's ontology, for:

> Even in supposing that the glorification of simulacra as a positive dimension of the univocity of Being constitutes an overturning of Platonism, the fact remains that, in the same way as for Plato . . . Deleuze's approach has to confront the thorny question of the names of Being. What, indeed, could be the appropriate name for that which is univocal? Is the nomination of the univocal itself univocal? (2000, 27).

Having turned to this question, Badiou comes to the conclusion that "a single name is never sufficient" to name the univocity of being; instead, "two are required." For "Being needs to be said in a single sense both from the viewpoint of the unity of its power and from the viewpoint of the multiplicity of the divergent simulacra that this power actualizes in itself." Whether otherwise Platonist or anti-Platonist, Deleuze remains within the Platonic tradition precisely because this "problem is constant from Plato . . . to Heidegger" and, beyond, to Badiou's own return to Plato (27).

But, prior to addressing the question Badiou invites us to, let us pause to examine the opposition between the "univocity" or "unity" of Being and the "multiplicity of the divergent simulacra." That Being in itself is a differential (non-)substance means that it involves both univocity—insofar as it is *one* function or relation: difference—and multiplicity—insofar as difference is a relation between at least *two* elements. The Spinozian–Marxian pantheism, that is, the subjection of the world to the signifier and economic value, indicates that in secular capitalist modernity, as Lacan put it, "the One is based only on (*tenir de*) the essence of the signifier" (1998, 5). As far as the historically specific Being of secular capitalism is concerned, its univocity emerges as an effect of the univocity of the signifier or exchange-value, the realm of metaphor or circulation, where one can give "one object for another," since all objects are there qualitatively the same: values (Lacan 1981, 103). In other words, the univocity of secular Being is introduced through the imaginary. Its multiplicity, on the other hand, emerges from the necessity of something that is not exchange-value, namely, objects of utility, required for the accrual of surplus-value. Unlike in Plato, neither the univocity nor the multiplicity is Being or its power. These are the two modes in which the attributes of the differential surplus manifest themselves empirically. Being in itself is a differential (non-)substance, which is to say undifferentiated univocity and multiplicity. Univocity and multiplicity as distinct categories emerge only on the empirical level.

Turning now to Badiou's question, the differential character of Being entails that its nomination requires three names. Secular Being needs to be said in a single sense (1) from the viewpoint of what appears to be true or real: beings and objects of utility, or the multiplicity of Being; (2) from the viewpoint of what appears to be false or imaginary: the sign or exchange-value, that is, the unity of Being; and (3) from the viewpoint of Being's own power, transcendence or differential (non-)substance itself, which alone is really true and real.[18]

If there is, therefore, a tradition that is neither Platonist nor anti-Platonist, this is the one that runs from Spinoza, through Marx, to Lacan. This line of ontology, even as it responds to the same question that has puzzled philosophy since Plato, does not simply overturn the Platonic hierarchy but collapses it as obsolete, since it reveals that the registers on which Being needs to be named are the following: (1) *being as the imaginary univocity of abstract thought, that is, as simulacrum (exchange-value or signifier)*; (2) *beings as the multiplicity of being (use-value or physical beings)*; and (3) *the primary, transcendent, yet immanent, differential (non-)substance that at once institutes the above duplicity and is the effect thereof (surplus).*

Žižek argues that the "very negativity" of the Thing-in-itself or of Spirit "must embody itself again in some miserable, radically contingent corporeal leftover," hence the Hegelian statement: " 'the Spirit is a *bone*' " (1989, 207). The present ontology indicates that in order to be embodied in empirical reality, the negativity of Being must embody itself *both* in some *corporeal* and in some *symbolic* leftover, both of which are equally "miserable [and] radically contingent." Hence, Hegel's statement must be rewritten as: "the Spirit is both *spirit* and a *bone*." Whereas Hegel claims that "the Thing has its essential being in another Thing," from Marx follows that *the Thing has its essential being in two other Things, languages and bodies* (Hegel 1977, 76).

The above argument does not entail that the modes are inferior distortions or misrepresentations of the attributes of (non-)substance. If Lacan can infer that Marx's surplus-value entails an equivalent function on the semantic level, and hence on the level of the subject, it is because on both levels the surplus presupposes abstract values and material bodies.[19] Surplus-enjoyment emerges out of the simple fact that secular reason, as we have seen, is circular, itself arbitrarily positing the ground of its truths. As a result, what in secular modernity is called 'objective knowledge' is in truth always inconsistent. It is this inconsistency that allows for, and requires, surplus-enjoyment, which is the enjoyment the subject derives from the sense experienced by its unconditional devotion to this knowledge, a devotion comparable to that of a religious believer. This sense is "*jouis-sens*," enjoyment-of-sense, that is, an enjoyment relying on the sliding of sense from the semantic to the sensual level: when 'objective knowledge' does not make sense, one can always enjoy the sublime sensation of one's unshakable, absolute devotion to it. While, on the one hand, surplus-enjoyment manifests itself empirically as this sensation, on the other hand, it simultaneously continues to inhere in the semantic sphere insofar as the subject procures the fantasy that fills in the gap in the Other and thus makes it appear consistent and as having an unambiguous will. Just as the accrual of surplus-value presupposes both exchange-value and objects of utility, the accrual of surplus-enjoyment presupposes both the signifier and bodies capable of sensation. The *modes* of the differential (non-)substance (surplus) are values *and* physical beings because *its attributes are value and sensation.*

The *Being* of secular capitalist modernity is neither value (Idea) nor beings (simulacra), for both are its own simulacra, equivocally attesting to the power of Being, which in itself is the *differential (non-)substance of value–sensation.*[20] Marx's third term (surplus-value), his surplus to the two Platonic terms (Being and simulacrum) is a *metaphysical* category that empirically is both *univocal simulacrum* and *multiple being,* so that neither the one nor the other is more real or true.

The statement that "truth is the standard both of itself and of the false" presupposes this ontology. On the economic level, surplus-value is the standard both of value (itself) and of objects of utility (false). On the semantic level, surplus-enjoyment is the standard both of sense qua sensation (itself) and of sense qua meaning (false). The crucial point that differentiates Spinoza from all Platonism is that "truth" and "itself" entail a redoubling, so that three terms are necessarily involved: truth, itself, and the false, or self, itself, and the other. This redoubling is necessary because the attributes of substance, although the same as those of the modes, cannot manifest themselves on the empirical level as modes except by splitting themselves into what appears to be true (multiple being) and what appears to be false (uniform value), whereas, in truth, they are both equally true, since the standard of both is truth (the attributes of substance). It is this ternary conception of truth that differentiates Spinoza and Marx from the entire Platonic problematic which is effectively obsolete in secular truth.

The identity of the attributes in substance (*natura naturans*) and its modes (*natura naturata*) is an inexorable postulate of any Spinozian ontology, as the first part of the *Ethics,* particularly propositions 21–23 make clear. Deleuze stresses this point in the following passage:

> [T]he attributes are strictly the same to the extent that they constitute the essence of substance and to the extent that they are involved in, and contain, the essences of mode. For example, it is in *the same form* that bodies imply extension and that extension is an attribute of divine substance. In this sense, God [i.e., substance] does not possess the perfections implied by the "creatures" [modes] in a form different from that which these perfections have in the creatures themselves: thus Spinoza radically rejects the notions of eminence, equivocity, and

> even analogy (notions according to which God would possess the perfections in another form, a superior form . . .). The Spinozian immanence is therefore no less opposed to emanation than to creation. And *immanence* signifies first of all the *univocity of the attributes*: the same attributes are affirmed of the substance they compose and of the modes they contain. (1988, 52)

At least based on this passage it is hard to see how Badiou arrives at the claim that Deleuze remains within the Platonist tradition because he "upholds the ontological thesis of univocity" of Being only at the cost of "the fictive character of the multiple" (2000, 27–28). Be that as it may, Badiou himself intentionally remains a Platonist by subscribing to Russell's "materialist argument" that "multiple being is anterior to the statements that affect it" (Badiou 2000a, 104). As long as one sustains a hierarchy or priority between (true) being and (fictive) statement, it makes no difference whether the multiple is on the side of being or of the statement. In both cases, as Badiou himself argues, one operates within the logic of Platonism, for which value is inconceivable. One must go beyond Platonism to conceive of Being in such terms that there is no priority between bodies and values (including statements), for they are both the effect (and cause) of the real. Proper materialism, what I would call *metaphysical materialism*, falls into neither the idealist nor the 'materialist' pitfall to mistake either ideas or beings for the real.

To linger further on Badiou and, as Peter Hallward puts it, his "*unusual fidelity to Plato . . . once you have renounced its transcendent aspect*," the question persists: What remains in Plato that would allow for the knowledge of value as empirically introduced infinity? (Badiou 2001, 119). But instead of repeating the point about Platonism's inadequacy to secular reason, it would perhaps be more useful to address the desire underpinning Badiou's exhortation to return to Plato. This desire, as Badiou himself admits, has three objects. First, that Plato shows that philosophy is inseparable from the four realms in which truth, as Badiou argues, can emerge: science, art, politics, and love. Second, that Plato persists on the category of truth, which is indispensable insofar as "philosophy doesn't add up to very much without the category of truth." And, third, that, once Plato is considered as a philosopher "who is interested not at all in the transcendence of the Ideas, but in . . . the question 'what is thinking?,' " then, the Platonic question becomes not only "What is an internal articulation between Ideas?" but also "What is its internal alterity, its impasse?" (2001, 120). The first two objects concern the "antimodern or anticontemporary" "category of truth, which is indeed "suspected, criticized, that is, denied, by most contemporary trends" (120). The third object concerns the "internal alterity" of thought, its failure to be identical with itself, or what since Freud we can call its unconscious. All three objects have been fostered as the treasures animating the desire of all bodies of knowledge on which the present work draws: Spinoza's monism, in which truth triumphantly reigns over itself and its other; Kant's radically anti-skepticist project in which reason nevertheless remains antinomic; Marx's unmitigated pursuit of the "eternal laws of [a] commodity-exchange" that remains throughout paradoxical (1990, 301); Freud's rationalist courage in encountering the unconscious and desire; and last but not least, a figure that haunts Badiou's own work, as both its object of desire and a point of resistance, Lacan with his anti-postmodern persistence on truth and the real in an otherwise thoroughly fragmented subject. Whence then the desire, if not demand, and even need, to return to Plato, as evidenced in Badiou?

While we shall address this question more closely in the second part of the present work, let us raise here the further relevant question: whence this impulse to turn away from Being to the event as the One? In his attempt to articulate an "Ethics of Truths" or of the "event," Badiou is eventually forced to differentiate his position from Heidegger and his *Ereignis* (event), so that Nazism is precluded from constituting an ethical event (2001, 40–41). To do so, Badiou supplements his theory with three conditions required for an event and a process of truth to be ethical, the first being that it must be real, as opposed to a "*simulacrum of truth*" (73). The two oppositional examples through which Badiou establishes this distinction are, not accidentally, Heidegger and Marx. In Badiou's words, what "led Heidegger astray" is the same fallacy that marks "the Nazi seizure of power in 1933," which, "although formally indistinguishable from an event," is "radically incapable of any truth whatsoever," "since it conceives itself as a 'German' revolution," that is, as a "closed particularity of an abstract set [*ensemble*] (the 'Germans' or the 'Arians')," which, as such, is exclusionary. By contrast, the "genuine event . . . relates to the particularity of a situation only from the bias of its void," which does not allow the situation to become a "closed" and "abstract set" (73–74). Given that "the fundamental ontological characteristic of an event is to inscribe, to name, the situated void of that for which it is an event,"

"Marx," unlike Heidegger and Nazism, "is an event for political thought because he designates, under the name 'proletariat,' the central void of early bourgeois societies" (69). In other words, the crux of the distinction lies not in the opposition 'One versus Event,' since, to repeat, both Marx and Nazism (by which, in this context, we are also to understand Heidegger) are "formally indistinguishable from an event." Rather, the distinction concerns the inclusion or not of the "void, the multiple-of-nothing" or "absolute neutrality of being" that "neither excludes nor constrains anyone," so that it does not ever allow the All or the One to form itself as a closed, and hence exclusionary, set (73).

Here it is necessary to address the relation between ethics and ontology. *The structure of that which an ethics defines as ethical is the same as the structure of that which an ontology defines as Being*. Being, that which is in itself and which remains unrealizable as such within the ontic (empirical) world, determines the ethical, that which should be. To repeat Lacan's words, "the status of the unconscious," which is that of Being, insofar as it never manifests itself as such, is "ethical, and not ontic" (1981, 34).

Indeed, in his ontology Badiou concurs with Lacan (and, for that matter, Marx), and counts himself among those who "rule out that Being can be thought as All" (2000, 97). Unlike them, however he thinks that the proper alternative to the categories of the All or the One enabling us to speak of Being is "grace" or the event (97).[21] For Badiou, these two pairs of concepts define all philosophy, insofar as "during this (short) period of our philosophical history, all in all there have only been (there are still only) two serious questions: that of the All (or the One) and that of grace (or the event)" (98). Badiou's postulate, however, that something "formally indistinguishable from an event" turns out to be a simulacrum of truth if it does not prevent the All from forming itself, relegates the whole question of both Being and the ethical from the event and its form to the All and its own form, namely, whether it is an All or a not-All. The strong way of putting it is that in the last analysis, the so-called "event" or "grace" does not pertain to a category epistemologically or ontologically other than that of the All or the One, but is rather its negative supplement, Being's "unnameable Real," to recall Žižek's words cited in the preceding note. Being is not-All, and it leads nowhere to substitute the term for the "event," when one is then forced to add that it must be not-All in order to be distinguished from other occurrences that are otherwise formally indistinguishable from it.

For a proper ontology, as well as a proper ethics, it is however necessary to add to the Lacanian not-All that Being is also a differential substance that itself posits both that which appears to be the universal One and that which appears to be multiple being. Otherwise, the equivocity of these two manifestations of Being is subrepted, typically resulting in the known hierarchical primacy of that which appears to be universal over what appears to be multiple being. At a certain point, Copjec writes that "Lacan hit Kant . . . not [by] deconstruct[ing] or dispers[ing] the universal" but by "rather redefin[ing] it as that which disperses being" (2002, 4–5). This is only partly true, for Lacan redefined the universal (Being) as that which both disperses Being into what appears to be multiple being, and as that which posits what appears to be the universal One. To repeat Lacan's words, "the One is based only on (*tenir de*) the essence of the signifier" (1998, 5). Being manifests itself equally as the universality of the signifier and exchange-value and as the multiplicity of things and use-value. This condition is presupposed for Copjec's own postulate that the being's "various appearances" be "not appearances of one being that acts as their ground" (2002, 127). For in a movement that starts with a universal that disperses Being, the universal remains prior to multiple being, and hence the latter is nothing more than "appearances of one being that acts as their ground."

At any rate, Copjec is right in differentiating Lacan from Kant by pointing out that for Kant, "the sublime ideas of reason posit a superior force or a superior measure from whose heights the subject can look down and find herself inferior, insufficiently strong or great," so that this measure constitutes "the various self-surpassing appearances of the subject . . . as appearances of one being," at the cost of "enslav[ing] the subject to a force or a measure to which she can never quite measure up and to which she is compelled to sacrifice her efforts and pleasure in an attempt to do so." Lacan, by contrast, Copjec continues, "introduces the concept of the 'feminine not-all' " as "the extraction of Kant's . . . absolute measure of the all" (2002, 126).[22] Again Lacan's gesture is fully Marxian, as it is Marx who, in Karatani's words, "by treating capital itself, and therefore money itself, as a commodity . . . identifies a paradox in which a class of the meta-level descends to the object level to occupy the same locus as the members; in other words, to become a member of itself" (1995, 70). To translate this statement back into Copjec's terms, "by removing the exceptional magnitude [capital] . . . from the all," by including what was presumed to be the "unmeasurable measure against which all others are measured" within the set of all other measures (commodities) as a member of the set, Marx revealed that in the universe of capitalism, the contradictory appearances of use- and exchange-value are possible only because Being is the tension between the "in itself" and the "for itself" (and, hence, "for the other"), inherence (sensation) and differentiality (signifier), the two attributes of Being.

In short, the crux of the matter with regard to a properly secular ontology (and consequently ethics) is the not-all character of Being—to which we shall return in the second part of this work—something which is not covered through its replacement by the "event."

But there is also a fourth object in Badiou's desire for a return to Plato, one named in a different context, not accidentally entitled "Philosophy and Desire." There Badiou states that "three principle orientations can be distinguished in philosophy today": "the hermeneutic," "the analytic," and the "postmodern" (2003, 42). The "hermeneutic orientation . . . always consists of the interpretation of speech acts"; the "analytic orientation" endeavors to "discover those rules that ensure an agreement about meaning"; and the "postmodern orientation promotes the idea of a multiplicity of sentences, fragments, and forms of discourse in the absence of homogeneity," its "objective" being "to deconstruct the idea of totality" (46, 43, and 44). It follows that all three current orientations or philosophies of meaning are grounded on "two fundamental axioms": a "negative," that "the metaphysics of truth has become impossible," and a "positive," that "language is the crucial site of thought because that is where the question of meaning is at stake," so that "the question of meaning replaces the classical question of truth" (47).

By negating metaphysics and truth, these three orientations, as Badiou argues, indeed "cannot give philosophy the means to sustain its desire." This Badiou defines "in a quadruple form," as the desire for "revolt"—insofar as "there is no philosophy without the discontent of thinking in its confrontation with the world as it is"—"logic"—insofar as philosophy always believes "in the power of argument and reason"—"universality"—insofar as "philosophy addresses all humans as thinking beings since it supposes that all humans think"—and "risk"—insofar as "thinking is always a decision which supports independent points of view," as opposed to the world of established opinions (2003, 47 and 39–40). Thus, the three philosophies of meaning effectively sustain the "four principle obstacles" "philosophy . . . encounters . . . in the world" against its four desires, namely, "the reign of merchandise, the reign of communication, the need for technical specialization and the necessity for realistic calculations of security," respectively (42).

Thus, as Badiou concludes, "if philosophy is to sustain its desire in such a world, it must propose a principle of interruption . . . not because all this must be interrupted—but because thought at least must be able to extract itself from this circulation" of commodified pragmatist opinions "and take possession of itself once again as something other than an object of circulation" (2003, 49). The sole "unconditional requirement" of this "interruption can only be . . . something which is submitted to thought with no other condition than itself and which is neither exchangeable nor capable of being put into circulation." Such an "unconditional requirement cannot be solely supported by the proposition of the polyvalence of meaning. It also needs the reconstruction or re-emergence of the category of truth" (49).

The author of the present work could not agree any more with Badiou's line of argument so far. But to contribute to such a "reconstruction or re-emergence" of truth, Badiou deems it appropriate to turn to Plato's statement in *Cratylus*: "We philosophers do not take as our point of departure words, but things." Badiou seals his unreserved solidarity with this position by further stating: "Whatever may be the difficulty or obscurity of this statement, I am for philosophy's revivifying the idea that it does not take as its point of departure words, but things" (2003, 50). Now, as is known, the thing taken not as word or representation or, in a more Kantian jargon, not as appearance, is the notorious thing-in-itself, beyond our perception and representation thereof. And even if one reads Kant as a philosopher who still believed in a transcendent objectivity or thingness of the thing beyond appearance, the "Thing-in-itself," as Žižek puts it drawing on Hegel's criticism thereof, "is effectively a pure 'Thing-of-Thought [*Gedankending*],' a pure form of Thought: the transcendence of the Thing-in-itself coincides immediately with pure immanence of Thought" (1989, 172).[23] The "Thing," Žižek continues, "is itself nothing but a lack, an empty place. . . . [B]eyond the phenomenal appearance there is only a certain negative self-relationship because of which the positively given phenomenal world is perceived as 'mere appearance,' " and therefore, as Hegel inferred: "*The supersensible . . . is appearance* qua *appearance*" (Žižek 1989, 193; Hegel 1977, 89).

In other words, Badiou's invocation of the thing as philosophy's point of departure can be understood as either utterly preposterous, according to the traditional reading of Kant with its essentialized thing, or as an assertion of the fact that the object of philosophy is not representation and meaning but the "lack, an empty place . . . beyond the phenomenal appearance," in short, the gaze, insofar as "if beyond appearance there is nothing in itself, there is the gaze" (Lacan 1981, 103). Indeed, the proper object of philosophy is not representation or meaning but the gaze, which is why beyond the three principle orientations in philosophy today mentioned by Badiou, there is also (Lacanian) psychoanalysis. But, in spite of all his references to Lacan's work, Badiou's work, as we shall also see in the second part here, is predicated on precisely the elimination of the function of the gaze. For his part, Badiou means the thing-in-itself in the sense attributed by Žižek to Kant, thereby reminding us of the fifth, equally omitted in Badiou's catalogue, principle orientation in philosophy and generally in contemporary thought: essentialism. Not accidentally, the latter experiences today a fervent revival extending from mainstream discourse to the discourse on DNA, biogenetics, etc. The zeal with which essentialism is welcomed in the postmodern era is, in my opinion, due to the same reasons that explain Badiou's increasing relative popularity. The postmodern soliloquy on the self-referentiality and dispersion of meaning has reached that point at which people are ready to take anything that appears as an access to the real. Which is why today fundamentalism—religious and scientific alike—is the inseparable companion of the general deconstruction of truth and its reduction to speech acts, rules, or culturally conditioned figments. The irony, however, is that the essentialist thing, far from being real, is one of the most deceiving illusions.[24]

Truth is to be found both in what appear to be words and in what appear to be things in themselves, their distinction being itself an effect of the transcendental differential (non-)substance of secular capitalist modernity, which replaced the theocratic Word and its equation with the Thing, up to and including the Thing-in-itself, God. The issue concerning philosophy today is neither overturning nor restoring any Platonist position but understanding that an irrevocable break with (anti-)Platonism has occurred more than three centuries ago, and that Spinoza, Marx, and Lacan offer us some of the clearest articulations of this break through their ternary nomination of Being.

Wherein Consists the Break of Secular Modernity?

Unlike Platonism, upright or overturned, which has no applicability to secular reason whatsoever, Christianity succeeds in approaching somewhat closer the secular capitalist problematic. For, albeit partly a variant of Platonism, Christianity departs from it by introducing the Holy Trinity, which establishes an immanent causality between Father and Son, through the mediation of a third term, the Holy Spirit, of which both are manifestations. Similarly, in Marx, value is the standard both of itself and of use-value, through the mediation of a third term, surplus-value. It is due to this analogy that Marx feels compelled to "take flight into the misty realm of religion" in order to describe the mechanism of the accumulation of surplus-value (1990, 165).

As is known, Hegel saw in Socrates the "*Inventor of Morality*," that is, the historical instance that allowed for the emergence of a subject who is the ultimate judge of himself (Hegel 1956, 269). In Hegel's words, Socrates "posited the Individual as capable of a final moral decision, in contraposition to Country and to Customary Morality," thus introducing "the inner world of Subjectivity" in a "rupture with the existing Reality." For this reason, Socrates amounts for Hegel to the herald of Christianity with its concept of guilt. There are reasons, however, to hesitate before this assertion. Indeed, as Hegel maintains, the "higher principle" of autonomous subjective morality opposed in classical antiquity the "Country" and "Customary Morality" and "proved [to be] the ruin of the Athenian state," whose "peculiarity" consisted in "that Customary Morality was the form in which its existence was moulded," since it presupposed "an inseparable connection of Thought with actual life" (270). Socrates signifies for Hegel such a radical, yet insidious transformation that the "deeply tragical character" of the Athenians' decision to "condemn[]" Socrates "to death" lies in the fact that belatedly "the Athenians had to make the discovery, that what they reprobated in Socrates had already struck firm root among themselves," which is why they eventually "condemned the accusers of Socrates, and declared him guiltless." Thus, Hegel concludes:

> that higher principle which proved the ruin of the Athenian state, advanced in its development without intermission. Spirit had acquired the propensity to gain satisfaction for itself—to reflect. Even in decay the Spirit of Athens appears majestic, because it manifests itself as the free, the liberal. (1956, 270)

But, one could argue, "Morality" connected to "Spirit" or "Thought," in its "rupture" with "existing Reality," far from effecting the "ruin" of Christianity became its very pillar, as many critics of religiosity and of the Christians' internalization of the church's dogmas have recurrently pointed out. Among them, Spinoza deemed religiosity as tantamount to "superstition," which is "engendered, preserved, and fostered" by the fact that people are "kept fluctuating pitiably between hope and fear by the uncertainty of fortune's greedily coveted favours" (1951, 3–4). Are we to agree with this Spinozian view of the disciplining function of the link between morality and thought as a mechanism for the internalization of law and guilt, and hence for social cohesion, or are we to consider, as is inadvertently implicit in Hegel's argument, the entire era of Christian theocracy as a long process in which Christians had sooner or later to make the discovery that what they reprobated (nonbelief) had already struck firm root among themselves, as a result of which the ruin of the theocratic state had eventually to arrive, yielding to secular modernity? Put in other terms, where is the break to be located? Between Socrates and Christianity, whereby Christianity and the secular modernity form a continuity that shares internalized authority and noncoercive coercion as its fundamental disciplining mechanism? Or, considering Socrates and Christianity as a long process toward renewed ruins, are we to locate the break between Christianity and secular modernity, as is indicated by the emergence of various new concepts since the early modernity, ranging from "conscience" and "subjectivity" to "hegemony," "ideology," the link between knowledge and power in the concept of "discourse," and, farther, to the link between the body and power in "biopolitics"? Or, finally, should we consider in this regard all history since Socrates as a continuum with no such break, and patiently await the moment at which secular subjects will make the discovery that what they reprobate has already struck firm root among themselves? The brief version of all these questions is: Is internalized authority exclusively a disciplining mechanism or also necessarily the cause of the very ruin of this authority? It's a tough call, with portentous consequences.

I am of the opinion that there has been a break, and this is to be located at the advent of secular capitalist modernity. For what changed radically at that moment is that the agency whose task it is to "hoodwink the subjects, and to mask the fear . . . so that men may fight as bravely for slavery as for safety," ceases to present itself as the belief in either religion or in the truth of any "tyrant," and starts to present itself as 'objective knowledge' (Spinoza 1951, 5). The peculiarity of the latter consists in presenting itself as being voiced not from a place of enunciation that involves authority and power. The unforeseen consequence thereof is that, whereas individuals in the past did indeed "count it not shame but highest honour to risk their blood and their lives for the vainglory of a tyrant," the secular subject does not perceive itself as ever fighting for any "tyrant," that is, for any authority (5). The crucial shift rendering modernity incommensurable with its own past consists in the emergence of the subject's self-understanding as "free." This consciousness is not unrelated, as we shall see in later chapters, to the concomitant, overarching shift, on which this work focuses, from spirit to value. Preliminarily we could say that, even as Christianity relies on the immanent relation between Father and Son, the nonexistence of value precluded the truth of the sons of the Son from adjoining itself to the truth of the Father, whereas the truth of the secular subject adjoins itself to that of "objective knowledge," just as surplus-value adjoins itself to capital.

The capitalist subjection of economic exchange to value engendered also a major epistemological shift by introducing infinity into the empirical field. Both the circulation of capital and capital itself are structurally infinite. In Marx's words, "the circulation of money as capital is an end in itself, for the valorization of value takes place only within this constantly renewed movement," buying in order to sell, so that the "movement of capital is limitless" (1990, 253). As for value or capital itself, it is "an automatic subject" or "self-moving substance," which is "money which is worth more money, value which is greater than itself," and hence also "limitless" or infinite (255–57). Rather than being any longer transcendent, the category of infinity inheres in secular empirical reality.

This fact eludes the standard versions of idealism and materialism alike, including the Nietzschean line of thought, whether in its deconstructionist or its Foucauldian developments. Foucault's historico-epistemological edifice in *The Order of Things* is predicated on this omission. Having identified the eighteenth century as the culmination of the "Classical paradigm," in which "the negative relation to infinity . . . was posited as anterior to man's empiricity and to the knowledge he may gain of it," Foucault turns to Marx's century:

> The experience taking form at the beginning of the nineteenth century situates the discovery of finitude not within the thought of the infinite, but at the very heart

> of those contents that are given, by a finite act of knowing, as the concrete forms of finite existence. (1970, 316)

The order of things is rather the other way around. Knowledge, in its customary slowness compared to the pace of autonomous economic structures, begins in the nineteenth century to articulate what had already been happening since the advent of secular capitalism in the seventeenth century. Thus, it now discovers both finitude and the infinite "at the very heart of those contents that are given," as the "concrete forms of finite existence," thereby also discovering that "the thought of the infinite" is not transcendent, let alone anterior, to finitude. If with Spinoza "God [i.e., substance] does not possess the perfections implied by the 'creatures' in a form different from that which these perfections have in the creatures themselves," then infinity is a quality that pertains to God only insofar as it pertains to the "creatures," and can therefore be known through the knowledge of empirical life. With the advent of secular capitalism, infinity descends to earth in the form of value. Which is why already Spinoza, and later Kant, as Heidegger rightly argued, can posit infinity only from within finitude; Spinoza from within nature, Kant from within phenomenal experience (see Heidegger).

In this subsumption of infinity within finitude lies, as I show elsewhere, the specific secular–capitalist break, the effects of which we indicate with our reference to biopolitics—an unprecedented, intrinsically modern mechanism. But here we shall remain within the problematic of secular ontology and ethics.

History of Differential (Non-)Substance

When we say that both modes in which the attributes of the differential (non-)substance manifest themselves empirically are equally not inferior to the attributes, then we also mean that the temporality of each mode is equally real. We live as much in the synchronicity of exchange value and the signifier, in which the instant and eternity coincide, as in the diachrony of linear and finite time, in which matter is subject to decay and, eventually, as far as living beings are concerned, to mortality. What does this mean regarding our concept of historical time? How do the two temporalities relate to one another in history?

With regard to value in the semantic field, Saussure pointed out that even though there is nothing positive in any differential system, and everything is constituted purely synchronically, negatively, and differentially, value itself is something that transcends the system's differentiality, arbitrariness, and synchronicity, and produces facts. As Saussure puts it: "the statement that everything in language is negative is true only if the signified and the signifier are considered separately" (120). When, by contrast, "we consider the sign in its totality, we have a "value" that is defined, on the one hand, through the "combination" of two dissimilar, arbitrarily chosen things (signifier and signified) that can be mutually exchanged, and, on the other hand, through being set in an equally arbitrary comparison to similar things (the values of all other signs). Only taken together do this combination and this comparison determine a sign's value, which itself is "positive in its own class," "a positive fact"—in fact, "the sole type of facts that language has" (120–21).

For instance, in French, "*mouton*" signifies "*sheep*," while in English it signifies only a piece of sheep "ready to be served on the table" because there is a second sign, "*sheep*," whose value stands for the living animal. This different value of "*mouton*" in the two languages is a "fact," in the sense that one cannot refer to a living sheep in English arbitrarily using the word "*mouton*" (Saussure 115–16). History may change the value, and hence the use, of the word in either language, which is to say, its value—although its signifier and signified are each purely arbitrarily defined—once it is established, is a "fact" that can change not arbitrarily, but only if at a point in history a new sign is introduced whose value effects the value of "*mouton*." Signifier and signifieds are purely arbitrary effects of synchronic differentiality, but their "combination" or "value" is the effect of both this differentiality and historical factors. This is "how . . . *value* differ[s] from *signification*" (114).

The "linguistic institution" is a purely synchronic system, whose "function" lies in "maintaining the parallelism between the two classes of differences [signifiers and signifieds]" (Saussure, 121). Nevertheless, the same institution produces as its own effect something that transcends itself insofar as it is "a positive fact" that, as such, can be effected only by something transcendent to the arbitrariness of synchronic differentiality, namely: historical contingency. For historical or "diachronic facts" are "particular," they are "events which are not only outside the system [of language] . . . but are isolated and form no system among themselves" (95). Therein lies the difference between the laws that govern the synchronic and the diachronic "facts" of language: "synchronic facts . . . evidence a certain regularity but are in no way imperative; diachronic facts, on the contrary, force themselves upon language but are in no way general" (95). One cannot therefore "speak of laws in linguistics," if by "law" one means "social law," which "has two basic characteristics: it is *imperative* and it is *general*," that is, universal (91). For only the diachronic facts are imperative, and only the synchronic facts are universal. By the same token, one cannot speak of 'synchronic facts' either, for facts are by definition imperative and not universal, in short, diachronic. This is why Saussure later concludes that the only fact in language is value, whose engendering involves, in addition to its synchronic constitution, a diachronic factor (production time) as its cause.

It is wrong, therefore, to infer, as is traditionally the case, that diachrony is the only factor in history. What Saussure argues is (1) that the facts (values) that can undergo change within diachrony are themselves produced out of synchronic differentiality (among signifiers and signifieds). And, more crucially, (2) that both the immutability and the mutability of a language are due to its synchronic, arbitrary character.

In Saussure's words, unlike a "symbol," which "is never wholly arbitrary"—e.g., the "symbol of justice, a pair of scales, could not be replaced by just any other symbol, such as a chariot"—"language is a system of arbitrary signs and lacks the necessary basis"—the rational justification of the combination between signifier and signified marking the symbol, since "there is no reason for preferring *soeur* to *sister, Ochs* to *boeuf*, etc."—which would provide "the solid ground for discussion" about why a sign should change (Saussure, 68). This lack "protects language from any attempt to modify it" and makes it immutable (73). Nevertheless, experience teaches us that diachronically there is a "more or less rapid change of linguistic signs," paradoxically caused by the absence of this same "basis," which also gives no reason for its value not to change either, so that "the two facts are interdependent: the sign is exposed to alteration because it perpetuates itself" (74). The "fact," which transcends the arbitrariness of the universal, is something that can change by a diachronic cause, but the cause of this cause is itself the synchronic, immanent causality of the differential system itself, with its arbitrary character and absence of "necessary ground." Or, in other words, *the sign is subject to diachronic mutations precisely because it is a synchronic, differential, and arbitrary system.*

Similarly, diachronic change is an effect of the signifier's synchronicity. In other words, what we call historical causality presupposes a logical or immanent, not transitive, causality. On a certain level, historical facts are random events that, to repeat Saussure's words, "are isolated and form no system among themselves." But if they can occur it is because historical temporality (and hence causality) is simultaneously a synchronic, differential, and arbitrary system that "lacks the necessary basis" on which to ground the combination between a brute fact and its meaning (signified) and thus to prevent any possible random change that would either attribute a new meaning to extant facts or make extant facts disappear and new ones emerge.

Hence, historical change in differential substance has not been explained prior to having explained the immanent cause presupposed for any transitive fact to occur. This is why the modes (i.e., also the facts) of the substance, as Spinoza argued against the Aristotelian tradition, are not contingent but necessary. This is to say that there is change in time, or as Lacan puts it, "new things do emerge in the symbolic order," not because of any diachronic law, such as the popular "progressivist tendency" of history, but because there is a multiplicity of modes in which the same substance can manifest itself, or, what amounts to the same, because the potentiality of substance is from the outset actual (1991a, 61).

Corollary to the standard unidimensional reduction of history to diachrony is the tendency (increasingly dominant in the parts of the world absorbed by the reproductive sectors of production—information, services, etc.) to reduce history to a pure synchrony in which there is room neither for historical change nor for mortality. This latter reduction underlies the dominant Western postmodern self-perception as the end of history and as a universe immune to death. Both historical change—in fact, the need thereof—and mortality are relegated to the directly productive sectors of production, the parts of the world which Žižek, as we shall see in the next section, refers to as being "excluded" from the universe of "relative prosperity." This widespread self-perception in the postmodern areas of advanced capitalist reproductive sectors of production is facilitated by the specific modality of the labor expended on reproduction, which easily lends itself to the illusion that it is not labor proper—this being clothed in the imagery of the industrial laborer—and, hence, that the participants live exclusively in the time of circulation—the time of selling and buying, i.e., the synchronic time of exchange-value—and not in the time of production—the linear, finite time in which concrete material objects are produced.[25] The latter time has become the exclusive prerogative of the "excluded."

This spatio-cultural, geo-political distribution of the secular-capitalist historical temporality has immense consequences on both biopolitics—a subject that, as mentioned, I address in another book—and on ethics, as we shall presently see.

Ethics of Differential (Non-)Substance

By arguing that the crux of the matter lies not in the distinction between All or event but in that between All and not-All, I do not mean that the "event" or, to refer to Lacan's relevant concept, the "act" are terms that should drop out of our vocabulary.[26] On the contrary, as my introduction here amply testifies, such terms are indispensable in the articulation of any ethics. Rather, I mean that the primary structure is the not-All, which is the matrix of both Being and the ethical act. Antigone's purely differential, non-evaluative language is such a not-All system, in which the prohibition imposed by the formal typing has been raised, so that the system is forced to take into account its own self-referentiality, and hence to become conscious of the arbitrariness of any hitherto established values.[27] The homologue state on the economic level would be a moment at which neither money nor any other commodity could constitute an exception as the means of exchange and measure for the other commodities' value. Both this economic hypothesis and the ethical act present the moment at which that which is the true state of affairs on a transcendental level (would be or) is realized within the empirical level.

Let us now turn to some points of contention within the literature on a possible ethics deriving from psychoanalytic theory. As Žižek writes, of course "an Act is always a specific intervention within a socio-symbolic context," but "this, however, does not mean that it is fully determined by its context." For "an Act retroactively changes the very co-ordinates into which it intervenes," that is, it entails the restructuring of the "socio-symbolic context," and, we could add, it is in fact the subsequent occurrence or not of this restructuring that determines whether or not an "Act" will always already have been an ethical act (2002, 152). Consequently, as Badiou writes, the criteria that allow us to identify whether an act or "event" is "good" or "evil," cannot be defined from the perspective of the "opinions" circulating within the established "socio-symbolic context," but can instead be defined only from the perspective of the "truth-process" of which this act or "event" is constitutive (2001, 60). "Good" and "Evil," far from being categories that pertain to the socio-symbolic context—the "objective" processes that support the function of the human as an "animal" pursuing its "interests"—Badiou continues, "exclusively concern[]" and presuppose "the rare existence of truth-processes," which are "transfixed by an immanent break," an "event" or act," and in which "the human animal finds its principle of survival—its interest—disorganized" (60). We saw in the introduction this structure in Antigone's "break," whose voice is clearly enunciated from a place in which her "interests" and "principles of survival" are thoroughly disorganized, and whose words can be judged only as "evil" from the existing socio-symbolic context or discourse (Creon's city-state) and could be accepted as ethical only after a fundamental restructuring of this context (in this case, the imminent advent of the Athenian democracy). This is why the ethical domain is inseparable from the political. It is no accident that Antigone's act meets Badiou's criterion of an "emancipatory politics," which "always consists in making seem possible precisely that which, from within the situation, is declared to be impossible" (2001, 121).

To address an actual and more recent case, let us turn to the debated events of 9/11 and its aftermath. The attack on 9/11 occurred within the specific "socio-symbolic context" of postmodern, global capitalism, which Žižek aptly describes as being determined by "the fundamental divide . . . between those included into the sphere of (relative) economic prosperity [the Western world] and those excluded from it [what in the old days used to be called the third world]" (2002, 149). Like Marx's "proletariat" of the bourgeois, industrial capitalism, the "excluded" constitute today the void of postmodern, global, informatized capitalism. It follows, therefore, that "the present model of late capitalist prosperity *cannot be universalized*," since, as "George Kennan" put it "with a brutal candour more than half a century ago," "we [in the U.S.A.] have 50 per cent of the world's wealth but only 6.3 per cent of its population," so that "our real job in the coming period . . . is to maintain this position of disparity," and "to do so, we have to dispense with all sentimentality" and to "cease thinking about human rights, the raising of living standards and democratization" (Žižek 2002, 149; citing Kennan [1948], in Pilger, 98). Consequently, Žižek continues, "any reference to universal human rights as an 'unfinished project' to be gradually extended to all people is here a vain ideological chimera—and, faced with this prospect, do we, in the West, have any right to condemn the excluded when they use any means, inclusive of terror, to fight their exclusion?" (150). *A fortiori*, "terror" might be the sole means left by the current "socio-symbolic context" to the "excluded" for them to name themselves as the void presupposed for "the sphere of (relative) economic prosperity."

Unlike the act of 9/11, which named or inscribed the "central void" of global capitalism, the American patriotic reactions to it presuppose "the closed particularity of an abstract set"—for which there is a rich array of names, ranging from a "We (in the U.S.A)" to "democracy"—formed by the said "divide." The "means" with which the excluded "fight their exclusion," as Žižek argues, "cannot be contained within the limits of democracy (conceived as a positive system of legitimizing power through free elections)," since this same "democracy" is predicated on the aforementioned "divide," across which these "means" can only appear as 'incomprehensible Evil' (2002, 153). Only from a radically different "socio-symbolic context" could the "means" of the 9/11 act be comprehended, which is why, as Žižek rightly puts it, "[t]he Act occurs in an emergency when one has to take the risk and act without any legitimization, engaging oneself into a kind of Pascalean wager that the Act itself will create the conditions of its retroactive 'democratic' legitimization" (153).

If, however, the event of 9/11 is prevented from "creat[ing] the conditions of its retroactive 'democratic' legitimization," it is not because the given so-called democracy does not see or hear the void—9/11 was one of the loudest ways one has ever attempted to name the current void. Nor is it because it does not want to include it within itself—we do not speak for nothing of *global* capitalism. Rather, it is because it *already* includes it *as the inferior side of the divide*—in the same sense that Plato included the simulacrum in the Idea, as its inferior side. The fact that the hierarchy between the two sides, the set of "relative prosperity" and its "void," remains intact for this "democracy" is what preempts the naming of the "void" from laying the ground for an ethical act.

Herein lies the ethical, and hence political importance of the ontology presented here. The hierarchy marking the sides of any divide can be challenged only through the recognition that *either side is the empirical manifestation of a third function* that requires both sides equally for its manifestation—in this case, global capitalism.

As the process of production is increasingly exported to the "excluded," the included are increasingly absorbed by the reproductive sectors of economy (e.g., services, education, information), whereby their relation to the products of the "excluded" becomes exclusively that of exchanging them and consuming them. The process of direct production, which is increasingly alien to the included, takes place in a temporality radically other than that of the circulation of exchange-values. For while in production, an object is not a differential value, but a physical thing with inherent qualities (specific materials, shape, etc.), which in turn requires a specialized kind of labor for its production. Nothing is arbitrarily exchangeable or substitutionable within the process of production. Far from being a value or symbol, which is by definition immortal, not subject to physical decay, both the material of the objects and the laborers who produce them wear out and eventually perish. While the included who labor on material that is reminiscent more of exchange-value (information, language, image, etc.) rather than physical objects of utility, perceive time as a synchronic infinity in which they are immortal, the excluded are left alone to deal with diachronic finite time and mortality. The world of global capitalism consists of two universes that, more than being simply the one of non-prosperity and the other of "relative prosperity," are the one of multiple (mortal) beings and the other of the univocity of the (immortal) simulacrum—with the latter claiming for itself the position of superiority. Only this recognition on the side of "democracy" could bestow on the event of 9/11 and its act of naming this "democracy's" void their potentially ethical character. This is why, as Žižek argues, an effective "resistance to American imperialism" can come not from the "Third World" but from the West itself, from "a unified Europe"—and, why not, from North America itself—as "a counterweight to Americanized globalism" (2002, 145).

However, there is a leap in Žižek's argument that because "democracy itself cannot provide [the] guarantee" that "the absolute (self-referential) act" would not deteriorate into "terrifying excesses" that, therefore, "*there is no guarantee* against the possibility of the excess" and that "the radical risk *has* to be assumed, it is part of the very field of the political" (Žižek 2002, 152–54). As the analysis of the ethical act throughout the present work shows us, on the contrary, whatever other risks it may involve, it is not true that it "always involves a radical risk, what Derrida, following Kierkegaard, called the *madness* of a decision," if "decision" is meant in the Carl-Schmittian decisionistic sense, which indeed includes the risk of terror (152; see Derrida 1995; for Schmitt's analysis of political decisionism, see Schmitt). As the comparison between Nazism and Marx's naming of the proletariat, as an All and a non-All structure, respectively, showed us, the act is not to be relegated to the "*madness* of a decision" since there are formal criteria distinguishing it from the madness of terror. Even if you begin with Marx but decide to make something like the dictatorship of the proletariat, for which all bourgeois tradition is the enemy, you form an exclusory All and—not accidentally, but by structural necessity—end up with Stalinist terror.

Beyond the not-All character of the ethical act, the next fundamental question regarding ethics concerns the epistemological status of the categories "good" and "evil." In the aftermath of the Enlightenment, the dominant assumption is that subjects act in certain ways and subject themselves to a certain political power because, having left behind them all superstitious, supernatural, and theological fictions and having received the light of reason, they are capable of assessing what is truly good for them. This assumption ignores the fact that one's good is not something that is transparent or innocently determined. My actions and the form of political power to which I am willing to subject myself arbitrarily pose their first and final cause, for which, and from the perspective of which alone, these actions and power appear to be good. I can rationally know what is good only insofar as I irrationally believe in a specific end toward which my whole existence—and, depending on the case, the existence of the whole world—is oriented. The good and the gaze under which it appears to be good, too, posit one another in the mode of immanent causality.

To be sure, there would be no gaze that sees my good as good if it were not "a gaze imagined by me in the field of the Other." But as soon as it is imagined, it functions as if it were an external gaze, giving material consistency to the Other, which otherwise does not exist. The Other emerges as a reality with a set of values only under the precondition that I imagine a second degree Other, a gaze, which makes out of the Other a consistent whole or All. True, "there is no Other of the Other," but this is all the more why I must imagine it in the field of the Other in order to be able to say: 'this is my good' (Lacan 1998, 81). The ethical act is alien to a society's distinction between good and evil because it embodies the recognition that there is no Other of the Other. The sole good that the ethical act can acknowledge is its own mandate to name the void of the situation.

To establish a new system of values differentiating good from evil, the recognition that there is no Other of the Other must (once again) be effaced. The relation between the ethical dimension of the subject and its dimension as a judge of good and evil is analogous to that "between [the] two points, the initial and the terminal" in the "*pulsative* function" marking the unconscious. "Everything that, for a moment, appears in its slit" (in the present case, the fact that there is no gaze in the Other and that, consequently, the meaning of everything the Other says to the subject is inconsistent) "seems to be destined, by a sort of pre-emption, to close up again upon itself," "because the second stage, which is one of closing up, gives this apprehension a vanishing aspect" and subjects the apprehended to "an 'absorption' fraught with false trails," which allows the imaginary to attribute a gaze to the Other (Lacan 1981, 43, and 31–32).

In other words, the category of good does not pertain to ethics but to established values, whether they are social norms or those of an individual conscience. To put it in the terms of transcendental analysis, good and evil are not transcendent categories; rather, they are the empirical manifestations of another transcendence, the gaze. Reconfiguring Badiou's aforecited thesis, "Good" and "Evil" are the empirical effects and manifestations, on the plane of socio-symbolic contexts, of "an immanent break" between socio-symbolic contexts—even as Badiou would not want to see his "immanent break" be associated with the Lacanian gaze. Paraphrasing Spinoza, we could say that the gaze is the standard of both good and evil. The gaze is the proper level of the ethical insofar as it is the precondition of good and evil.

From Libido to Enjoyment

The central role of immanent causality in secular knowledge makes us not only empathize with Karl Kraus's (1874–1936) indignation but also wonder why he targeted it solely against psychoanalysis' introduction of the libido. His criticism applies equally to all possible cognition of any differential substance, since in any such cognition "it would be wasted effort to try and prove that libido isn't involved."

For "libido" is an economic category, a purely "quantitative magnitude" or value that can increase or decrease, and—like Marx's "self-valorizing" capital, which is always "greater than itself"—is not even "actually measurable," while it can be displaced or "diverted from [its] aim" or specific investment, in order to "force [its] way towards" another aim or investment (Freud 1959, 22; 1999,

XIII, 98; Marx 1990, 255 and 257). In all this, libido's primary raison d'être is to safeguard that all "individuals" belonging to a "group" are "in harmony" or agreement ("*Einvernehmen*") with all other individuals of the group, and, *a fortiori*, that "everyone is equal" with anyone else so that, from an economic point of view, they, like commodities, are all exchangeable (Freud 1959, 24 and 26; 1999, XIII, 100 and 102). Libido is to subjects what value is to commodities. Moreover, since "all values," to recall Saussure, are "governed by the same paradoxical principle" that links each value to both a "*dissimilar*" and a "*similar*" thing, "each individual is bound by libidinal ties on the one hand to the leader," just as each commodity is bound to capital, "and on the other hand to the other members of the group," just as each commodity is bound to the other commodities, in comparison to whose values its value is determined (Freud 1959, 27; 1999, XIII, 104; see Marx 1990, 125–63).[28]

Unbeknownst to him—though, I would venture to guess, most likely he would have nothing against it, if he had recognized it—Kraus's target is any differential system, including, not least, capitalist economy. His method, however, is ineffective, for no critique of capitalist economy is possible without having understood its logic, which involves immanent causality, the very causality that for Kraus is straight-out illegitimate.

To give credit where it is due, however, Kraus is, nevertheless, correct in objecting to "the book-keepers of compulsive actions" and their debates as to whether "Goethe's sorcerer's apprentice" sublimates "masturbation or bed wetting," for such debates certainly misconstrue the nature of libido. In spite of libido's remarkable mobility and transformability, it, as Freud puts it, "always preserv[es] enough of [its] original nature to keep [its] identity recognizable," whether it manifests itself as the "the longing for proximity" (and, ultimately, as sexual drive) or as "self-sacrifice" (and, hence, as death drive) (Freud 1959, 22–23; 1999, XIII, 98). In both cases, the "identity" of the libido lies in providing the preconditions because of which a society (the Other) can sustain itself, or, in Freud's words, it lies in being a "power" because of which "a group is . . . held together" (1959, 24; 1999, XIII, 100). And although Freud unambivalently equates this "power" with "Eros, which holds together everything in the world," a year earlier, in *Beyond the Pleasure Principle* (1920), he had stated equally unequivocally that, from an " 'economic' point of view," beyond sex and the "pleasure principle" we must presuppose "die Existenz von Todestrieben [the existence of death drives]" (Freud 1959, 24; 1999, XIII, 100; 1961,

3; 1999, XIII, 60). In Freud, as Deleuze puts it, "beyond Eros we encounter Thanatos" (1994, 114). For, to recall Lacan's words, if the libido can at all have a "rapport à la sexualité [relation to sexuality]" and the so-called sex drive, it is only because "toute pulsion est virtuellement pulsion de mort [every drive is in effect death drive]" (1971, 215; translation mine).[29]

In order to avoid precisely such misunderstandings as committed by the "book-keepers of compulsive actions," Lacan eventually replaced the term *libido* with enjoyment (*jouissance*), stating that "by making his way through a tissue of puns, metaphors, metonymies, Freud evokes a substance, a fluidic myth titrated for what he calls *libido*." But, Lacan continues, "what he is really performing . . . is a translation which reveals that" it is "*jouissance* that Freud implies through the term primary process" (1990, 9).[30] For "la *libido* est . . . organe [the libido is . . . organ]"—in the sense of the organ insofar as it is lacking, that is, it is *objet a* or gaze—and "le sujet parlant a ce privilège de révéler le sens mortifère de cet organe [the speaking subject has the privilege of revealing the mortifying sense of this organ]"—i.e., the fact that its true nature is that of the death drive—because of which the subject becomes "l'objet du désir de l'Autre [the object of the Other's desire]," thereby yielding to the Other the access to enjoyment (Lacan 1971, 215; translation mine). It is no longer the subject, but the Other ('objective knowledge') who enjoys, insofar as the subject's unconditional, self-sacrificial devotion to the Other allows the inconsistent and arbitrary reasons offered by the Other to function as if they were necessary causes (truth).

To repeat Lacan's words, with the advent of secular capitalism, "l'impuissance à faire le joint du plus-de-jouir à la vérité du maître . . . est tout d'un coup vidée [the impotence of adjoining the surplus-enjoyment to the truth of the master . . . is suddenly voided" (Lacan 1991, 207). Once economy becomes capitalist and the sign secular, whether we engage in economic exchanges or speaking, "we are within values." In economy, although value "differentiates itself as original value from itself as surplus-value," surplus-value adjoins itself to capital, so that "both become one, £110" (Marx 1990, 256). Similarly, on the level of the subject, although the Other's enjoyment differentiates itself as enjoyment (i.e., the Other's self-sustenance supported by the [subject's] illusion that it speaks objective truth) from itself as surplus-enjoyment (the subject's fantasy that it is the object of the Other's desire, to which it devotes itself, thereby producing the illusion that sustains the Other), surplus-enjoyment adjoins itself to the truth of the master (Other), so that both become one—an objective cause, and no longer an arbitrary reason.

This mechanism of enjoyment accounts for hegemonic discipline, whose majestic feat consists in being paradoxically experienced as noncoercive.

A History of God in Secular Reason (From Philosophy to Non-Anti-Philosophy)

The present argument, with its focus on the "eternal laws" of capital, does not entail that since the appearance of secular, differential (non-)substance nothing has changed in history, either in thought and consciousness or in economy and politics. Even if we can legitimately call all phases of Western secular economy and politics capitalist and hegemonic, several considerable mutations have occurred as is evident in the fact that we speak of mercantile, industrial, and postindustrial or postmodern informatized global capitalism, as well as of the absolutist state, the democratic state, and the crisis of the state in the age of corporate global capitalism. And in the realm of thought and consciousness, similar changes have occurred, revealing themselves in their most clear and condensed form, as always, in the relation between truth and its first cause or ground.[31]

Only a few years after Spinoza's death, Leibniz (1646–1716) wrote that "ideas are in God from all eternity, and they are in us, too, before we actually think of them," thus implying something that one could already call the unconscious (1996, bk. 3, chap. 4, sec. 17, 301). To be sure, one could argue the same about Plato's Idea. And the following passages from Leibniz recall as much Socrates' maieutic method as Austin's performative function of language: "[W]e are said to have the idea of a thing even if we are not thinking it, provided we can think of it *if the occasion presents itself*," since "it is . . . one thing to retain," and "another to remember, for the things we retain are not always the things we remember, *unless we are reminded of them in some way*" (Leibniz 1965, 7: 263; 1966, 37; emphasis mine).

An irreducible difference, however, remains between the tranquil equanimity with which Leibniz accepts the contingency of thought and the haphazard nature of remembrance *and* the rage experienced by Kraus and the other critics of psychoanalysis in the face of the same fact. This difference is due to the historically disparate conceptions of *God* between the seventeenth and the twentieth centuries—a disparity, crucially, not in the image one has of God per se but in the role that God can legitimately play in grounding truth at a historical moment. Albert Einstein (1879–1955), for instance, was, as is known, far from atheist, but whether he conceived of God in an essentialist, deistic, or any other sense, he never invoked—nor could he invoke, unlike Descartes—God as a proof of the truth of his theory.[32]

If the first (Cartesian) moment in the process of secularization consists, crucially, not in challenging the existence of God, but in the demand to ground this existence through human reason, and the second (Spinozian) moment in the recognition that such a grounding is always arbitrary, then, in the next (Kantian) phase, this Spinozian insight becomes a mantra. For the demand now becomes that reason perform a self-reflexive interrogation of its own transcendental preconditions, thereby leading to the consciousness of its antinomic or paradoxical nature, which, by logical necessity, prevents reason from being capable of proving whether God exists or not.[33] The process of secularization, including the notorious project of the Enlightenment, therefore, far from aiming at the certainty of God's nonexistence, is impelled toward grounding a radical uncertainty as to whether God exists.

Although already implied in Kant's need to differentiate between "pure" and "practical" reason, this profoundly agnostic character of secular thought is expressed at its clearest in the nineteenth-century rigorous distinction—what we could call the Kierkegaardian moment—between knowledge and the paradoxical human revelation or Faith. At that moment, the question of God is relegated to Faith, whereby the secular era becomes for Kierkegaard the one in which Christianity finally realizes itself fully.[34]

However true Kierkegaard's conclusion may be, there nevertheless remains a world of difference between pre-secular Christianity and the epistemological function belief can legitimately have in a society that simultaneously understands itself as secular and as guided by reason. Whereas, in Christianity, only a knowledge derived from belief was legitimate, the gradual separation of knowledge from faith, completed in the nineteenth century, makes it inconceivable—even if people can legitimately still believe in God—that, whenever knowledge regresses into the infinity of transitive causality, it could henceforth legitimately invoke God as its first cause and guarantor. To return to Einstein, that he was a believer, far from grounding the theory of relativity, becomes an oxymoronic anecdote meant to startle and possibly bemuse (a religious scientist!). Or, alternatively—for oxymora, too, are antinomic—Einstein's religiosity becomes an argument that, after all, even if in epistemology there is an abyssal gap between knowledge and belief, a person can nevertheless be both a believer and a scientist, perpetuating the Kantian/Enlightenment division between public and private spheres.[35]

In the aftermath of the sharp severance of knowledge from belief, the first cause grounding a system of knowledge is forced to be split: on the one hand, it is proven to be, by logical necessity, ungroundable by reason itself (Kant), and, on the other, it is always, arbitrarily and tautologically, by equal logical necessity, posed and, hence, immanently presupposed by any system of knowledge (Spinoza).[36] The more permeative the consciousness of the simultaneous logical *impossibility and necessity* of a ground for knowledge becomes, the more intense the denial of this paradox and the louder the reassuring cry that "God" (and, later, both truth and ideology) "is dead" becomes. Postmodernism could be seen as the culminating symptom of this Spinozian-Kantian paradigm.

In other words, whereas God is for Leibniz a concept through which one could still prove the force of reason, by proving His necessary existence, for Kraus's or Wittgenstein's modernism this hope has been irrevocably lost, and God has become nothing more than the frustrating stumbling block of reason, which the latter, nevertheless, cannot dispense with. Hence the stark difference in their reactions to the unconscious.[37]

Freud's break consists in his demand to acknowledge this same paradox—the at once impossible and necessary character of secular reason's ground—as a *legitimate part of reason itself*. This postulate inevitably led him to displace the split character of this ground onto the subject itself ($), which now consists of consciousness and the unconscious.

Like Descartes', Freud's gesture, however, constitutes a break only insofar as it—unlike Descartes' *cogito*, which demanded that reason ground its own ground (God)—recognized that, as far as the question of ground goes, secular reason shares with pre-secular reason the fact that it, too, remains grounded on a ground (the unconscious) that it cannot ground, just as the pre-secular reason did not ground God, since the latter's truth and existence was revelatory—with the crucial difference that the truth of the unconscious is not revelatory. But, as far as Freud is concerned, the psychoanalytic archaeological excavation can unearth the truth of the unconscious that lurks in the depths of the subject's Acheronta. This is to say that Freud challenged the increasing secular severance of knowledge from belief, but, other than this, he remained himself partly trapped within the Platonic paradigm by ascribing to the arbitrary unconscious ground the status of the pre-given, transcendent Idea that awaits somewhere to be recalled. Freud did not fully and systematically acknowledge the performative, immanent, and transferential constitution of knowledge's ground, and hence the radical degree of its arbitrariness. For Freud, immanent causality remained an object of suspicion or doubt, capable both of undermining his theoretical enterprise (and consequently, of inviting justifiable, if not properly argued, criticism) and of propelling the further development of psychoanalysis. Freud's work, *in itself*, is an astonishingly large production of some of the most arbitrary and ungrounded interpretations and self-contradictory hypotheses, marred with more logical leaps and unacknowledged tautological loops than even Descartes' thought.[38]

If the Freudian "unconscious," in spite of its conspicuous logical inconsistency and the circular logic it employs in its attempt to unify knowledge and belief, nevertheless continues to be regarded as a hallmark in the history of thought, this is due to the simultaneous critique and legitimization thereof, produced by Lacan. Unlike Freud, for whom the unconscious was lurking in the depths of the subject, awaiting to be exhumed, Lacan revised the concept as that which does not exist but in its effects. It is the effects that posit, with inexorable inevitability, their own first cause, up to and including Being. Hence, Lacan's conclusion that "God is unconscious" became equally inevitable, insofar as Lacan's God is neither the Platonic nor the theocratic, nor even the Leibnizian, but the Spinozian, the immanent cause of all things (1981, 59). (Which, reading Spinoza against himself also means that *God's will* or end is arbitrarily posited through *fiction*.) This, and not Dostoyevsky's or Nietzsche's "*God is dead*," Lacan argues, is "the true formula of atheism," thereby drawing to its furthest logical consequences secular reason, including both Spinoza's and Freud's thoughts (59).

The "fictitious," being the "structure" of "every truth," is not "that which deceives," but "the symbolic," that is, the world of established opinions (Lacan 1992, 12). The real, by contrast, "is placed" in Bentham's "thought . . . in opposition to the English term 'fictitious,' " as the failure of the fictitious and its opinions, on the level of which alone truth can emerge (12).[39] This level of truth does not exist in Aristotle, as is evident in the fact that "Ethics in

Aristotle is a science of character: the building of character, the dynamics of habits and, even more, action with relation to habits, training, education," in short, a science of sustaining already established "habits" and opinions. "Happiness" is thereby expected from the humans' best possible adjustment to these habits (10).

The break with this tradition, Hegel tells us, had already been introduced by Socrates and his rift between external reality and internal conscience, which Christianity was to perpetuate. In truth, however, neither Socrates nor Christianity broke with the fundamental tenet of the Aristotelian tradition, throughout which the "good" is defined as a "pleasure . . . [that] is to be found on the side of the fictitious"—understood as the symblic order and its norms, rather than its failure—and hence, as "a certain tempering, a lowering of tone, of what is properly speaking the energy of pleasure" (Lacan 1992, 12–13). From the Aristotelian to the Christian ethics, the good remains predicated on the homeostatic principle of pleasure and its "tempering" tendency, which allows the human being to fit itself within the mold of habits. This conception of "good" "embodies the idea that pleasure has something irrefutable about it, and that it is situated at the guiding pole of human fulfillment, insofar as, if there is something divine in man, it is in his bond to nature," so that "what is properly speaking human fulfillment" is understood, as "involv[ing] the exclusion of all bestial desires" (13). The "whole large field," Lacan continues, "of what constitutes for us the sphere of sexual desires is simply classed by Aristotle in the realm of monstrous anomalies" (5). This is equally true of Christianity, which also demands the tempering, ideally the elimination, of all "bestial desires."

"Since Aristotle's time" and his tradition, however, Lacan continues, "we have experienced a complete reversal of point of view" due to the secular introduction of value (1992, 13). For the "theory of values . . . allows" us "to say that the value of a thing is its desirability," whereby "the point [becomes] to know if it is worthy of being desired, if it is desirable for one to desire it" (14). At this point, "nature" itself becomes a system of values, so that desire loses its naturalness or bestiality and becomes, as Alexandre Kojève (1902–1968) had pointed out in his reading of Hegel, "always desire in the second degree, desire of desire" (14; see Kojève). The "result is a kind of catalogue that in many ways might be compared to a second-hand clothes store in which one finds piled up . . . different judgments," whose truths or conceptions of good are as exchangeable as all other goods (commodities) (Lacan 1992,

14). The human subject is no exception to this "catalogue" of goods, since it is always a question of being oneself desired. The moment desire becomes the desire to be desired, desire effectively becomes the desire to be a "good"—a commodity. This is why "the economic role of masochism," the specific perversion that allows one to experience one's own pain as an exchangeable "good," becomes central as the background against which a theory of ethics can be formulated (15).

The moment nature becomes a system of values, good and truth can be nothing more within the "fictitious" or the symbolic order than yet another kind of goods or opinions. Truth, in its properly philosophical sense can therefore emerge only from that place "in opposition to the English term 'fictitious,' " the place of the real. This is why, as Lacan puts it, "the ethics of analysis . . . involves effacement, setting aside, withdrawal indeed the absence of . . . the dimension of habits, good and bad habits" (1992, 10).

The reversal of the Aristotelian point of view through the introduction of value means nothing less than the cooptation of what for Hegel still remained the rebellious Socratic-Christian disregard of established norms. For now, the truth or good of the individual conscience or of an alternative, even revolutionary in its intentions, group cannot escape the universal commodification of truths and goods. In the system of value, nothing can escape integration and appropriation as yet another exchangeable value, as the existence of the multicultural vast array of culinary, fashion, lifestyle, religious and other commodities testifies to. Everything always finds its appropriate label and is offered for purchase, from sectarian to gender identities. The Aristotelian and Hegelian traditions gradually yielded to the Nietzschean and, farther, the deconstructionist tradition, with cultural relativism, identitarian politics, and all the new movements in its aftermath, that enthusiastically rallied to the support of this development. The notorious end of philosophy, assured to have been completed somewhere between Nietzsche and Heidegger, simply designates a shift within the philosophical tradition towards a catholic commodification of truth. Today we evidence not the end of philosophy but a new, yet by now well-established, tradition of philosophy proper to the commodifying tendency of value.

The break with the entire philosophical tradition therefore can emerge only out of this Spinozian-Marxian ontology, for which exchange-value is only the one mode of the attributes of substance. Everything is commodifiable and exchangeable only insofar as everything is a non-substitutionable singularity. And both aspects are what *appears* to be real and what *appears* to be really real, respectively, under the gaze that makes them appear so, and which *is* the sole real. Beyond the "fictitious" symbolic order, whose opinions only appear to be true, and those truths that appear to a particular conscience to be really true, there is a Truth of which both are its modes and are, therefore, necessarily determined by It to be as they are.

In the era of value, a properly philosophical truth—as opposed to its relativist conception as one among other "goods"—can be articulated only on a level beyond the opposition between truth and false. This level is designated by the Lacanian gaze.

Lacan announces neither an inversion nor the obsoleteness of philosophy, but a new object of study in the place of philosophy's traditional object, truth—be it understood as either the opposite of the false or as yet another "good." This new object is neither non-truth nor against truth (anti-truth), nor even directly truth, but the truth presupposed for all of the above. By this token, if Spinoza designates the commencement of properly secular philosophy, Lacan designates the commencement of something that cannot be called simply the "end of philosophy" or "anti-philosophy," even if the latter is the term Lacan used in order to describe his work. To name Lacan's 'philosophical' attitude, we would rather have to take recourse to the Greimasian logic and produce the term: non-anti-philosophy.[40] For the Lacanian gaze entails not that truth is the opposite of the false nor that there is no one, universal, truth, but that truth is what makes both theses appear true, whichever of the two might be the one that appears truly true.

God in (or out of?) Cultural Studies

Another aspect in Descartes' work traditionally understood as constituting a break or innovation, and fervently emulated by subsequent philosophers, concerns his primary methodological step of excluding or bracketing everyday life and experience as a means of freeing himself from all tradition and established opinion, the presumed obstacles in the path to truth. The truth, however, as is known, is that, far from causing a break in tradition, Descartes' exclusion of everyday life destined philosophy to remain hermetically trapped within the spiritualizing and intellectualizing monastic tradition, which, as Michel Foucault (1926–1994), Carlo Ginzburg, and others, have pointed out, had hitherto excluded everyday practices from the field of the representable. While secular philosophy was entering modernity in this anachronistic, monastic mode, new secular institutions and discourses were simultaneously emerging to represent, define, and control philosophy's excrement: everyday life.[41]

Hence the eventual emergence of cultural studies, as a field that finally postulates that all culture (including what in the past was labeled "low" culture), in its relation to both power and subjectivity, become an object of theoretical study. From the outset, the project of cultural studies—welcomed and institutionalized in the U.S.A. more broadly and rapidly than in Europe—is predicated on a syncretic analysis of "high" and "low" culture in their relation to the constitution of subjectivity and power. In practice, however, a concurrent anti-intellectual trend—also marking, at least so far, primarily the U.S.A. rather than Europe—often reduces cultural studies to an inversion of the canon of traditional humanities, making out of it a field that excludes "high" culture, with metaphysics eminently figuring in the list of such outcasts. Thus, cultural studies become literally "anti-philosophy."

The said anti-intellectualism is justified through the assumption that the deconstruction of a fiction—fervently, if not frenetically, performed and reperformed in mass media and academic institutions alike—is the same as the elimination of the function this fiction used to fulfill in the past. However, when a metaphysical fiction has been demolished in the theoretical discourse, this does not mean that it ceases to be operative within the various strata of culture, everyday practice, and being. This anti-intellectualism, both in institutional curricula and in mainstream culture, safeguards for the new generations a theoretical ignorance of the tradition of metaphysical fictions and their functions, so that the latter are unrecognizable by them in everyday culture and practices. The current development of cultural studies effectively preempts its revolutionary analytical potential opened up by its own innovation. The more obsolete a metaphysical fiction is declared, the more unknown it remains, and the more insidious its function in our culture becomes, since the repression or exclusion of metaphysics from the representable—mistaken as the "end of philosophy"—gives it free rein to operate undercover, as "low" culture once used to do.[42]

If the first cause and the *telos* of both the world and the knowledge thereof, and hence the truths of metaphysics, are all sheer fictions, arbitrarily posed, then their sole function lies indeed in sustaining (or undermining) any given power. But, far from making them any less effective or obsolete, this insight only points to the indispensable function of fictions in determining both individual and collective practices, as well as in sustaining secular power and political authority, whether or not the individuals in question have ever heard of the names of the metaphysical, theological, and other concepts involved.

If "God is dead" entails that "God is unconscious," then "metaphysics is dead" must also entail that "metaphysics is unconscious."

There is no point in repeating here what the rest of the present work argues regarding the above insight. This short section was simply meant as an explicit exhortation to cultural studies to reconsider its mission and course of action.

The Break of Extimacy

Let us recapitulate the present brief intellectual history of secular capitalist modernity in terms of fiction and its epistemological function. The Cartesian moment demands that reason grounds the existence of God and thus establishes secular reason as one that, unlike theocracy, incorporates the hitherto exterior (revelatory) first cause of knowledge within itself. Insofar as it is enabled by Descartes' logical leap, the ground in question is fictitious and, hence, according to the traditional understanding of truth, external to reason. But this fact remains at this moment unacknowledged. Next comes Spinoza who recognizes reason's first cause (God's existence) as a fictitious, tautological effect of reason itself, thereby abolishing exteriority altogether. The fictitious is necessarily part of reason, just as the false is part of truth. With Kant (and Kierkegaard), who separates pure reason or knowledge from both the thing-in-itself and practical reason (or belief), we arrive at the moment at which the exteriority of fiction is posited in a radical way, insofar as it is now deemed to be irrelevant to the interiority of reason. In the meantime, Hegel challenges the distinction both by explicitly reducing the thing-in-itself to pure thought and by conceiving of substance and/or subject as (tautologically) self-positing, thus performing in this regard a kind of an at least partial return to Spinoza (albeit within the frame of his otherwise anti–Spinozian theoretical edifice). Subsequently Marx posits "capital" as the sole "self-moving substance" and "subject," which, "constantly assuming the form in turn of money and commodities," is a "self-valorizing value" that is "the starting-point and the conclusion of every valorization process," "an end in itself" (1990, 255–56 and 253). With Marx, nothing in the world is external to value, since both money and all things and people (commodities) are nothing more or less than the fictitious manifestations or modes of existence of the truth, which is surplus-value.

In this alternation between monism and dualism, Freud's break consists in demanding the acknowledgment of reason's fictitious exteriority (unconscious), the cause and effect of interiority (reason or consciousness), as a factor of interiority itself, in the opposite direction than that of Descartes. That is, not as that which interiority should ground but as that which grounds interiority itself, albeit only illogically or arbitrarily. While Descartes had inverted the theocratic direction of the causal relation between revelation and reason, Freud now inverts Descartes' direction of causality between exteriority (fiction) and interiority (reason). Thus, Freud establishes secular reason as a reason that is simultaneously secular and marked by the pre-secular/pre-Cartesian demand that the first (fictitious) cause (God or the unconscious) be that which grounds reason and not that which reason must ground.

Lacan's moment is a second and more catholic return to Spinoza via Freud. Lacan relates consciousness (internal) and the unconscious (external) in terms of properly immanent causality. Thereby, he denies any causal priority to either, as becomes evident in his aforementioned understanding of the relation between repression (a function of consciousness) and symptom (a function of the unconscious) not as two moments distinct in diachronic time, but as two simultaneous operations that are the two sides of the same process (see the section "Causes or Reasons?"). Crucially, however, Lacan goes beyond Spinoza's intentions, for whom the fictitious final cause, his monism notwithstanding, remained something of which reason had to free itself. By correlating this Spinozian to the further Spinozian thesis that "truth is the standard of both of itself and of the false," and drawing on Bentham and others, Lacan conceived of a third function—the real—as something that is *extimate*, that is, transcending the opposition between interiority and exteriority.[43] In fact, it is that which in the first place institutes the distinction between interiority and exteriority, while itself being their effect.

Thus, whereas for Freud the unconscious evokes the underworldly images of an "*Acheronta*," for Lacan "*the unconscious is the discourse of the Other*," in the plain light of the surface (1981, 131). This discourse is enunciated in objective *external* reality, and yet, its place of enunciation is paradoxically also *in* the subject, insofar as it is the latter that substantiates it and gives it its meaning by imagining the gaze from which it speaks.

(Burning with) Enjoyment

Equally extimate is another key concept in Lacanian psychoanalytic theory, enjoyment (*jouissance*), the heir to Freud's libido.[44] "Enjoyment" designates the relation between the subject and the Law or Power. But, crucially, "Law" and "Power" refer here not to any empirically given, sociopolitical laws and forms of power, but to the absolute Law and Power—the gaze—tautologically posed through the very movement of immanent causality, executed by interiority and exteriority, consciousness and the unconscious, or the subject and the discourse of the (social) Other. In other words, the Law and Power in question are also extimate, as well as metaphysical, rather than empirical, categories. And yet, enjoyment, far from being a nonsocial or apolitical function, is the stylobate of Western secular societies and politics.

Since Žižek's work has largely focused on the political function of enjoyment, I will begin the following exposition of enjoyment with a passage from *The Sublime Object of Ideology* (1989). An advantage of this passage lies in foregrounding the Kantian sublime as one of the major sources—along with Hegel's "enjoyment [*Genuß*]," as distinct from "desire [*Begierde*]," and Marx's surplus-value—for Lacan's concept of enjoyment.[45]

The "Sublime," Žižek writes, is "opposed" to "Beauty . . . along the axis pleasure-displeasure," insofar as "a view of Beauty offers us pleasure," while, in Kant's words, "the feeling of the Sublime" is "a pleasure" only insofar as "at the same time," it is "a feeling of pain" (1989, 202; Kant 2000, 119). It follows that the sublime "is 'beyond the pleasure principle,' it is a paradoxical pleasure procured by displeasure itself (the exact definition—one of the Lacanian definitions—of enjoyment [*jouissance*])" (202; brackets inserted by Žižek). Moreover, Žižek continues, Lacan defines "the sublime object" as " 'an object raised to the level of the (impossible-real) Thing," the "unattainable Thing-in-itself," which for Kant is inaccessible to our understanding and, hence, to representation (202–203). The Sublime can, therefore, be so far defined as

> the paradox of an object which, in the very field of representation, provides a view, in a negative way, of the dimension of what is unrepresentable. It is a unique point in Kant's system . . . at which the . . . gap between phenomenon and Thing-in-itself is abolished in a negative way, because in it the phenomenon's very inability to

> represent the Thing adequately *is inscribed in the phenomenon itself.* (1989, 203)

To obtain an adequate definition of the Sublime, however, one needs to go beyond the traditional understanding of the Kantian Thing-in-itself, and to enter the realm of Spinoza's pantheism of value, where God or substance (Thing-in-itself) is tautologically self-posited out of value's sheer differentiality. If we follow Žižek and accept that Kant "still presupposes that the Thing-in-itself exists as something positively given beyond the field of representation," then we should also admit that Hegel is here closer to Spinoza than Kant, insofar as he maintains, in Žižek's words,

> that there is *nothing* beyond . . . the field of representation. The experience of radical negativity, of the radical inadequacy of all phenomena to the Idea . . . is already *Idea itself as 'pure,' radical negativity . . . for this Thing-in-itself is nothing but this radical negativity. . . .* In short, we must limit ourselves to what is strictly immanent to this experience [of the Sublime], to pure negativity, to the negative self-relationship of the representation. (1989, 205–206)

The Sublime is the Thing-in-itself or the real, which is nothing other than the "negative self-relationship of representation," the tautological redoubling of representation or the relation of representation to itself (consciousness), the effect of which is the real (unconscious) as *"nothing but this radical negativity."*

And yet, this real, which has negative ontological status, that is, does not exist in itself, does nevertheless exist in its immense effects on the field of positively given experience, including, not least, the fields of ethics and politics. Politics is that field that is always organized, as Lacan says, on the basis of a conception of what is "good" and "how goods are created" and "furnish the material of a distribution" (1992, 228–29). Drawing on both the double meaning of "good" and Kojève's reading of Hegel's dialectic of the master-slave relation, Lacan stresses that "to exercise control over one's goods is to have the right to deprive others of them," and, hence, that the "domain of the good is the domain of power" (229).[46] But whereas for Kojève, just as for Jean-Paul Sartre (and, for that matter, Nietzsche), the whole issue of both politics and ethics is reduced to a struggle for more wealth, that is, for more power over the others, Lacan argues that "in all this wealth finally . . . there is from the beginning something other than use-value" and goods, namely "*jouissance* use," which opposes "utility," one's interest, and the pleasure principle (229).[47] Insofar as the subject, as both Hegel and Lacan argue, is constituted through the other, to say that one's "control over one's goods" is " to deprive others of them," amounts to saying both that "the power to deprive others is a very solid link from which will emerge the other as such" and "defending one's goods [against the other] is one and the same thing as forbidding oneself from enjoying them" (229–30).[48] For this threatening other lurking to take hold of one's goods, the "depriving agent[,] is an imaginary function . . . the little other, one's fellow man, he who is given in the relationship . . . of the mirror stage" (229).

The Lacanian reading of Hegel indicates that in the so-called dialectic of the master-slave relation, the slave, far from being the true free master, is the master of himself, the very agency that forbids himself from enjoying his goods. The real, the Thing-in-itself or enjoyment, is the (negative) relation not only of representation or consciousness to itself but also of the subject to both itself and the others, and hence all the others, namely, the Other.[49]

Having defined enjoyment in the above terms in his seventh seminar (1959–1960), four years later, in his eleventh seminar, Lacan offers the arguably clearest explication of the structure of enjoyment through his analysis of the famous dream, cited by Freud in *The Interpretation of Dreams*, of the father whose son is burning. Here is Freud's account of this dream and its surrounding conditions:

> A father had been watching beside the child's sick-bed for days and nights on end. After the child had died, he went into the next room to lie down, but left the door open so that he could see from his bedroom into the room in which his child's body was laid out, with tall candles standing round it. An old man had been engaged to keep watch over it, and sat beside the body murmuring prayers. After a few hours' sleep, the father had a dream that *his child was standing beside his bed, caught him by the arm and whispered to him reproachfully: "Father, don't you see I'm burning?"* He woke up, noticed a bright glare of light from the next room, hurried into it and found that the old watchman had dropped off to sleep

> and that the wrappings and one of the arms of his beloved child's dead body had been burned by a lighted candle that had fallen on them. (1998, 547–48; 1999, II, 513–14)

Freud's concern in analyzing this dream in 1900 lies in verifying his theory of dreams as wish-fulfilling. More than forty years after Freud's *Beyond the Pleasure Principle* (1920) and the introduction of the death drive, Lacan's concern in his analysis of both the dream and Freud's interpretation thereof lies not in repudiating Freud's theory but in showing, that, *a fortiori*, the wish that the dream fulfills pertains not, as Freud sees it, to the imaginary level ("to show the child as once more alive"), but to the real of the subject (Freud 1998, 548; 1999, II, 514). The wish being fulfilled by the father's dream concerns not the momentary, imaginary revival of the child—"the dream is not a *phantasy* fulfilling a wish"—but the restitution of "the missed reality that *caused* the death of the child" in the first place (Lacan 1981, 58–59; emphasis mine). The real, the missing first and final cause of the child's death, lies on the side of the dream, not of reality, or, as Lacan says: "we cannot conceive the reality principle as having . . . the last word" (1981, 55). The dream "show[s] the child as" both "once more alive" and as once more dying ("*Father, don't you see I'm burning?*"), so that he can give his father an explanation of his death: 'I am dying because I am burning, and the reason why I am burning,' as follows from the fact that he says this "*reproachfully*," 'is precisely that you, father, do not see that I am burning.' The phrase, "*Father, don't you see that I'm burning?*" which, in Lacan's words, "is itself a firebrand," is in all its sweltering reproachfulness more than welcome, for it allows the father to be precisely *reproached* for his son's death, to be found *guilty* for it (59). The son's death becomes through the dream the father's own, meaningful and just, punishment, so that life itself, including death, becomes once again meaningful and just.

The cause of the son's death is for the father "the *tuché* . . . the real as encounter . . . insofar as it is essentially the missed encounter . . . the trauma . . . that which is *unassimilable*" (Lacan 1981, 55). Wittgenstein would say that what Lacan calls "*tuché*" or the "real" is in truth an absent cause, an imaginary reason that has nothing to do with the event of the child's death, and which is deemed as its reason only because of the father's agreement. What he thereby misses is that knowledge of the scientific or physical cause preceding an effect (and this is particularly true when the effect involves loss, as in the case of death) does not suffice to make life appear meaningful. For the "meaning of life," as Kant knew all too well, demands and presupposes a first and a final cause, not just a random cause in a series of causes that would regress to infinity without such a limit. In our everyday life, including our night sleep, we are motivated by the desire for the distinction between "good" and "evil" and the reconfirmation that life is both meaningful, organized by the distinction between "good' and "evil," and just, rewarding the "good" and punishing the "evil"—even if this is possible only at the cost of losing our innocence and being ourselves the "evil-doers."

This "missed reality" or cause is the surplus that the father must add to the set of signifiers describing his reality in order to render it meaningful. Or, to put it differently, the surplus-enjoyment produced by the subject's semantic labor (the "dream work [*Traumarbeit*]") adjoins the signifier to produce a coherent narrative that reconfirms and sustains the mastery of the signifier (Other).[50] What is more, surplus-enjoyment also determines the subject's identity. Precisely because there is no cause prior to the father's/dream's producing one, this cause will determine, in Lacan's words, "the counterpart of what will be, once he is awake, his consciousness"—namely, a specifically guilty consciousness (Lacan 1981, 59). For "*the effects are successful only in the absence of cause*" (128). No cause can be as effective on the subject as a cause that is absent—that is, a cause that the subject itself must labor in order to produce. To borrow another term from economics, one has a personal investment in a cause that is one's own product.

The question about not the mechanical but the first and final cause of an event is essentially a question pertaining to theodicy, the field of metaphysical justice. In the case of the father whose son is burning, the question could go like this: "Yes, but why was it my child, of all children, who had to die?"—regardless of the physical causes of this death. As Spinoza made amply clear, the secular discourse is incapable of providing an answer to this question, which is why it is a discourse that is by structural necessity inconsistent, lacking a gaze that pins down its desires and intentions. In such a state of affairs, only the subject's own surplus-enjoyment can allow, on the one hand, the Other to enjoy (an appearance of) consistency, and on the other, the subject itself to find enjoyment-of-sense (*jouis-sens*) in sensing that life makes sense, even if only at the cost of the subject's own culpability. The father's sacrifice evidences his unconditional devotion to the faith that life is meaningful and just.

If in secular reason God is unconscious rather than simply dead, then theodicy posits itself also on the level of the unconscious. In tangible terms, this means that one does not need to believe in God in order to raise questions concerning theodicy. Consequently, the more rationalistic a discourse is, and the more it demands from its subjects to accept science as the ultimate truth, the more semantic sacrifices the subjects are forced to make in order to find an answer to these, officially illegitimate, questions of metaphysical justice. And the more the subjects are forced to take upon themselves the responsibility for the discourse's inconsistency, the more noncoercively does the discourse sustain itself and its authority.

Surplus-enjoyment transforms contingency (the absence of first or final cause) into necessity, just as surplus-value transforms contingent objects into the necessary prerequisite for the accumulation of capital. The speaking subject relates to the circulation of signifiers in the same way that the laborer relates to the circulation of exchange-value. Capitalism and noncoercive authority go hand in hand.

The necessary nature of this symbiosis is already indicated in Marx, who saw that the "sublime quality" of the object, in Karatani's paraphrase, "exists not in the nature of the object in itself, but in its 'universal exchangeability' " (2003, 212). For it is only through the object's universal exchangeability that the negative self-relationship of representation emerges on the level of economy. Only taken as exchange-value can the object be represented by an amount of money, whereby the negative self-relationship between its representation as a relative exchange-value (the object's value that is to be determined) and as an equivalent exchange-value (money, the value that determines the object's value) emerges. No sooner does this occur than the impression is produced that there must be a thing-in-itself (a physical object of utility or use-value) that representation fails to represent adequately, since it represents only exchange-values. In truth, however, there is no thing-in-itself beyond representation, but, rather, use-value is this negative self-relationship of representation. Which is why, as I have argued extensively, in secular capitalist modernity substance is a differential (non-)substance. Capital entails the transformation of everything into the contrary of what it is in itself. For, as Marx put it, "money is the alienated *ability of mankind*," so that:

> That which I am unable to do as a *man*, and of which therefore all my individual essential powers are incapable, I am able to do by means of *money*. Money thus turns each of these powers into something which in itself it is not—turns it, that is, into its *contrary*. (Marx 1976, 325)[51]

One of the contraries of the human subject, insofar as it is a secular subject, is precisely God. Capital turns the human "individual essential powers" into something that they are not in themselves: their own first and final cause. Which is why only through the logic of immanent causality and transferential knowledge can we understand the mechanisms through which capital and its Other produce a subjectivity that sustains them—a precondition also in order to undermine them.

God, Nobody, or Mr. Nobody?

If, due to the absence of a first cause or ground in the Other, subjectivity and human practices, as well as truth and the authority of the Other, are dependent upon the above mechanism of enjoyment, then, the positivist understanding of the world as a chain of a consistent transitive causality cannot ever approach the real agencies that operate in both the subject and the functioning of society and political power. For what is ultimately at stake in the debate between the two modes of causality and the two kinds of knowledge they ground (positivist and transferential cognition) is nothing less than the question of agency.

Wittgenstein is aware of the stakes in his critique when he articulates the difference between "sciences" and psychoanalysis as analogous to the difference between the statement, "I found nobody in the room," and the statement, "I found Mr. Nobody in the room," respectively (1958, 69). Wittgenstein astutely discerned that a discourse that drew to its ultimate consequences the logic of nonpositivist sciences, such as psychoanalysis, would end up saying, not " 'We do not know who did that,' but 'Mr. Donotknow did that'—so as not to have to say that one does not know something" (Wittgenstein 1976, 402; cited in Bouveresse 1995, 33–34). Indeed, when the father recognizes himself as the cause of his son's death, as essentially the person "who did that," what he effectively does is to accept an explanation that is no less rational than the explanation

" 'Mr. Donotknow did that,' " so as, precisely, "not to have to say that [he does] not know something"—for the "something" in question is nothing less than the missing cause and ground of the Other. And, indeed, psychoanalysis is the pioneer in the realization of this language that follows from drawing to its ultimate consequences the logic of the secular, differential substance that constitutes this Other while also rendering impossible the answer: "It was God's will" (except as yet another mode of enjoyment).

To the surplus-enjoyment and its "Mr. Nobody" applies precisely what Marx said about religion, when he characterized it as "the *opium* of the people." Here is once again this famous passage:

> To call on [people] to give up their illusions about their condition is to *call on them to give up a condition that requires illusions.* The criticism of religion is therefore in *embryo* the *criticism of that vale of tears* of which religion is the halo. (1975, 244)

Objecting to the "enlightened" misunderstanding of Marx's comment, Karatani remarks:

> Marx attempts to say that it is impossible to dissolve any religion unless the "real suffering" upon which every religion is based is dissolved. There is no reason to criticize religion theoretically, because it can only be dissolved practically. . . . [T]o criticize its "illusion" means no more and no less than "to call on [people] to give up a condition that requires illusions." And religion will be upheld so long as this state of affairs endures. (1995, 187–88)

While, however, both Marx and Karatani intend to say that religion cannot be abolished as long as the material conditions of people's life make them suffer, the present line of argument points to the fact that along with the material, the differential, as it were, conditions must also change for "religion" to be abolished. For secular beings suffer on both levels of exchange, the economic and the semantic. "It is impossible to dissolve" the culprit Mr. Nobody and the subject's willingness to identify itself or others with him as the cause of the Other, "unless the 'real suffering' "—caused by the very secular absence of such a cause, "upon which every" surplus-enjoyment or Mr. Nobody "is based"—is "dissolved." While "enlightenment man . . . put in question religion as a fundamental imposture . . . it can be said that throughout the world, and even where the struggle against it may be at its sharpest, religion nowadays enjoys universal respect" (Lacan 1981, 264). It is precisely in this sense that "psycho-analysis," even though "it proceeds from the same status as Science *itself*," may "be reduced to the rank of . . . religion" (265). Psychoanalysis is religion insofar as both can function "as a sacrament," that is, they can "wash away sins," relieve the subject from its identification with Mr. Nobody. Of course, the irreducible difference between psychoanalysis and institutionalized religion is that for the latter Mr. Nobody is sustained as an objectified gaze external to the subject also after the dissolution of the sin. On the other hand, "psycho-analysis is not a religion" but a science insofar as both its specific body of knowledge and generally "the corpus of acquired scientific knowledge . . . is, in the subjective relation, the equivalent of . . . *objet petit a*," that is, the gaze and object-cause of the subject's desire. Psychoanalysis, like any other science, is "engaged in the central lack in which the subject experiences himself as desire . . . in the gap opened up at the centre of the dialectic of the subject and the Other," with the sole, but crucial difference, that—unlike science, which must operate by forgetting, even, when necessary, covering up the fact that it is a gaze—psychoanalysis is oriented toward "the *liquidation* of the transference" with that gaze, which is, in a Moebius-like twist, what makes it a sacrament (265 and 267). In other words, science and religion, too, are not opposites or contraries but supplements. Which is why Spinoza's "scientific" thought inevitably leads to the emergence of psychoanalysis as a religion-science.

The positivist, purely "scientific" critiques of "reasons" are futile, since "there is no reason to criticize" surplus-enjoyment "theoretically, because it can only be dissolved practically." The "scientific" model of "objective knowledge," by repressing the question of the final cause and acting as if it were irrelevant to an "enlightened" subject, far from contributing to the dissolution of the "illusion" of Mr. Nobody, does its best to safeguard that "this state of affairs endures." A society that represents itself as postideological and "scientific" only fosters the myriad Mr. Nobodies with which each of us in our solitude sustains the state of affairs. And, what is perhaps worse, it increasingly pushes people to take recourse to institutionalized religion. Thus, the postmodern paradox of global capital is that the most ardent proponents *and* opponents of the state of affairs both tend to be religious fundamentalists.

Given its centrality, it is to the gaze that the second part of the present work is devoted.

Part II

Kant with Marx

Surplus, Or, Gaze

. . . the absolute totality of all possible experience is itself not experience. Yet it is a necessary problem for reason, the mere representation of which requires concepts quite different from the pure concepts of the understanding, whose use is only immanent, i.e., refers to experience so far as it can be given. Whereas the concepts of reason aim at the completeness, the collective unity, of all possible experience, and thereby go beyond every given experience. Thus they become transcendent.

—Kant, *Prolegomena to Any Future Metaphysics*

The internal opposition between use-value and value, hidden within the commodity, is . . . represented on the surface by an external opposition, i.e., by a relation between two commodities such that the one commodity, *whose own* value is supposed to be expressed, counts directly only as a use-value, whereas the other commodity, *in which* that value is to be expressed, counts directly only as exchange-value. Hence the simple form of value of a commodity is the simple form of appearance of the opposition between use-value and value which is contained within the commodity.

—Marx, *Capital*, Vol. 1

A triumph of the gaze over the eye.

—Lacan, *The Four Fundamental Concepts of Psychoanalysis*

Commodity Fetishism: Toward an Epistemo-/Ontology of Surplus

Its notoriousness notwithstanding, the philosophical (by which I mean, non-anti-philosophical) consequences of Marx's "commodity fetishism" are still to be explicitly drawn, even as they have been lurking implicitly for more than a century now in the work of several thinkers.

Alfred Sohn-Rethel was among the first ones who pointed out that "the formal analysis of the commodity holds the key not only to the critique of political economy, but also to the historical explanation of the abstract conceptual mode of thinking" (33). Paraphrasing this passage, Slavoj Žižek teases out the implications even more emphatically: "[T]he apparatus of categories presupposed . . . by the scientific procedure . . . the network of notions by means of which it seizes nature, is already present in the [objective or external] social effectivity, already at work in the act of commodity exchange" (1989, 17). If, in Sohn-Rethel's words, the "formal analysis of the commodity" and "the abstract conceptual mode of thinking," or, in Žižek's words, "the apparatus of categories presupposed" by thought, that is, the transcendental preconditions of thought (let us refer to them as Thought) and the forms structuring "the act of commodity exchange" are the same, then, the conclusion deriving from commodity fetishism is that the structures of Thought coincide with those of external or objective reality, and hence of being, in its ontic sense (being for itself and for the others). And if the ontic being, with Spinoza, embodies in its modes the attributes of Being in itself (Being in the ontological sense), then the structures of Thought coincide with those of Being.

Marx's commodity fetishism entails that both Thought (and hence epistemology) and Being (ontology) are historical effects (and hence causes). This implication of commodity fetishism is theoretically fully realized in Lacan's conception of the real (Being in itself) as both the cause and the effect of the historically given categories (the imaginary and the symbolic).

Marx also subscribes to the Spinozian monism, according to which everything that exists in empirical reality (values and bodies) embodies the attributes of one and the same transcendent (non-)substance, so that the structures of Thought and Being indeed coincide. In fact, if this were not the case in Marx, he would not have been able to conceive of commodity fetishism. The latter, therefore, is the key to both a secular epistemology and ontology. But to arrive at this Marxian epistemo-/ontology, we have to make a detour through the Kantian antinomies, which, as Joan Copjec has pointed out, constitute the background of Lacan's formulas of sexuation (see Copjec 1994, particularly 201–36).

The Rule of Representation and Sex (From Kant's Rule of Reason to Marx's Rule of Exchange-Value)

The universe, society, or, for that matter, just an individual subject, when taken as an "All" or "totality," become transcendent to experience, Kant argues, and, thus fail to constitute a whole in two regards and in two ways: in the way of the dynamic antinomy, with regard to causality (e.g., the cause of everything in the world); and in the way of the mathematic antinomy, with regard to extension (e.g., the limits of the world).

With regard to causality, reason can prove as true two contradictory statements: the thesis that "causality in accordance with laws of nature is not the only causality . . . it is necessary to assume that there is also . . . freedom"; and the antithesis that "there is no freedom; everything in the world takes place solely in accordance with laws of nature" (1998, 484–85; B472/A444–B473/A445). In truth, however, Kant argues, there is no antinomy here, for "if natural necessity is merely referred to appearances and freedom merely to things in themselves," then, "no contradiction arises if we at the same time assume or admit both kinds of causality . . . to one and the very same thing, but in different relations—on one side as an appearance, on the other as a thing in itself" (1977, 84–85; §53).

Before proceeding to the next antinomy, let us stop here to note that the dynamic antinomy becomes the cornerstone of Kant's political philosophy, grounding "civil society" on "freedom" *and* "obedience," as the double cause or law determining the actions of all enlightened citizens. Unconditional obedience and absolute freedom are addressed to the very same subjects, but in different relations: on one side, as "members of the community," where "argument is certainly not allowed—one must obey"; and, on the other side, "as a member of the whole community or of a society of world citizens," where one "certainly can argue without hurting the affairs for which he is in part responsible as a passive member" (1959, 87). Thus, there is no contradiction in the imperative: "Argue as much as you will, and about what you will, but obey!," or, in Frederics II's more revealing paraphrase: "Let them reason all they want to as long as they obey" (as cited in Foucault 1997, 34).

Qua "world citizen" of the "whole community," the subject is a kind of Being-in-itself whose knowledge remains free from, or transcendent to, the laws of the concrete "community," so that this knowledge is inconsequential for these same laws—as members of the concrete community, subject must obey. "Transcendence" (e.g., "world citizens") in the realm of the dynamic antinomy effectively means an exception *inconsequential* for the concrete totality (e.g., "civil society") established by the antinomy. Enlightenment institutes the right of free thought and expression, as it safeguards that thought and expression have no political consequence.

Since Kant, this is arguably the basic rule of Enlightenment, which means both of democratic societies *and*, as we understand through Žižek's contribution, of Stalinism, insofar as in Stalinism, too, "argument is not allowed—one must obey" within the concrete community, but one can also, qua traitor of the party, have access to the universal and transcendent realm where one can represent oneself as a subject freed from the laws of Stalinism ("I have been acting as a subject corrupted by bourgeois ideology," and so on). I would disagree therefore with Žižek's argument that Nazism and Stalinism were both "alternate modernities." While Nazism can arguably be said to constitute such an "alternate modernity," Stalinism was rather a caricature-like historical staging of the logical premise of canonical Western democracy, drawn to its ultimate conclusion.[1] Or, in terms of Eric Santner's distinction, Stalinism was the "punctual" of the "structural" of Western modern democracy, that is, the moment that exemplified in a condensed form the otherwise dilutedly manifest structure of Western modern democracy.

Returning to the pure form of the dynamic antinomy, its function is to articulate the failure of reason presupposed so that an unconditional law (e.g., "you must obey") imposes itself on a totality that is always heterogeneous, insofar as it presupposes as its exception a transcendent realm (e.g., that of "world citizens") where this law has no validity. We could therefore formulate the dynamic antinomy as follows: "Everything is subject to the law x, under the precondition that there is something that is not subject to this x."

Turning now to the mathematic antinomy, with regard to the world's extension, reason offers two answers: the thesis that "the world has a beginning in time, and is also limited as regards space" and the antithesis that "the world has no beginning, and no limits" (1998, 470–71; B454/A426–B455/A427). Both statements, however, are false, insofar as the categories of time and space pertain only to appearances and not to things in themselves: "[S]pace and time, together with the appearances in them" are "nothing existing in themselves and outside of my representations" (Kant, 1977, 82; §52c). The world can be said to be infinite or finite only qua appearance, *not in itself*. While we think that we are considering the world, in effect we are asking a self-referential epistemological question about the limits of "the series of conditions for given appearances," having as our referent our *knowledge of* the world rather than the world itself (Kant, 1998, 470–71; B454/A426–B455/A427). Hence, "enclosed in boundaries" or "infinite with regard to both time and space" is the series of conditions required for our knowledge of the world, and not the world itself, which cannot form a totality, whether infinite or finite (1977, 82; §52c). Consequently, "I cannot say the world is *infinite* . . . nor . . . that it is *finite*"; instead, "I will be able to say . . . only something about the . . . magnitude (of experience)"—not the magnitude of the world, which may or may not coincide with that of our experience (1998, 526 and 528; A 520/ B 548 and A 523/B 551).

Since the object of the mathematic antinomy turns out to be cognition itself, it forms a homogeneous realm coextensive with spatiotemporality, and with no transcendent exception. Rather than posing transcendence as a distinct and delineated exception, this antinomy raises the unanswerable question whether the world in itself coincides with that of our cognition or whether it also exists outside and independently from our experience thereof, as a Thing-in-itself.

It follows, Kant concludes, that the mathematic antinomy provides us with "a *regulative* principle of reason," as opposed to a "constitutive cosmological principle . . . of the absolute totality of the series of conditions, as given in itself in the object." Consequently, to mistake the magnitude of our experience for that of the world in itself amounts to "the subscription of objective reality to an idea that merely serves as a rule" of reason (Kant, 1998, 520–21; A 509–10/B537–38).

What escapes Kant is the fact that the complete *rule of reason* derives from *both* ways in which reason fails, the dynamic and the mathematic—which, at least initially, entails that *both* antinomies provide us only with a "regulative principle of reason." Both antinomies tell us something about experience and appearances (representation), not about Being in itself, as is evident in the fact that when applied to political philosophy, the dynamic antinomy *arbitrarily* designates a realm of experience (the "scholar" as the freely reasoning subject) as the Being in itself. *Pace* Kant himself, his antinomies of reason effectively articulate the paradox that thought operates within two temporalities—*logical* and *linear* time, or *synchrony* and *diachrony*—depending on whether it examines causes or extension.

As we saw in the section "Science of Differential Substance," when we examine causality we operate within synchronic time, because causality is always immanent, that is, cause and effect are simultaneous. The same is true also of historical causality: the failure of the 1848 peasant German revolution, the late constitution of the German nation state in 1871, the German defeat in World War I—all these events can be said to have contributed to the emergence of the Nazi phenomenon only after the latter has occurred. But the moment they are identified as causes of the said phenomenon, a hypothesis has "*freely*" (i.e., arbitrarily) been presupposed and posed as the *absolute* law determining this causal series of events, namely, that a country's failure to keep up with the modern European development toward what Karatani calls the triad of "capital, state, and nation" (in short, Habermas's "delayed modernization") is doomed to result in a monstrosity of the Nazi type (2003, 203). Only this arbitrary presupposition makes out of these otherwise contingent events a necessary causal link, as is evident in the fact that Nazism can also be reduced to other causes (as in the famous *Dialectic of Enlightenment* by Horkheimer and Adorno). The dynamic antinomy expresses the same paradox as that expressed by the double meaning of the word *arbitrariness*: both necessity and freedom. Logical time always presupposes an absolute *and* free—in one word, ideological—positing of a transcendental presupposition (e.g., "delayed modernization"), without which the law of causality established within phenomena would not apply. This ideological presupposition is what Lacan calls the Master-Signifier.

By contrast, when we examine extension, we operate within linear time and consider everything in its diachronic succession. Thus, when confronted with the question about the limits of the world, since we cannot empirically know them, we are forced to admit the infinite regress in the series of our experience of the world, and to be unable to constitute the totality of the world, since there is no arbitrary presupposition we can pose in this matter. And the complete "rule of reason" consists in reason's quality to perform both operations, the synchronic and the diachronic.

It was structural linguistics that drew attention to this paradox of the "rule of reason." As Copjec puts it, Kant's regulative "rule of reason" is the "rule of language" or of the "signifier," which is a "genuine contradiction," insofar as "it enjoins us not only to believe," in our diachronic mode, "that there will always be another signifier to determine retroactively the meaning of all that have come before"—or, in more explicitly Kantian terms, that there will always be another condition in the regress of the series of conditioned—but "it also requires us to presuppose," in our synchronic mode, " 'all the other signifiers,' the total milieu that is necessary for the meaning of one," as "the simultaneity" or totality of all signifiers or "phenomena" (1994, 205 and 220). In short, *the rule of reason is the postulate of an infinite regress in the diachrony of signifiers antinomically coupled with the demand for the synchronic totality of all signifiers, which, however, cannot be formed but through the arbitrary positing of an exception.*

Seen from this perspective, we could say that when Kant defines the totality of enlightened society as the division between world citizenship and civil citizenship, he is committing what he himself derogatorily calls "transcendental subreption," that is, the projection onto "objective reality" of the "idea" that "serves as a rule" of reason. Transcendental subreption makes out of the "regulative principle of reason" a "constitutive cosmological" or, more precisely in Kant's own case, socio-political "principle." Just as in Marx's commodity fetishism, "it is nothing but the definite social relation between men themselves which assumes here, for them, the fantastic form of a relation between things," in what we could call Kant's *principle* or *category fetishism*, it is nothing but the definite categories of thought themselves that assume here the fantastic form of a relation between the members of society (Marx 1990, 165). And, yet, the irony is that, *pace* Kant who thinks that transcendental subreption is an error, it works, and "enlightened societies" are indeed organized according to the dynamic antinomy, precisely because of commodity fetishism, that is, the fact that Thought and Being share the same structures. There is no projection, but identity between the two structures.

It is no accident that after Kant, and prior to structuralism, it was Marx who identified the same paradox of the rule of reason in capitalist economy. This rule postulates, on the one hand, that "the relative expression of value of the commodity is incomplete, because the series of its representations never comes to an end," regressing to infinity, since there are "innumerable other members of the world of commodities," including ever new ones. But, "on the other hand," Marx's rule of exchange-value also indicates that "the general form of value . . . can only arise as the joint contribution of the whole world of commodities," since "a commodity only acquires a general expression of its value if, at the same time, all other commodities express their values in the same equivalent" (1990, 155–56 and 159). For the totality of the field of exchange-value to form itself, one commodity (money) must form the exception against which the exchange-value of any other commodity can be directly measured, without comparison to all other (indefinitely many) commodities.

The rule of reason or of the signifier and the rule of exchange-value coincide. This rule governing signifier and exchange-value alike consists of both antinomies, the dynamic and the mathematic, or both temporalities, diachrony and synchrony, of which only the latter can account for causality (and hence knowledge).

Now, even though Thought and Being are governed by the same laws, it would be indeed a "transcendental subreption" to claim that the rule of reason or exchange-value is the rule of Being-in-itself, a "cosmological principle" in the strictest possible sense. For it is explicitly a rule only of representation, whether semantic (reason) or economic (exchange-value), that is, a rule that applies only to the one of the two empirical manifestations of Being, the *univocal simulacrum* (exchange-value), and *not* multiple being (use-value). To arrive at a *proper cosmological principle,* we must have available *both the rule of reason and some rule that applies to use-value.* We'll come to this.

The above-described perfect symmetry between Kant and Marx, however, is only ostensible, as it is undermined by one of Marx's ingenious subversions, itself resulting from the fact that Marx does not treat the paradox corresponding to the dynamic antinomy as a "constitutive cosmological principle."

As far as Kant is concerned, representation (the object of the mathematic antinomy) is governed by diachrony and its infinite regress, thus being incapable of forming a totality, and it is only through Being in itself—the Being that (in the realm of the dynamic antinomy) escapes representation and forms its exception—that representation can appear as a synchronic totality (e.g., as the concrete community governed by a set of laws, or, to put it in more directly representational terms drawing on Lacan, as a symbolic order governed by a set of laws imposed by a Master-Signifier). On the other hand, in Marx's scheme, representation remains, as in Kant, nonfunctional as long as the diachrony and its infinite regress are operative—the exchange-value of the commodity cannot be established by comparison to all other (indefinitely many) commodities—but, unlike Kant's scheme, in Marx, as long as the commodity cannot be expressed as an exchange-value and, thus, transform itself into an abstract symbol, it remains trapped within the existential realm of beings or objects of utility (use-value). What is more, like Kant, Marx requires an exclusion for the realm of exchange-value to constitute itself as a totality, yet, what is excluded in Marx is not Being, but one of these commodities taken as *pure* exchange-value, as pure symbol (money).

To bring Kant, Marx, and Lacan together, Marx is the first to grasp that the excluded Master-Signifier, required for representation to constitute a totality, is not Being but *pure* signifier, the *signifier signifying signification* itself.

In Marx there is (we could also say, in Marx, the mathematic antinomy yields) an infinite multiplicity of being (use-value or objects of utility) and (the dynamic antinomy yields) a unity of symbol or signifier (exchange-value), established through the exception of the pure signifier (money or Master-Signifier). By contrast, in Kant, in properly Platonic fashion, there is (or the mathematic antinomy yields) a multiplicity of signifiers (infinite regress in the "series of conditions for given appearances") and (the dynamic antinomy yields) a unity of being (free Being in itself) which functions as the asymptotic real reference of the representational field and, thereby, unifies it as a totality that, however inadequately, always tends to represent it.

Marx's first subversion—for, as we shall see, he performs also a second one—consists in conceiving of being as multiple and of representation as unity. Qua exchange-values (signifiers), all commodities are interchangeable, that is, qualitatively the same, and only as objects of utility (being) do they reveal their qualitative multiplicity.

Before we proceed to Marx's second subversion that concludes his radical break with Platonism (including anti-Platonism), let us include another of Lacan's contributions in this brief intellectual history of the rule of representation. The rule of representation yields in Lacanian theory the formulas of sexuation. Sex qua real (i.e., as distinct from gender or any other representable identity of the subject) is the failure to represent the subject as a totality or unity. The male or dynamic failure consists in forming a totality, but with one exception—the "I" or ego, in control of the subject. The mathematic or female failure consists in not forming a totality, in conceiving of the subject as not-all, multiple, and decentered. If the totalizing function, with regard to sexuality, is the "phallic function [Φ]," then, Lacan says, the male totality or "man as whole acquires his inscription (*prend son inscription*), with the proviso that this function [Φ] is limited due to the existence of an x by which the function $\Phi\chi$ is negated (*niée*)" (1998, 79). To return to Kant's political philosophy, via Copjec, the (male) public sphere of law and obedience forms an all through the "*prohibition*: do not include freedom in your all" (1994, 235). On the other side, Lacan continues, the female sex does "not allow for any universality," it remains "a not-whole, insofar as it has the choice of positing itself in $\Phi\chi$ or of not being there (*de n'en pas être*)" (1998, 80). Whereas the male sex is doomed to be invariably subjected to the phallic function, the female sex can either subject or not subject itself to the phallic function—which is not to say that it can do the one without being always liable to doing the other. This explains the inherent impossibility of answering Freud's notorious question "*Was will das Weib?* [What does woman want?]."

To remark briefly on Žižek's apt characterization of the particularism of postmodern, postcolonial discourse as "abstract nominalism," where, for instance, there is no abstract woman but only particular women inscribed by race, ethnicity, historicity, etc., the logic exhibited in this discourse is a caricature-like (hysteric) historical staging of the logical premises of canonical Western female sexuality, the failure of reason in the mode of the mathematic antinomy, with its infinite regress and its reluctance to form a totality.[2] We can therefore say that postcolonial particularism, far from challenging Western patriarchal totalization, is its female underside and companion. We shall return to this point, because it has great consequences not only for feminism but also ethics.

Sex pertains to the level at which reason or representation fails. As we saw, the cause of reason's failure is its self-referentiality. But nothing on the level of reason's failure, the level of the two antinomies, indicates its self-referentiality. Here reason fails either because it must pose an exception in order to form a totality or because the totality is not formed at all. This is why *we must differentiate strictly between two levels: the level of the failure of reason (whose structure is revealed through Kant's/Marx's antinomies) and the level of the cause of this failure, which is reason's self-referentiality* (whose structure we shall see below). It is only on the level of reason's self-referentiality that the thing-in-itself, Being, is posited. *Sex is neither representable nor Being*. It is a lacuna between representation and Being, to which it points, but with which it must not be collapsed, as is often the case in many contemporary rearticulations of Lacanian theory. To put it in the terms of Miller's distinction mentioned in the first part, sex is R2 and Being is R1.

The failure of representation yields sex, which, in turn, is representation's failure to pass directly through its failure from appearance to Being.

Set Theory and Being (Marx's Materialist Metaphysics)

The direct passage from representation to Being is to be found in Marx's second subversion. The truth underlying and allowing for the antinomy of the rule of representation, and hence for sexuation, is that of *set theory*—a theory that escaped Kant but not Marx.

Examined from the perspective of set theory, the obstacle preventing a set from forming a totality is not the infinite regression in the diachronic series of its elements but the *self-referentiality of its synchronic totality*. In set theory, the set of all sets is defined as not-all (i.e. as not constituting a totality), not because we perpetually encounter yet another set, but because it cannot be decided whether it itself (the set of all sets) is included as a member of itself or not. Foregrounding the centrality of set theory in Marx's analysis of capital, Karatani writes that, just as "Cantor . . . treated infinity as a number," whereby the set of all numbers (infinity) became a member of itself, and hence not-all, Marx, too, I repeat Karatani's words, "by treating capital itself, and therefore money itself, as a commodity . . . identifies a paradox in which a class of the meta-level descends to the object level to occupy the same locus as the members; in other words, to become a member of itself," whereby capitalism becomes a not-all, "deconstructive" system with no "transcendental center" (1995, 69–70). In Marx's words, if "gold confronts the other commodities as money [it is] only because it previously confronted them as a commodity," and nothing could have "won a monopoly" as the "universal equivalent" if it itself, "like all other commodities," had not "also functioned as an equivalent" (1990, 162–63). To ground his point, Marx offers examples of societies in which gold, furs, and other commodities/objects of utility were used as money, but we, in late capitalism, do not need such examples, as we know that even paper money occupies "exclusively the position of the equivalent form" while remaining a commodity sold by credit companies. By contrast, the classical economists whom Marx criticized had conceived of money, in properly "dynamic" fashion, as a "barometer," an exception that is not itself a member of the world of commodities (Karatani 1995, 70).

The paradox of set theory bears a great resemblance with both antinomies, which is why it is often not properly distinguished from them, and, hence, why we must here stress its distinctive character.

As far as the dynamic antinomy is concerned, set theory differs from it insofar as it treats the exception to the set simultaneously as a member of the set. For Kant, the exception (freedom) is inconsequential for the laws governing the citizens of the concrete community ("they must obey"). By contrast, set theory entails that, since the exception is simultaneously a member of the set, the "exception" is in truth extimate and must therefore have consequences on the set. In Lacanese, the not-all of set theory entails that the exceptional Master-Signifier must simultaneously be considered as a member of the representational set it establishes. Once considered thus, *the Master-Signifier becomes the gaze,* that is, the transcendental exception presupposed for the Other to appear as a consistent field of representation, and which, however, does not exist but only insofar as it is "imagined by me [the subject] in the field of the Other" (Lacan 1981, 84). Just as money is both inside and outside the set of all commodities, the gaze is both within the field of appearances (vision or representation) and not in it.

Let us unpack this point further. With the shift from the dynamic antinomy to set theory, we also shift from the Master-Signifier, as the pure signifier, signifying signification itself, to the gaze as the "*objet a*," the "object" or "organ," which is simultaneously a symbol, specifically the "symbol of a lack," for the organ it symbolizes is "separated" from the subject, "it is lacking" (Lacan 1981, 103). In other words, the shift in question is one from pure signification to the *coincidence of signification and object*. Just as money is both pure symbol and a use-value (being), the gaze is both symbol (of lack) and (lacking) object. If the Master-Signifier is "the phallus" (Φ), the gaze is the "symbol . . . of the phallus, not as such, but in so far as it is lacking" (–Φ), insofar as there is no such transcendental "barometer," as money or the gaze, of the Other, but only the arbitrary elevation of an immanent commodity or gaze to that level (103). Extimacy emerges on the level of set theory, not on that of the antinomies. On the level of the real (R1), Thought (signification) and Being (object) coincide. To say, therefore, that *Thought or Being is self-referential is the same as saying that they are extimate in relation to one another.*

Let us exemplify further the difference between the dynamic antinomy and set theory by considering the relation between death drive and pleasure principle in psychoanalysis. As Gilles Deleuze rightly puts it:

> What we call a principle or law is, in the first place, that which governs a particular field; it is in this sense that we speak of an empirical principle or law [such as the pleasure principle]. . . . But there is another and quite distinct question, namely, in virtue of what is a field governed by a principle; there must be . . . a second-order principle, which accounts for the necessary compliance of the field with the empirical principle. It is this second-order principle that we call transcendental. (1994, 112–13)

This "transcendental" principle is the death drive. Therefore, Deleuze concludes, here, Freud "is concerned not with the exceptions to this principle but with its *foundations*" (113). Correct. However, the crucial and undecided point lies in Deleuze's further assertion that the death drive is "something not homogeneous with" the pleasure principle—does this statement entail that the death drive is to be ostracized from the empirical field, just as freedom is from Kant's civil society? (112). While for the dynamic antinomy the death drive is simply not homogeneous with the pleasure principle, in terms of set theory it is both heterogeneous and homogeneous, since it is both an exception to and a member of its field. Here we also see the difference between Lacanian psychoanalysis and ego-psychology, whose reason fails in the mode of the dynamic antinomy.

As for set theory's resemblance to the mathematic antinomy, a proper conceptual distinction between the two kinds of the not-all (infinite regression and set theory) sheds light to a common confusion or, at least, linkage between femininity and the issue of ethics. Copjec herself bears testimony to this tendency, stating that "if it is woman who is privileged in Lacan's analysis this is because" she is the one "who is guardian of the not-all of being" (2002, 7). Woman only *appears* to "remain closer to the truth of being," insofar as this truth is representation's own self-referentiality, but woman sees not *this* not-all but the not-all of the infinite regress—which is why the postcolonial "abstract nominalism," too, is not "closer to the truth of being." The failure of postmodern, postcolonial "abstract nominalism" lies in its assumption that it suffices to point to the illegitimacy of the Master-Signifier in order for it to cease to function. By failing in the mode of the mathematic antinomy, "abstract nominalism" also fails to understand that it is precisely insofar as there is no Being (no positive thing-in-itself hiding behind appearances) that there is Being, that precisely because there is no Being that Being (and the gaze) functions. I would also argue that it is highly contestable that Lacan himself indeed privileges woman, although I would accept that his own work is conducive to the confusion between the two not-alls, as, to my knowledge, he makes no explicit distinction between them. Be this as it may, I maintain that a consistent Lacanian theory entails that, while the not-all of the infinite regress relates to the female sex, it is the not-all of set theory on which a proper theory of ethics should be based.

In the era of secular reason and capitalist economy, the status of Being is that of the unconscious, that is, Being has no ontic existence but only ontological (which is also to say, ethical). From the ontic perspective, Being is (non-)Being, or, by analogy to the unconscious, Un-Being. Something that has only ontological existence, like the unconscious, is a relation or function. *Being is,* specifically, *the function of self-referentiality.* The Spinozian-Marxian path led us to differential (non-)substance; the comparison between Kant and Marx brings us to self-referential (non-)Being—the two terms designate the same thing.

Marx grasped Being in capital's self-referentiality, the gap between capital and itself, namely: in surplus-value. For surplus-value is that which is presupposed for money to become specifically capital, that is, the "value which is greater than itself." To recall Marx's words:

> [T]he money [exchange-value] and the commodity [use-value] function only as different modes of existence of value itself [surplus-value], the money as its general mode of existence, the commodity as its particular or, so to speak, disguised mode. (1990, 255)

Albeit radically different from one another (use-value being, for instance, an apple qua eatable object, i.e., a concrete object of utility; exchange-value being an apple qua the equivalent of, say, $1.00, i.e., an abstract object or symbol), in comparison to surplus-value they nevertheless are of the same ontological status, both belong to the ontic or empirical field of appearances. By contrast, as we have seen, pure value (i.e., surplus-value) is something else entirely, a thing transcendental to experience, which is never given in it as such. Just like the Nothing in psychoanalysis, the Surplus has not an ontic but only a transcendental or ontological existence, and is nevertheless functional within the ontic field; in fact, it is its very precondition (which is why it is called transcendental and not simply transcendent).[3]

If the first step toward a properly materialist ontology lies in taking Kant's concept of the Thing-in-itself, as Žižek suggests, "more *literally* than Kant himself," the second step consists in taking "Hegel's position . . . that there is *nothing* beyond phenomenality" more *literally* than Hegel himself—which is what Marx and Lacan did (1989, 205). Beyond phenomenality, beyond the two modes of existence of value, there is pure value or the gaze, a Nothing that is Surplus.

You might, then, say: Ah, okay, surplus-value may be a transcendental thing that cannot manifest itself empirically as such, but when it does, it does so only as exchange-value, capital. No, as Marx emphasizes, surplus-value has two "different modes of existence," the "general" and the "disguised" or "particular," for it "has its origin both in circulation and outside circulation," that is, both in exchange-value and in use-value (Marx 1990, 268). This is why the endless circulation of capital, represented through the formula M—C—M′ (money exchanged with a commodity which is again exchanged for more money), can simultaneously be represented through the formula C—M—C, the "selling [of a commodity] in order to buy" another commodity that one needs for the satisfaction of some need, so that we could say that M—C—M′ "finds its measure and its goal" as much "in a final purpose which lies outside it, namely consumption [of commodities as use-values], the satisfaction of definite needs," as it does in the "vocation . . . to approach, by quantitative increase, as near as possible to absolute wealth" (Marx 1990, 252). In other words, the process of circulation is simultaneously two processes: "selling in order to buy" (C—M—C), and "buying in order to sell" (M—C—M′) (252). Another way of putting it is to say that if there were no needs because of which one seeks certain commodities in order to satisfy them, nobody would engage in the process of buying in order to sell, or, if capitalism is capable of producing 'imaginary needs,' this is possible only because we are beings that have real needs.

To avoid misunderstandings regarding the accumulation of surplus-value, the latter does not presuppose that labor is necessarily underpaid. Labor is, on the one hand, sold (through the sale of the commodity) as a "definite quantit[y] of *congealed labour-time*," that is, as sheer exchange-value which, as such, is arbitrarily established in its synchronic relation to the exchange-value of all other commodities. On the other hand, labor is purchased from the laborer as a concrete kind of labor (use-value—e.g., the labor of the mason, the weaver, the teacher, and so on) at the price determined as appropriate for this specific kind of labor, according to "historical and moral" conventions, themselves defined by what a society deems to be "the means of subsistence necessary for the maintenance" of this specific kind of laborer (Marx 1990, 130 and 274). In other words, surplus-value presupposes (and entails) that the cost of labor (when bought) is defined according to the laws of diachronic contingent facts (in precisely the Saussurean sense we saw in Part I), while its price (when sold) is determined differentially, in its synchronic relation to the price of all other commodities. In short, surplus-value presupposes and entails—not necessarily low wages, even if this is empirically often the case, but—the rule of representation as the governing law of its ontic manifestations.

Exchange-value and languages represent Being as it *appears*, while use-value and bodies represent Being as it *really* appears. Commodity fetishism, therefore, is about how both Being and Thought are a Nothing that manifests itself as something either qua appearance or qua real appearance, or, conversely, that Being and Thought are the effect of the fact that the empirical world consists of appearances and real appearances, languages and bodies. If one does not add this transcendental or ontological level of Being and Thought as Nothing, one remains constrained within a phenomenological reading of the commodity fetishism.

As we have seen, Badiou argues that the crucial question of ontology is not that about the hierarchy between being and its simulacrum, but whether "the nomination of the univocal [is] itself univocal" (2000, 26). I would like to reexamine his line of argument in the present context. To recapitulate, Badiou argues that "a single name is never sufficient" to name the univocity of Being; instead, "two are required," for "Being needs to be said in a single sense both from the viewpoint of the unity of its power and from the viewpoint of the multiplicity of the divergent simulacra that this power actualizes in itself" (27). In the (anti-)Platonist tradition, multiplicity lies with the "divergent simulacra" that the power itself of Being actualizes, whereas "unity" *is* this "power" actualizing the multiplicity of the simulacra. The simulacra that represent the power of Being are multiple, whereas the power of Being itself is One, and it is the One that determines the multiple. What Marx tells us, by contrast, is that Being is a Nothing, a Zero, which is simultaneously a surplus, and which needs to be said in a single sense both from the viewpoint of the unity of its exchange-value (the One abstract form that renders all beings equivalent) and from the viewpoint of the multiplicity of use-value, the multiple concrete and divergent empirical manifestations of Being. Neither the unity of exchange-value nor the multiplicity of use-value, neither being-for-others nor being-in-itself is the "power" that determines the other, as they are both determined by the power of Being and Thought (Surplus) of which both are the empirical "modes of existence."

Marx makes us realize that the real problem of Platonism, anti-Platonism, and Badiou alike is that, appearances to the contrary, their ontologies are ultimately reducible to bipartite schemes. By contrast, in secular capitalism we have: (1) *being as the imaginary univocity of abstract formalism, the simulacrum of the signifier or of exchange-value*; (2) *the multiplicity of being or use-value*; *and* (3) *the immanently transcendental Being (surplus), which is the gap or void that at once institutes the above duplicity and is the effect thereof.*

Because, with Marx, Being is the effect of the empirical world, itself presupposed for this same empirical world, Marx's ontology, the ontology of surplus, introduces a break through which metaphysics becomes properly materialist, what one can call a *physics of transcendence*. This *materialist metaphysics* obtains the concrete universal, that is, the overlap of the particular and the universal, as is manifest, in economic exchange. Use-value (particular) and exchange-value (universal) overlap as the two modes of existence of the transcendent surplus.

If metaphysics, as Žižek rightly complains, is marred by the inability to make the transition from the epistemological deadlock to the ontological, this is precisely because, even after Marx's analysis of the commodity and his articulation of commodity fetishism, metaphysics remains reluctant to draw the conclusion that Thought and Being share one and the same form. Thus, metaphysics has also always failed to understand that a *formal restructuring in economy* goes hand in hand with a *formal epistemological and ontological restructuring*.

To be sure, at least since the Enlightenment, no political revolution ever omitted reference to a concomitant cultural revolution. But I do not know of any revolution, however Marxist in its conception it may have claimed to be, that ever took into account the surplus—except, of course, for the resolute intention to eliminate it. But you can eliminate surplus-value only if you also eliminate surplus-enjoyment, which also means to substitute hegemony and ideologically based modes of noncoercive coercion for straightforward coercion. (Stalinism was a historically necessary consequence of the bolshevist determination to eliminate the surplus). Given that, as I have shown, capitalism is not an ontological necessity but one of the theoretically infinite manifestations of Being and Thought within the realm of the possible as determined by them, the only other alternative for Marxians, therefore, is to rethink communism as an economic, political, and cultural system that includes the surplus on all levels.

From Absolute Knowledge to the Gaze

Marx's' pantheism subsumes all reality, with no exception, under value, whereby the realm of "social effectivity" structurally overlaps with the realm of signification, both consiting of what appears to be true (exchange-value or signifier) and what appears to be really true (use-value or being). As a result, the production of surplus is the precondition for the production of secular truth, and vice versa. Science too, insofar as it produces some truths, produces and is the product of its own surplus. There is truth only where there is surplus-enjoyment, and hence ideology; so, why would science—a highly ideological field—not produce truths? If one grasps that truth and surplus (ideology) are intrinsically correlative, then one ceases to hope for a cognitive field outside ideology. One introduces a new set of questions altogether, which is why Lacan had to introduce neologisms, such as *objet a*, and to redefine existing words, such as the *gaze*.

We recall from the introduction here that in his critique of "Neo-Spinozism" Žižek writes that the so-called absolute knowledge "is . . . defined by the reduction of deontology to ontology," which is the fundamental practice of all "objective" or "scientific" knowledge (what Lacan calls the "University discourse"; see Lacan 1991) (Žižek 1993, 217). By presupposing that every system of knowledge (science included) is an "ideological field" grounded on a Master-Signifier, Lacan, in opposition to Deleuze, infers that in the face of any knowledge, the subject always encounters the same lack that is "encountered by the subject in the Other," which leaves the subject wondering: *"He is saying this to me, but what does he want?"* (Lacan 1981, 214).

A response to this latter question can emerge only if the subject knows the intention (Master-Signifier) of the Other, and—given that this is impossible, since the totality of the Other is always inconsistent, offering the subject antinomic intentions—the presumed intention can be produced only insofar as the subject can imagine a gaze (surplus) in the Other.

Žižek's criticism of "Neo-Spinozism" equally applies to Alain Badiou, whose attempt to rescue truth, his self-differentiation from Deleuze notwithstanding, falls within the paradigm of "Neo-Spinozism." Badiou's path toward truth endeavors to bypass the ideological nature of representation by means of a recourse to logical formalism and "mathematics," as the direct revelation of the "ontological situation," that is, as a presumably pre- or supra-representational field ("objective" or "Absolute Knowledge") in which universal truths and Being reveal themselves transparently, without any ideological distortion (2003, 170).

Let us begin examining Badiou's attempt to bypass ideology by noting that Badiou, "following Hegel" and his " 'dialectic,' " rightly asserts that "one is to understand that the essence of all difference is the third term that marks the gap between the two others" (2004, 3). It follows that one must object to the maxim of the present relativist "*democratic materialism,*" according to which "*there are only bodies and languages,*" that "*there are only bodies and language, except that there are truths*" (1 and 3). Thus, Badiou rightly places truths in the gap between bodies and languages, thus far having formulated an argument that makes the present argument appear as its repetition. And yet, the two positions differ diametrically, as Badiou's truth is embodied in the unity of the One, the power of Being, which can be positively given—as it does in mathematics—whereas truth, in the present argument, remains a disembodied gaze, since this gaze is a Nothing, which can be filled in only with a gaze imagined by the subject. Another way of stating the difference between Badiou and the present argument is to say that, for the former, truth is to be located on the level of the statement and to be articulated in the mathem (the minimal unity of mathematical formalism, by analogy to the linguistic semem), whereas, for the latter, truth is to be located on the level of the enunciation, and to be articulated through the function of the object (gaze) insofar as it is lacking. Of course, what remains to be defined is the distinction between the statement and the enunciation, to which we shall return below.

In his attempt to go beyond the currently celebrated pluralistic skepticism, Badiou exemplifies the existence of universal truths, in *Logics of Worlds*, through concrete examples in each of his known four functions of humanity, science (mathematics), art, politics, and love. Three of the four examples of universal truths express three, more or less directly recognizable, tautologies.

To begin with Badiou's "mathematical example," there are two kinds of numbers. The first consists of numbers such as "2,3,5" or "17 and 19," which "are prime," that is, "divisible only by [themselves] and by the unit 1." The second consists of numbers such as "4 (divisible by 2), 6 (divisible by 2 and 3), or 18 (divisible by 2, by 3, by 6 and by 9)," which "are not [prime]" (2004, 9). Euclid defined "prime numbers" by saying that they "are in greater quantity than any quantity proposed by prime numbers" (*Elements*, Book 8, prop. 20). A mathematician in the aftermath of Cantor would by contrast say: "There are as many prime numbers as numbers." The discrepancy between the historical truth expressed in Euclid's *Elements* and the historical truth expressed in the post-Cantorian parlance "of the lexicon . . . of the infinite," Badiou continues, "seems to herald a triumph of the relativist, the pragmatist partisan of an irreconcilable multiplicity of cultures" (9–11). Euclid's statement "is formulated in a lexicon entirely other to that of the infinite," so that to speak in the post-Cantorian terms "is for a Greek, even a mathematician, to speak an entirely unintelligible jargon." Nevertheless, Badiou argues, both the Greek and the post-Cantorian statements, although they are historically and culturally differentiated material bodies of writing, are nevertheless linked to a universal "formalism," "an eternal truth." This is "the structure of numbers," which Badiou sees in "that they are composed of prime numbers, which are like the 'atomic'—indecomposable—constituents of numericality" (11–12). We began with two historically removed statements, which, at least in one of their aspects, are nevertheless reducible to one and the same premise, namely, that numbers are above all defined as prime or not. And since this is our initial premise, we inevitably conclude that all numbers—therein consists their "numericality," that which makes them numbers—are composed of prime numbers. Undoubtedly true, since it is tautological. If we had begun with the single premise that the formula of every natural whole number is: 0 (+ 1, multiplied by n), where "n" is any natural whole number, then, regardless of the amount of the statements from which we would have derived our initial premise, we would inevitably conclude that numericality consists in being composed of 1(s). The sole criterion in our choice is whether the selected premise uses terms recognizable by all statements from which we derive it, in the context of Badiou's example, by both Euclid and post-Cantorian mathematicians, as the divisibility of numbers by prime numbers indeed does.

Similarly, to take Badiou's "artistic example," there is no doubt that "in the immense process of pictorial creations, from the hunter," who paints a horse in the "Chauvet cave," to Picasso and "the modern millionaire, it is indeed Horseness which, quite exactly, we see" as the eternal truth of painting horses (2004, 15 and 17). Here are some more transhistorical and transcultural truths: a horse is a horse, a painting is a painting, and art is art.

As far as love is concerned, Badiou defines it as a truth, specifically the truth of sex, for, "far from governing the supposed relation of the sexes, [love] *is what makes the truth of their disconjunction.*" Since "every truth is an infinite, but also generic, fragment of the world in which it emerges," bringing together the infinite and the finite or the universal and the particular, the same must be true also of truth qua love. Sure enough, love, too, "creates trans-temporal and trans-worldly truths, truths that bear on the power of the Two . . . to cut an existence, a body, a banal individuality, directly onto the sky of Ideas" (1996, 12; 2004, 24 and 27). In short, "as Deleuze would have put it," Badiou concludes, "love is this disjunctive conjunction . . . between infinite expansion and anonymous stagnation" (27). If truth is infinite and finite, and love is truth, then, love is also infinite and finite.

There are only bodies and languages, except that there are truths—*except that there is also the question*: Okay, he is saying this (that numericality consists in being composed of prime numbers; a horse is a horse; love is mortal and immortal) to me—*but what does he want?*

I am not convinced that the invocation of analytic judgments can at all help us counter the assaults of democratic materialism and its pragmatist relativism against universal truths.[4] We may all agree that a piece of land is a piece of land, but this agreement is a mute statement in my disagreement with my neighbor as to whom of us two this piece of land belongs. Universal truths matter only insofar as they can be asserted at the point of the *juncture between stated synthetic a priori judgments and enunciated desires.*

Otherwise, the assertion of truths is doomed, like Kant's "world citizens," to remain inconsequential for the field of knowledge and experience. Therein I see the danger in Badiou's sharp severance of the realm of truth from that of "opinions." For Badiou, philosophy pronounces statements only from "the anonymous situation" of "the point of view of truth," whereas "situations from the point of view of knowledge" are the domain of "experiences and the encyclopedia of knowledge," a domain in which philosophy cannot trespass (2003, 171). Yes, but, also according to Badiou's own theory, it nevertheless befalls philosophy to state what in politics, as in any other function of humanity, can constitute a universal truth. This intrinsic intertwining of philosophy and politics, affirmed in Badiou's own work, would however be thoroughly preempted if philosophy told politics: 'Only tautologies are universal truths in politics, the rest is a matter of "a distribution of predicates," which, in turn, is a matter of "experience and the encyclopedia of knowledge" ' (2003, 171). For, if this were the case, then politics would have nowhere else to draw but on this "encyclopedia of knowledge," which presently happens to be predominantly written by the pluralist relativism of democratic materialism.

To be sure, Badiou is not Kant, which above all is to say, his agenda lies far from an attempt to prevent political intervention. Well, that's exactly why Badiou's fourth example, the "political," is not tautological. The truth of politics, far from being something to the effect that 'politics is politics,' consists of four other "truths," which

> articulate four determinations: will (against socio-economic necessity), equality (against the established hierarchies of power or wealth), trust (against anti-popular suspicion or the fear of the masses), authority or terror (against the "natural" free play of competition). (2004, 23)

While I would say that this definition of the universal truth of politics leaves no room for doubt or complaint as far as its character as a synthetic a priori judgment is concerned, Badiou, ironically, means it as an a priori analytic judgment, where all the predicates of the above definition of politics are included in the concept "politics." These four truths, Badiou argues, are the "common" transhistorical and transcultural truths shared by a variety of political phenomena as far apart as "the Chinese empire experimenting with its centralization," in ca. "80 BC," "the post-war Stalin, and the Mao of the 'Great Leap Forward,' and then the red guards and the Great Proletariat Cultural Revolution" (2004, 19).

All these cases reveal one common element: "a kind of matrix of State politics that is clearly invariant, a transversal public truth that can be designated as follows: a really political administration of the State submits all economic laws to voluntary representations"—hence, the first truth: will—"fights for equality and combines, in the direction of the people, trust and terror"—hence the other three truths (19). The obvious objection, because of which it becomes immediately transparent that the said truths do *not* derive analytically from the concepts either of "politics" or of the "State," is that if "State" comes to be defined this way it is only because Badiou's historical examples, however, apart from one another, share the same ideology, which Badiou describes as "the will to abolish 'the old rules and the old systems,' " without which "the passage to communism is illusory" (20). Conversely put, the politics of democratic materialism, for instance, does not share this "generic kernel of political truth" as an element common between itself and the other examples. Nevertheless, this does not prevent democratic materialism from being one of the most evasive and permeative forms of politics ever known, expanding itself, as Badiou admits, to "biopolitics," even if it opts to hide it under "the scientific name" of its "progressive reverse": "bioethics" (2).

Badiou is not unaware of the partiality marking his choice of examples and, hence, his definition of political universal truths. Early in his book, Badiou asks: "What name can we give to the theoretical ideal under whose aegis this examination [of democratic materialism] is carried out?" (2004, 2). Having argued that the "nostalgias" and "delectable bitterness" of an "aristocratic idealism," as is known from "Nietzsche" to "Heidegger" and from the "surrealists" to "Guy Debord and his nihilist heirs," will not do the job, on the ground of the fact that "there is no philosophy of defeat," Badiou responds to his own question: "Philosophy in its very essence, elaborates the means of saying 'Yes!' to the previously unknown thoughts that hesitate to become the truths that they are" (3). Not accidentally, this statement is a paraphrase of Mao Tse-tung's assertion, cited few pages later: "We will come to know everything that we did not know before" (7). Now, neither is Badiou's affinity with Maoism a secret nor do I have a principled objection to the fact that he carries out his examination of democratic materialism and of politics "under the aegis" of the Maoist "theoretical ideal." My point is that his universal truths of politics can be derived *analytically* from his examples of empirical politics only *under the precondition of a specifically Maoist definition* of politics, which may or may not share common elements with other politics, but certainly does not with *all*.

To react to this objection by declaring any non-Maoist politics as nonpolitics would be a rhetorical acrobatics exhausting itself on the level of nomenclature and having absolutely no consequences on the reality of politics. Whether or not we want to include democratic materialism within the political function, people live in democratic materialism and they would have no problem to continue to do so conceding, if that's what we want them to do, not only that they are not, but also that they have no intention to be political.

Crucially, the objection I raise here is not against the fact that Badiou establishes universal truth in politics from a specific ideological perspective, but, quite the contrary, against the fact that he does not do so also in the other three fields. I must admit, however, that by committing this political exception, Badiou conspicuously displays to us the symptom encoding the problem of his other three examples. While the latter are analytical statements, Badiou's political universal truths are not, since the concepts "will," "equality," "trust," and "authority or terror," as defined by Badiou, can by no means be directly derived from the concept "politics," or even that of the "State." They are synthetic a priori judgments that derive their possibility from their being enunciated from the place of a specific ideological gaze and desire. And qua symptom, these judgments show us that every truth, whether political, artistic, scientific, or amorous, presupposes, therefore, a (ideological) gaze—a belief that itself is not part of the truth that it states, but its presupposition. The epigraph of *Logics of Worlds* already betrays the text's contradiction:

> The agony of France was not born of the flagging of the reasons to believe in her: defeat, demography, industry, etc., but of the powerlessness to believe in anything at all. (André Malraux)

As long as we are not in the state of the "powerlessness to believe in anything at all," we believe in something, and therefore we had better be conscious of our belief. The issue, however, is not some pseudo-Freudian observation of the type: Badiou is not aware of his ideological belief. Far from this, the issue is Badiou's conviction that the way to bypass the problematic of representation (the fact that it is ideological, always grounded on some belief) and its potential relativist hazards lies in the tacit inclusion of belief in the statement as part of its (ostensibly) analytic content. Badiou's logic here seems to be: if we have arrived at the present mess through a quasi-interminable series of acts known as analysis of ideology, then, to extricate ourselves from the mess, we must eliminate the realm of ideology, and to do so, we must act (as if we were) speaking from the position of Absolute Knowledge.

I propose that the way to counter the relativism engendered by democratic materialism out of representation lies, by contrast, in (1) *a precise distinction between the statement and the enunciation,* (2) *the consideration of the enunciation as a synthetic a priori judgment,* and (3) *the explicit inclusion of belief in this judgment, as that which renders the synthetic judgment necessary (a priori),* as opposed to an *a posteriori* (empirical and contingent) synthetic judgment.

Let us begin with the distinction between statement and enunciation. A preliminary distinction would be that, while the statement states a condition, the enunciation points to the desire underlying the act of stating the condition. Importantly, however, the distinction in question, as Robert Pfaller has aptly shown on the ground of Freud's classical example of negation (*Verneinung*), does not lie between the statement "it was *not* my mother" and "it is the mother"—resulting from the logic that "utterances like 'You ask me who this person in my dream might be. It is *not* the mother,' must be immediately understood in the opposite sense: 'So it is the mother' " (Pfaller, 227; citing Freud 1963, 213). This understanding of the distinction entails what Pfaller calls "*transgression by explicit immanence,*" namely, the assumption, evidenced in Žižek's reading of Ridley Scott's film *Blade Runner,* that "it is only when, at the level of the enunciated content [i.e., the statement], I assume my replicant-status," and say " 'I am a replicant,' " that, "at the level of enunciation, I become a truly human subject," that is, 'I am not a replicant' " (Pfaller, 230; citing Žižek 1993, 41). By the same token, as Pfaller remarks, in order to be not in ideology it would suffice to acknowledge that " 'I am in ideology' " (235). This, however, is not the case insofar as "there is an ideology that is based precisely on propositions like this; there is an ideology that consists in saying things like 'I am in ideology' " (231).

To explain this, Pfaller turns to Spinoza's critique of Pascal's "(Hegelian) dialectical solution for the problem of human greatness," which Pascal offers in his statement: "Man's greatness comes from knowing he is wretched" (234–35; citing Pascal, 29; §114). Commenting on the third part of Spinoza's *Ethics*, Pfaller writes that Spinoza sees in "the Pascalian solution . . . nothing but an example of 'presumptuous modesty' " (235). "Human greatness cannot at all be achieved or reliably testified by its denial," for to be great, since "human greatness . . . is for Spinoza the same as human freedom," means that to "recognize that we are not free is . . . only useful as a positive knowledge, not as an empty admission without knowledge," that is, "it only helps if it means to see that what we considered to be our own effects are in fact not wholly our own—and if this is a first step to produce different effects that are really our own" (235). Pascal's negation only "pretends a transgression," insofar as it seems to "signalize[] the wish to transgress the closed sphere of human misery," but "at the same time it shows that it does not really want to transgress this sphere," and in fact wants the opposite, namely, "to maintain the certainty that there is no real space beyond [misery]; it expresses the fear that the space beyond might not be empty" (236). Because I fear that there might be a space of greatness outside our closed sphere of misery, I assure you that greatness is actually here, in our closed sphere, so that I make sure that you stay here, rather than going out there.

Freud's negation, as exemplified by Pascal, is revealed through Spinoza's critique to be structured as the famous joke Freud narrates in "*Der Witz und seine Beziehung zum Unbewußten* [The Joke and its Relation to the Unconscious]" (1905). Two Jews meet at a station, the one asks the other, "Where are you going?," and the other responds, "to Crakau," whereupon the first one roars: "When you say you are going to Cracau, you actually want me to believe that you are going to Lemberg. But now I know you are really going to Cracau. So, why are you lying to me?" (freely translated from Freud 1999, VI, 127). To paraphrase the joke in Pascalian terms: "—How does one go from misery to greatness?—By staying in misery.—When you say that one goes from misery to greatness by staying in misery, you actually want me to believe that one really goes to greatness. But now I know one stays in misery. So, why are you lying to me?"

Thus, in Pascal's Hegelian solution to the question of human greatness not only are we left with "an imaginary transgression," but *a fortiori*, as Pfaller concludes, "even the wish of transgression within it is imaginary" (236). The presentation of the outside as a void makes the enterprise of "going out" appear vain (since it would amount to going nowhere), and thereby endeavors to safeguard that no one will even want to "go out." Here we encounter the distinction between Hegelianist and Spinozian dialectics. As Pfaller puts it, the "Hegelian solution that Slavoj Žižek proposed for the replicant problem . . . presupposes topologically that the only transgression of certain spaces is a negative transgression; that the only beyond of a closed space is an empty beyond" or that "what limits the positive" is "something negative" (234). By contrast, "the Spinozian principle" of monism indicates "that something can only be limited by something else that is of the same nature," namely, also "positive" (234). Therefore for Spinoza, Pfaller concludes, "the solution of a problem of transgression can never consist only in the 'empty gesture' of a negation"; "if we want to transgress a space we must arrive at another space . . . (whereas a space that cannot be transgressed at all, cannot be transgressed by negation either)" (234).

This is why a Spinozian ontology entails that beyond the closed sphere of appearances there is not simply nothing but the Nothing as a positive function, which is of the "same nature" as the appearances, since the latter embody its attributes. This is the structure of the gaze, which, although, or rather because it is in itself void, requires an empirical embodiment whose gaze fills the void. Thus, when we transgress appearance, what we encounter is not the void but an empirical gaze. To transgress appearance or ideology is to arrive not at nonappearance or nonideology but at the very ideology presupposed for the multiplicity of all empirically given ideologies. *It is on the level of this second degree ideology that universal truth can be located, as the shared precondition of all ideologies.*

The lesson of this comparison between Spinoza and Pascal/Hegel is that, as Pfaller writes, the "dialectical concept of transgression by explicit immanence is a concept of ideological integration," as is known from Kierkegaard, according to whom, "a true Christian can only be the one who says 'I doubt whether I really am a Christian' " (236–37). In short, although Freud's assumption about negation—i.e., "the suggestion that behind the utterance 'I doubt whether I am a true Christian,' there lurks a true Christian"—is itself "a lie," nevertheless, "this lie is constitutive of Christianity: you are a true Christian if you have learned to perform this ritual of negation" (237). Far from obtaining transgression, negation is a constitutive part of ideological integration, "*not because what it denies were necessarily true, but because the gesture of negation is real*" (237–38).

Therefore, "the importance of the denial," as a necessary part of "ideology's customs," does "not lie on its constative level" but "on its performative level"—the level of the enunciation—which is to say, "what it says does not have to be true, but it must be said" (238). This is not to say, as is largely assumed, that the categories of truth and false do not pertain to the performative level or the level of desire. For, as Pfaller reluctantly admits, by inserting truth into quotation marks, "its [denial's] 'truth' lies in its performative level," namely, in the fact that I take this further step of denying or doubting what I am, thereby closing the ideological sphere of my existence, with me within it (238). Yes, it cannot be said that the desire to be a Christian, to be interpellated by a certain ideology, is in itself true or false—desire can only be real or unreal. But, it can be said about any given subject that his or her desire to be a Christian is true or false, that he or she is really interpellated by a certain ideology or not. Which is why we are capable of saying that the *true* Christian is the one who doubts that he or she is truly a Christian.

In recapitulating, as Pfaller puts it, "everything that negation says"—including "what it says on the level" of what Freud would mistake for "enunciation," that is, both "I am a Christian" and "I doubt I am truly a Christian"—"belongs to its enunciated content" (233). The true "level of enunciation" is "only the fact that it is a negation," that is, the necessary 'dotting of the i,' by means of which only one of the two constative statements, "I am Christian," proves to be the truth of my desire (233). Hence, although on the constative level both "I am a Christian" and "I doubt I am a true Christian" are initially wrong, on the performative level only one of them *is* true, thereby retroactively rendering the one of the two constative statements also true. Which is why we must subvert the old formula, according to which, as Pfaller argues, "everything that can be falsified or verified is a part of the constative level of the enunciated—not of the performative level of enunciation, where the question of truth does not play any role" (233). On the contrary, everything that is a part of the constative level of the enunciated, as Pfaller himself proved, can be falsified (except, as Badiou reminds us, for tautologies); it is only on the performative level of enunciation that the question of truth is raised, for only there can a statement be falsified *or* verified, and thus also verify one of the constative statements.

Even tautologies can be said to be always constatively true only insofar as they do not entail any performative level (desire), and no sooner does it become evident that they do entail a desire than they are no longer true—in fact, like any non-tautological statement, they become constatively self-contradictory and hence false. Take the tautology, "business is business," as a statement justifying a course of action on the part of an employer vis-à-vis an unproductive employee of hers. The statement can actually mean two antinomically opposed things: "Fire this unproductive employee even if he starves, because business is what matters" or "Do not fire this employee, even if he is unproductive, because after all business is only inessential business." While one needs to unpack a tautology and reveal its implied opposing synthetic a priori judgments, the latter (which are no longer tautologies) directly reveal themselves as constatively wrong, and yet, retroactively, through the sheer act of the enunciation, make the one of them true.

Pfaller's scheme needs one more step to be completed. For as it stands, it can always only affirm the affirmative of the two constative statements. Whether we begin from a tautology or from a synthetic a priori judgment, we always deal with two false judgments—the constative level fails in the mode of the mathematic antinomy. On the empirical level, two false constative judgments function no differently than two equally true judgments. For the constative level is the realm of how things appear, the realm of representation or of exchange-value, which is why one judgment is as 'good' as any other, each deserving its right to representation next to any other. This realm provides the rhetoric of democratic materialism, which wants to know nothing about desire, except how better to subject it to biopolitics. Once we enter the realm of the performative, we find ourselves falling in the mode of the dynamic antinomy, a fall that allows the object of desire to form itself, and us to declare 'I want this, and not the other,' 'I am this, and not the other.' This, as we know, is possible because something (the Master-Signifier) has been excluded. I identify myself as secular because I presuppose that somebody else somewhere in the world is a believer, thereby forgetting that a belief (e.g., in "belated modernism") is presupposed for any rational judgment I make. Thus, my desire is constituted, and I am interpellated by a specific ideology. This is the realm of how things really appear: "All opinions may have the same right to self-representation, but I recognize as really true only my own opinion. It is not that I cannot accept rationally your truth; it is simply that I personally identify with mine, which is why I am I, and you are you."

This is even more so particularly if I deny any identity, since the "I am not" is required for the closure of the sphere of the

"I am." Which is why, as Pfaller remarks, "ideology even has to provide the subjects with such a feature in order to enable them to 'transgress' [imaginarily] their ideology; it has to interpellate them as something 'beyond ideology,' 'beyond identity' " (240). Thus, we have phenomena such as "the 'Generation X'-movement' " or, simply, the more common and "less programmatic, cynical, liberalist pragmatism," in which "the absence of identity" becomes itself as "rigid" as any other identity, "that it again has to be imaginarily transgressed," to become a more "colorful identity," assuming various forms, such as "urban tribalism or romantic motorcycling as a pastime" (240). In other words, "interpellation beyond interpellation" is the dominant postmodern mode of interpellation, as employed by democratic materialism.

Democratic materialism entails cultural pluralism because the true ideological formula of Christianity is not simply "There would be no Christianity if I were not Christian," but also "There would be no Christianity even if I were Christian." But if something other than Christianity is the standard both of Christianity and non-Christianity, then, what is the difference between Christianity qua truth and non-Christianity qua false? None. For in the statement "truth is the standard both of itself and of the false," "truth" and "itself" are not the same. The "itself" of truth and the false have the same epistemological and ontological status: they are appearance as it really appears and appearance, respectively—which, in the case of the Christian, they are non-Christianity and Christianity, respectively. "Truth," on the other hand—the subject in Spinoza's statement—is of another epistemological and ontological level, which alone is really a Truth, unlike both "itself" and the "false," which are both false. This means that Christianity has nothing whatsoever to do with the Truth of the Christian and the non-Christian.

Let me exemplify this by returning once more to Lacan's reading of Sophocles' *Antigone*. There, Lacan draws on a distinction other than the one between dynamic and mathematic antinomy. This is the distinction, as we saw, between "discourse" and "language," the former being conceived as a teleological diachrony. *Language*, on the other hand, he defines as a not-all, not in the sense of the infinite regress but in that of *self-referentiality*, as deriving from set theory.

From either not-all, that of the mathematic antinomy and that of set theory, it does indeed follow that the two opposing judgments—"Polynices is bad" and "Polynices is good"—are equally false, insofar as Polynices is value-free, unless one poses the arbitrary and, hence, inadmissible presupposition that one's redemptive value is predicated on one's historical past, as judged by existing norms, themselves determined by the discourse's *telos*. As Kant writes, "[I]f two mutually opposed judgments presuppose an inadmissible condition," then, "despite their conflict . . . both of them collapse, because the condition collapses under which alone either of them would be valid" (Kant 1998, 517; A503/B531).[5] Thus, both the mathematic antinomy and language (the self-referential set) reveal that the judgments of discourse appear as true because of the "inadmissible condition" of excluding a third possibility ("Polynices is value-free"). Yet, unlike the mathematic antinomy—and this is crucial—language challenges discourse and its "inadmissible condition" not by means of a regression to infinity in the "magnitude (of experience)," which would show that the process through which we could arrive at the absolute and true condition is "indeterminately far." Here (in the mathematic antinomy), the absolute condition is posited as given, even if out of reach: the value of Polynices will become known only at some "indeterminately far" end of history or Last Judgment; until then, only the pluralism of values can legitimately reign. The objection of the mathematic antinomy is culturalist. By contrast, the not-all of set theory postulates the inclusion of the particular (my own culturalist ideology) within the universal (ideology as such): "*Any* value attributed to Polynices is possible only because of my value; if I do not identify with a value, if I am not interpellated by a value, Polynices has no value either." Language shows *hic et nunc* that *any* discursive system of values is a not-all or self-referential, decentered set, in which any presumed center, and hence *telos*, is only arbitrarily posited. And, since any *telos* is as "good" (or, as rationally ungrounded and illegitimate) as any other, so that I could as well be interpellated by another *telos*, there must be another interpellation, a *second order ideology*, because of which I am interpellated by this *telos* and not another. *It is this surplus ideological belief, which must be included in the empirical and contingent synthetic (ideological) judgment in order for it to function as a priori, that is, necessary.*[6]

This second order ideology is pointed to through the secondary literature on *Antigone*, which, on the ground of this tragedy has advanced a variety of theses about the tension between a tribal societal organization and the institution of the polis-state, farther down to the tension between family and the state, the distinction between the private and the public spheres, the role of woman, and so on. In other words, the integration of the exception within the totality entails that what is at stake in the decision about Polynices' value is another value—the value of Sophocles' *Antigone*—that pertains to a second order ideology, which is the precondition for the first order ideology to appear consistent and true.

If several sets of ideology are tolerated within one and the same community, this only indicates that there exists a second order ideology, which is presupposed by all sets of ideology constituting this community. If there is an ideological set that does not presuppose this second order ideology, then it is not tolerated by it, which is why the ideological set of the said community does not hesitate, its claim to cultural relativism notwithstanding, to exclude it and, if necessary, to fight it. There is a second order ideology for which the Christian and the non-Christian are equally valorized, because they become irrelevant to Being and Truth. This is the ideology proper of capital in its absolute domination, for capital could not care less about the religion of its consumers and investors. The distinction Christian/non-Christian may become again relevant only at the moment of that specific crisis in which the absolute dominance of capital is challenged, and capital's inherently all-inclusive cultural pluralism is forced to exclude the ideology that challenges it, if it so happens that the opposition comes from non-Christians.

And, in the last analysis, or rather, in advanced capitalism, the opposed party does not need to be labeled by any specific ideology, as the category of "ideology" itself becomes its sole stigma. Capital presents itself as nonideological, so that its zealots need no labels whatsoever in order to differentiate themselves from its opponents. Names no longer matter, for the difference is simply expressed through the statement: "Either you are with us or against us." The zealots forget that if capital were nonideological, they would be incapable of action. If they are so eager to contribute to the accumulation of capital, it is because the latter *is* ideology in its purest form, insofar as it *posits directly itself*, and without the need to invoke anything else as its ideal, as its own *telos*.

Cultural relativism, far from being about ideological pluralism, is the best way to sustain most rigidly a unitary ideology. This is a conclusion that cannot be derived from the not-all of the mathematic antinomy, which can only deduce from its logic cultural pluralism and cannot consequently explain such phenomena as capital's periodic need to retreat from its all-inclusiveness.

The second order ideology is what we call the gaze or surplus, and it pertains to the performative level proper. All possible cultural identities tolerated within democratic materialism are wrong statements that performatively affirm as Truth none of the ideologies enunciated in their affirmative and negative statements, from Judaism, Christianity, Buddhism, and Islam, to any national, ethnic, racial, and gender identity, and from there to any recreational identity democratic materialism has produced and continues to produce as part of its (bio)politics.

This means that Truths (which are always universal) can be enunciated only from the locus where the set of ideologies tolerated by democratic materialism and the set of ideologies not tolerated by it meet—that is, clash. But all the culturally pluralistic force of democratic materialism is oriented toward occluding its ideological surplus, its second order ideology that sustains the appearance of a pluralism of ideologies within itself. *A fortiori*, similarly to Godard's futuristic Alphaville with its eclipsed words, the word *ideology* is no longer included in the Bible-dictionary of democratic materialism, except as an insult reserved for the other. Badiou's political lapsus moves toward a more ethical position than the one evidenced in his three other examples, insofar as it betrays its ideological surplus. There is no reason to save universal Truths unless they pertain to the level of the ideological surplus. If it matters whether democratic materialism will acknowledge universal Truths, it is only because it matters whether it will acknowledge its surplus ideology—not the pluralist brouhaha that sustains it, but the ideology because of which bodies and languages in the era of global capital, within both the sets tolerated and not-tolerated by democratic materialism, are increasingly subjected to the law that forces surplus to manifest itself exclusively as surplus-value and surplus-enjoyment.

Is It Possible Not to Hate Representation? (Another Look at *Empire*)

Even if through different strategies, Badiou's goal of bypassing representation and its ideology and seizing directly the thing is not dissimilar from the "Neo-Spinozist" goal. Both share "Heidegger's discontent" that, as Karatani puts it, "modernist thought[]" seeks "truth not directly but only via representation" (2003, 149). The most recent popular "Neo-Spinozist" attempt to arrive at truth without passing through the defiles of representation is evidenced in Hardt and Negri's *Empire*.

To enter *Empire*, though, we must first be familiar with two central Spinozian terms, *potentia* and *potestas*. In Michael Hardt's words in his foreword to Antonio Negri's *The Savage Anomaly*, "the distinction between Power [*potestas*] and power [*potentia*] reveals an opposition between metaphysics and history" (Hardt 1991, xiv). While "from the idealistic perspective of the *Ethics* Power [*potestas*] is recognized" by Spinoza "as an illusion and subordinated to power [*potentia*]," from "the historical perspective," Hardt continues, "power [*potentia*] is continually subordinated to Power [*potestas*]" (xiv). For *potestas* is the representation of power, which is always mediated by imaginary distortion, as we experience it in our everyday representations and practices of power. In "the metaphysical domain," as Hardt writes, "the distinction between Power and power cannot exist" (xiv). For, in the metaphysical domain, power (*potentia*) is considered as in itself, prior to its historical representations. It is first through the ideological distortions brought about by its actual representations in everyday practice that power appears in an illusory way, as *potestas*. Consequently, Hardt concludes, "from the point of view of eternity . . . there can be no distinction because there is only power [*potentia*]" (xiv). By contrast, from the perspective of everyday practice, albeit metaphysically speaking illusory and hence false, imaginarily distorted "Power" (*potestas*) is the sole, empirically given truth, while *potentia* as such remains unrepresented. Consequently, Spinoza was the first modern thinker to claim for the imaginary the status of a legitimate cognitive concept that has a major function within politics.

We can elucidate further the difference between *potentia* and *potestas* through the Marxian distinction between *Vertretung* and *Darstellung*, as highlighted by Karatani's insightful analysis of Marx's *The Eighteenth Brumaire of Louis Bonaparte*. There, Marx focuses on the "parliamentary system," which was implemented after the "revolution of February 1848" and the introduction of "universal suffrage for the first time." Drawing on the fact that in his analysis, Marx "pointed out the existence of the real social classes behind the representation" that was established by the "parliamentary system," Karatani continues, Engels "attributed to Marx the discovery that behind the ideological (i.e., political, religious, philosophical) representations [*Darstellung*] there exists the economic class structure, and that the struggle between classes is driven by the 'law of history,' " which, still faithful to Hegel, somehow always manages to bypass these distorted representations and to bring triumph on the just side of this class struggle, the proletariat (2003, 143–44; bracket inserted by Karatani). "Reading the text closely, however," Karatani continues, "what Marx discovered in the series of events was quite the reverse: The conjunctures developed independent of, or even contrary to, the economic class structure" (144). In other words, what Marx discovered was "the autonomous 'operations' of the events" whose "agent . . . was obviously the institution of the representative system *[Vertretung]* itself" (144; bracket inserted by Karatani). What is new about "the parliamentary system based upon universal suffrage," is the fact that "the representative system is thoroughly 'fictitious' as compared to the *Ständeversammlung*—an assembly of different castes/professions from preindustrial Europe, as Hans Kelsen later claimed" (144). Karatani refers to Kelsen's observation that "die Fiktion der Repräsentation [the fiction of representation]" consists in "der Gedanke, daß das Parlament nur Stellvertreter des Volks sei [the thought that the parliament is (presumably) only the representative (proxy or placeholder) of the people]," while in truth "die Abgeordneten von ihren Wählern keine bindenden Instruktionen anzunehmen haben [the appointed members of the parliament are not bound by the instructions of their voters]." As a result, "das Parlament [ist] in seiner Funktion vom Volke rechtlich unabhängig [in its function, the parliament is legally independent of the people]," in opposition to the "alten Ständeversammlung . . . deren Mitglieder bekanntlich durch imperative Mandate ihrer Wählergruppen gebunden und diesen verantwortlich waren [old *Ständeverssammlung* . . . whose members, as is known, were bound by the imperative mandates of their voter groups, toward whom they were held responsible]" (1929, 30; translation mine).

After the abolition of the *Ständeversammlung*, the representative system known as the parliamentary system, "is thoroughly fictitious," and as such, its function is not really that of "*Vertretung*," in which the link between representative and represented is not arbitrary but determined by actual power relations. Rather, the parliamentary system is a representation based on fictitious, and hence arbitrary relations, designated under the term "*Darstellung*." As Karatani puts it, Marx describes the "institution of representatives" as one in which "there is no apodictic rapport between the representer and the represented," so that "the acts and discourses of political parties" are "independent of the real classes" (2003, 144). As a result, as Marx writes, "the relationship between the *political* and the *literary representatives* of a class and the class they represent" or between the "spokesmen and scribes of the bourgeoisie, its platform and its press, in short, the ideologists of the bourgeoisie and the bourgeoisie itself, the representatives and the represented," is one in which the two sides "faced one another in estrangement and no longer understood one another" (Marx 1998, 51 and 102).

The relation between parliamentary representatives and the "real classes," which are no longer *vertretet* but *dargestellt*, is the same as the relation between *potestas* and *potentia*, the arbitrary, fictitious representation of power and power dynamics as they really are. As Karatani remarks, "the representative (qua discursive) system [*potestas*], exists autonomously" and, consequently, "classes come into consciousness only via this system" (2003, 145). Which is why, to repeat Hardt's words regarding Spinoza's power, from "the historical perspective, power [*potentia*] is continually subordinated to Power [*potestas*]." The consciousness of real classes about real relations of power [*potentia*] is fully mediated by the imaginary relations as articulated in the representations of power [*potestas*]. On the historical or empirical level, therefore, whatever is experienced as real relations of power (*potentia*) is already determined by the dynamism that orients imaginary relations of power (*potestas*). The real relations of power (*potentia*) can be accessed empirically not in themselves but always already as discourse, that is, as an always already oriented network of power relations, a web of forces that always already knows its direction and goal, depending on the fantasy that governs the imaginary relations of power (*potestas*), through which the consciousness of real people and real classes is constituted. Only on the metaphysical plane is *potentia* freed from any directionality, revealing itself as brute collision of indifferent forces with no overall orienting will.

Power, too, therefore, does not escape in Spinoza his universal principle of truth and its ternary structure. *Potentia*, the raw clash of forces with no aim, is a metaphysical function that, like God's metalanguage, cannot dictate any course of action. This Power-in-itself or *Potentia* (note my capitalization) can manifest itself empirically either as itself (*Vertretung*) or as false (*Darstellung*), either as *potentia* or *potestas*, as real appearance and appearance, or, finally, as the mirage of a 'non-ideological,' 'real' direction of history and tangible ideology. The former is for each of us what interpellates us, the latter what we recognize as illusion. And both are the two empirical modes of existence of *Potentia* (with capital letter).

The "Neo-Spinozist" assumption about power is structurally the same as its assumption about absolute knowledge. In both cases, "Neo-Spinozism" takes at face value Spinoza's belief that survival, the increase of one's power and self-interests, is a "scientific," nonideological truth. Once one subjects, according to Spinoza's pantheism, all knowledge to value and, hence, to the imaginary and ideology, then Spinoza's theory takes on a wholly new meaning. If God has no will and "God's power is his essence itself," then this power or essence is that of indifference, of intending nothing in all that exists or occurs (Spinoza 1985, 439; *Ethics*, part I, prop. 34). The increase of power, then, is increase of indifference and nonintentionality. *Ethics* is the proper title of Spinoza's book precisely because it leaves no room for "pathological self-interests." In Kantian terms, the Spinozian *God is an absolute antinomy* and nothing more. That the human being manifests the attributes of God in the same perfection only means that the human being is *torn between the pleasure principle and the death drive.*

Hardt's assertion, therefore, that Spinoza's ideal "democracy . . . is a return to the plane of the *Ethics*," in which "there is only power [*potentia*]," is untenable, for *potentia* has no *telos*, let alone the specific *telos* of "democracy" (Hardt, xvi and xiv). Nevertheless, this assumption constitutes the basic premise of not only Negri's *Savage Anomaly* but also Handt and Negri's *Empire*, written almost two decades later. The methodology of both works is predicated on a movement from the *Ethics*, which in Hardt's words, "subordinates Power [*potestas*] to power [*potentia*] in the idealistic terms of its utopian vision," to a strategic methodology that "poses the real tendency toward a future reduction of the distinction, when a democratic Power [*potestas*] would be completely constituted by the power [*potentia*] of the multitude" (Hardt, xvi). To avoid Spinoza's presumed idealism and utopianism one only needs to collapse the metaphysical and the historical, so that both *potestas* and *potentia* manifest themselves within the plane of history, where, in some "future" moment, *potestas* will no longer be distinguishable from *potentia*, as the former "would be completely constituted by" the latter. Here we evidence a double, and typically "Neo-Spinozist," reduction. On the one hand, there is the reduction of the metaphysical to that which is realized within the historical—a reduction justified and supported by a widely spread misunderstanding of both Spinozian immanence and materialism, which are taken to demand the reduction of everything to empirically given reality. Were this the case, there would be no surplus-value, and if Marx had nevertheless managed to have written *Capital,* he would remain as radically incompatible with this "Neo-Spinozism" as he is today—which makes it all the more bewildering that this "Neo-Spinozist" line of thought indulges in invoking "communism" in his name. On the other hand, there is the simultaneous reduction of constituted representation (*potestas*) to constituent Being (*potentia*). The latter becomes the explicit and persistent agenda of *Empire*:

> *Today the militant cannot even pretend to be a* representative, *even of the fundamental needs of the exploited. Revolutionary political militancy today . . . must rediscover what has always been its proper form:* not representational but constituent activity. (413)

Both "democratic Power" and "*revolutionary political militancy today*" would do away with "representational" mediations (*potestas*) if they simply "*rediscovered*" that they are "completely constituted by the power [*potentia*] of the multitude," the collective subject of history (413). Thus, *potentia* is presumed to manifest itself in historical reality in its pure (metaphysical) form, totally unalloyed by the deceiving power of *potestas.* And while they thus become equally historical forces, the superiority of *potentia* over *potestas* is equally undeniable. In *Empire,* while *potestas* pertains to representation, and is thus "constituted" and linked to "contingency," "second nature," and "relations of production" (as opposed to the means and forces of production), *potentia* is directly ontological, it is "being," "nature," "productive force," and "constitution."[7]

But, one might object, perhaps we should not be so disconcertedly alerted by this hierarchical discrepancy between *potestas* and *potentia,* since the historical and the ontological are equally material and objective, lying in the same plane of immanence. As Negri had written earlier:

> There is no longer nature, in Spinoza, but only second nature; the world is not nature but production. The continuity of being is not formed in a process that leads from a principle [nature] to a result [second nature], from a cause to an effect (on this nexus and in this direction); rather, it is revealed as given, as a product, as a conclusion. The result [second nature] is the principle [nature]. Produced, constituted being is the principle of production and constitution. (1991, 225)

We begin with a hyperbolic exaggeration ("there is no longer [constituting] nature . . . but only second [constituted] nature") to conclude that in truth there are both and on the same plane of immanence, insofar as they relate to one another in the mode of immanent causality, with the "constituted being" being itself "the principle" of "constitution." But where Negri really wants to arrive is the opposite of what is stated in the initial hyperbole:

> In the composition of subjectivity there is always progressively more of that sociability and collective intelligence that raise power [*potentia*] up against Power [*potestas*], that make Power an always more subordinated and transient form with respect to human, intersubjective productivity, with respect to the mature composition of subjectivity. (1991, 226)

It turns out after all that if something is subsidiary and ephemeral, "subordinated and transient," this is not constituting nature but, on the contrary, constituted *potestas*, the representation of power. Eventually, by the time we arrive at *Empire*, *potestas* is so pervasively defeated by the triumphant constituting *potentia* of the multitude that it is reduced to a negativity: "the non-place of Empire" (Hardt/Negri, 395). Thus, as we had already read in *The Savage Anomaly*, by "freeing itself from the relations of production [*potestas*] and showing itself as immediately constitutive," *potentia*, the "productive force," "displays the possibility of the world to be unfolded and analyzed and transformed according to desire" (1991, 229). And, since the multitude is the direct earthly embodiment of divine *potentia*, without being in the least mislead by *potestas*, its desire is also the manifestation of God's Will. The *telos* of history, therefore, is infallibly the increase of the multitude's power—q. e. d. In Hardt and Negri's words:

> One might object at this point, with good reason, that all this is still not enough to establish the multitude as a properly political subject, nor even less as a subject with the potential to control its own destiny. This objection, however, does not present an insuperable obstacle, because the revolutionary past, and the contemporary cooperative productive capacities through which the anthropological characteristics of the multitude are continually transcribed and reformulated, cannot help

> revealing a telos, a material affirmation of liberation. . . . The teleology of the multitude is theurgical; it consists in the possibility of directing technologies and production toward its own joy and its own increase of power. (Hardt/Negri, 395–96)

One is here tempted to quote that passage from Spinoza where he writes that people imagine that "God might love them above all the rest, and direct the whole of Nature according to the needs of their blind desire and insatiable greed," but "while they sought to show that nature does nothing in vain (i.e., nothing which is not of use to men), they seem to have shown only that nature and the Gods are as mad as men" (1985, 441; *Ethics*, part 1; prop. 36, appendix). Why should God be on the side of the multitude's "desire," which, as far as Spinoza is concerned, is "blind," and not on the side of the equally blind and "corrupt" desire of the "non-place of Empire" and its *potestas*? (passim). For even though *Empire* globalizes the multitude—to the indignation of many critics, such as Lotringer who remarks that "*Empire* involves an original kind of class struggle: *a struggle looking for a class*"—the damned "non-place" remains, and it cannot be a sheer negation, but must be *another place—with its own multitude and desire.*

Invocations of the "theurgical" in the context of a historical "telos" within a Spinozian frame of analysis are nonsensical when taken at their face value. Of course, like everything false, Hardt and Negri's statement speaks the truth about God's will and the multitude's desire, and, unlike my psychoanalytic reference above to pleasure and drive, it speaks it in directly political terms: *the fate or necessarily increasing power of political opposition in the era of the Empire is to mistake advanced capitalism for itself.*

This is *transformismo* in advanced capitalism. Originating in the 1870s, *transformismo* is the concept Gramsci adopted and extended in the years 1931–1932, in his *Prison Notebooks*, to describe the state of bourgeois hegemony in Italy. In *transformismo*, opposition and the possibility of undermining power, far from being real or effective, are ostensible and effectively absorbed by the hegemonic groups. The main referent in Gramsci's mind was the transformism of Leftist individuals or groups who go over to the Center or Right, as when ex-leftists or ex-anarchists become the members of conservative parties.[8] The term was later also used to designate not so much the explicit transformism of Left individuals or groups into more conservative ones, but, rather, a covert *transformismo* in which individuals or groups, as the historian Norman Stone puts it, "talk left and act right" (45). But *transformismo* essentially applies to all hegemonic politics, for as Geoff Waite puts it:

> One contributing cause/effect of *transformismo* is that bourgeois political parties, such as the current Democratic and Republican Parties in the United States [of America], tend to represent only oscillatory social groupings around a single unmolested core of dominant economic interests, rather than representing more fundamental class differences and antagonisms. Such parties typically share a static procapitalist ideology, while giving off the appearance of dynamically "debating" and "opposing" one another, thus suppressing and precluding radical alternatives to capitalism. This includes the violent production, in effect, of "terrorists" who are then immediately figured as "radical evil." (365)

Surpassing all hitherto existing applications of the term, Hardt and Negri's *Empire* forces us to realize that the distance between "real classes" and their representation has reached the point at which *transformismo* today includes, beyond those who overtly turned to the Right, those who talk [L]eft and act [R]ight, and the Democratic and the Republican Parties, also those who understand themselves as communist even as they also talk Right. The truth about the 'communist' multitude in its present state is that, while it imagines that it has passed on the other side of representation, it blindly follows the line imposed on its *potentia* by *potestas*.

The meandrous iridescence of *Darstellung* may prevent us from seeing *Vertretung* even "through a glass, darkly" (1 Corinthians 13:1). One more reason, then, not to mistake the former for the latter.

Conclusion

Raising a Question

Another Look at Ethics, or, Commodity and the Gaze

If, unlike the "Neo-Spinozists" and several "Neo-Lacanians," we want to remain within representation with its (double) failure and its self-referentiality as its sole nonrepresentable effects, and, if we also want to maintain the structural homology between economic and semantic exchange, how can we formulate a theory of ethics as also the ground for political action?

The intuitive Lacanian criticism of any theory that reduces the question of ethics to the encounter with the neighbor (e.g., notably, Levinas's face-to-face encounter with the other) is that in this account a third term is missing, which would take into account the death drive. The neighbor I encounter in the face of the other is, of course, not this concrete other, but not even this other qua my mirror image. Rather, it is the Thing-in-itself, my own sheer self-referentiality, for the primary moment in this encounter with the other is not me seeing the other but me being seen by the other and her desire—in short, in my encounter with the other I am being placed under her gaze. Therefore, the encounter with the other is in truth directly an encounter with the Other, insofar as her desire and gaze are only imagined by me in the Other—which is why the whole encounter is precisely self-referential.

And so what? What's so important about realizing that what we (mis)take for the face-to-face encounter with the other is the face-to-face encounter with the gaze imagined by me in the Other? This is the point that reveals Marx's political analysis of economy as also a veritable treatise on ethics. The attributes of Surplus, once it has taken up the specific mold of surplus-value, as is the case in capitalism, determines, to recall Marx's words, the commodity to represent its

> internal opposition between use-value and value, hidden within the commodity [itself] . . . on the surface by an external opposition, i.e., by a relation between two commodities such that the one commodity, *whose own* value is supposed to be expressed, counts directly only as a use-value, whereas the other commodity, *in which* that value is to be expressed, counts directly only as exchange-value. (Marx 1990, 153)

Similarly, in semantic exchange, and hence, in my encounter with the other, once the Surplus has been squeezed into the specific mold of surplus-enjoyment, it determines the subject to represent its "internal opposition . . . hidden within" itself, the opposition between me and the gaze I imagine in the Other, "by an external opposition, i.e., by a relation between two" subjects, me and the other.

It is particularly in literature and film that we become most sentient of the gaze of the Other, because of the ubiquitous existence of a narrator or a camera—a gaze imagined and, in this case, materialized by a subject, the author or director, and forced upon our perception. The presence of the Other is all the more palpable the more its gaze is omniscient, yet unidentifiable. In the fourth chapter of *The Trial*, Kafka, a master in constructing such narrators, grants us an indiscrete view into both their own and the mutually projected desires of K. and his landlady, Frau Grubach, during a short dialogue. Having insinuated that Fräulein Bürstner, K.'s attractive neighbor, is of lax morals, Grubach cannot meet K. but with the desire to be found by him innocent of slander, so that everything K. says, however "stern," becomes, in Grubach's eyes, "an approach toward forgiveness" (1992, 75). K., on the other hand, fearing that Grubach might evict Bürstner, encounters Grubach with the unflinching desire to keep his neighbor around.

The difference of their respective desires notwithstanding, for a moment it seems that the two can arrive at a satisfactory reconciliation. Frau Grubach declares "in her sobs": "It never entered my head to offend you or anyone else." K. soon reciprocates: "I didn't mean what I said so terribly seriously either." The two confessions converge toward a consensual declaration of communicative failure, which K. states not without relief—"We misunderstood each other"—and which now seems to open up the possibility of a successful communication. Having eventually understood that more than Bürstner's eviction, Grubach desires K.'s desire—the guarantee that he would not turn against her because of another woman—K. finally pronounces the declaration of love intractably cadged for by Grubach: "Do you really believe that I would turn against you because of a strange girl?" "That's just it, Herr K.," Grubach immediately retorts, "relieved in her mind [sobald sie sich nur irgendwie freier fühlte]," as if to seal the success of their communication (1992, 76; 1998, 97).

Whereupon the narrator ominously intervenes to warn us that this statement was in fact "etwas Ungeschicktes," something clumsy, a "tactless" intimation of the imminent disaster. Grubach indulges anew in her garrulous sponging for K.'s desire—"I kept asking myself. . . . Why should he quarrel with me because of her, though he knows that every cross word from him makes me lose my sleep?"—inevitably making K. think that "he should have sent her from the room at the very first word." Not "want[ing] to do that," K. "contented himself with drinking his coffee and leaving Frau Grubach to feel that her presence was burdensome." A futile hope, as Frau Grubach kept feeling nothing of the kind, so that "her dumb helplessness . . . exasperated K. still more." And his exasperation, in turn, could only preclude his desired outcome: "He began to walk up and down . . . and by doing that he hindered Frau Grubach from being able to slip out of the room, which she would probably have done" (1992, 76–77; 1998, 97).

It is paradoxically only as long as K.'s and Grubach's desires do not meet, as long as he thinks of his alluring neighbor and she of him, that their dialogue moves toward a resolution, albeit only seemingly so. In this ostensible resolution, K. recognizes Grubach's desire and declares with a rhetorical question his devotion to her. But this apparent resolution in effect unleashes, on Grubach's part, an emotional barrage of infatuated confessions, which can only exasperate K. who is in truth soliciting somebody else's (Bürstner's) desire. At this point, there is only a limited knowledge, and it is all possessed by K.: 'Grubach desires my desire.' She, by contrast, who actually was in the know when she was still feeling jealousy toward Bürstner, has in the meantime been led by K. to imagine that her fears about her rival were ungrounded, and naïvely indulges in a diffuse reassertion of the very desire to which K. responds only in order to achieve his goal: 'if you think that I desire you and not Bürstner, you will have no reason to kick her out of the house.' We could say that at this point K. knows the truth, and it is only Grubach who *imagines* a gaze in the Other. But this moment is also the turning point at which knowledge is retracted from both sides. K. now imagines that continuing "drinking his coffee" silently will signal to Grubach that "her presence was burdensome." But it is not K.'s eyes with which Grubach reads the signs. The persistence of her helpless and exasperating sobbing makes K. nervous, as a result of which he begins to "walk up and down," hindering Grubach's exit from the room and ignoring that by then her withdrawal is "probably [wahrscheinlich]" Grubach's own desire (1992, 77; 1998, 98). Now it is K. who may imagine a gaze in the Other, while it remains probable that Grubach has gotten K.'s real message regarding her presence in the room.

So far, the miscommunication between K. and Grubach notwithstanding, our communication with the omniscient narrator is transparent, leaving no void because of which *we* would need to imagine a gaze in the Other in order to interpret the scene. We are as omniscient as he, knowing the characters' unspoken thoughts and what each desires, detests, and even fears. But no sooner has the Kafkaesque text allotted us this reassuring and comfortable position, than it introduces "a knock": "It was the maid, who announced that Fräulein Montag," Bürstner's friend who was already moving into the former's room, "would like a word or two with Herr K." Taking the invitation as an unmistakable indication that Montag brings him a message from his neighbor, K. "turned an almost mocking eye [fast höhnischen Blick] on the startled Frau Grubach." The omniscient narrator reappears to explain further K.'s "eye" or, rather, more accurately "gaze" (*Blick*): "His look [Blick] seemed to say that he had long foreseen this invitation of Fräulein Montag's, and that it accorded very well with all the persecution he had had to endure that Sunday morning from Frau Grubach's boarders" (1992, 78; 1998, 98). In spite of the interpretative modesty expressed through the verb "seemed [schien]," the textual absence of other interpretations of K.'s gaze indicates that this is the sole possible one, particularly since the narrator's interpretation throughout *The Trial*, as Stanley Corngold puts it, "is forced on the reader, before the process begins, as an inescapably self-evident mode of understanding" (224). Thus, "seemed" does not mitigate the narrator's omniscience, the latter, however, is nevertheless undermined, since we still do not know *to whom* K's "look seemed to say" all this.[1]

Is it K.'s interpretation of (and, hence, intention in) his own look? Is it the interpretation from Grubach's jealous perspective? Is it that of the maid? Is it that of the exclusively superior knowledge of the narrator? Is it all of the above perspectives or none?

And here we encounter the void—because we do not know not *what* happens, but *who* is looking at what happens. We can safely know all about K.'s gaze, but only under the precarious precondition that we do *not know who we are* when we know. The relation between eye and gaze is the same as the relation between two lovers, for "when in love," as Lacan puts it, "*You never look at me from the place from which I see you*" (1981, 103).

On closer inspection, the instances of successful recognition of the other's desire in the above scene are moments of pain and/or discomfort: Grubach's fear of K.'s desire for Bürstner; K.'s exasperated compliance with Grubach's desire for him; and Grubach's probable recognition that she'd better retire. For the rest, the characters are satisfied in their feeling of engaging in a successful communication leading them to a reconciliation, eventually thwarted by K.'s final revengeful "look," even as we do not know who is the seer and recipient of this revenge. But in this rest part the dialogue is essentially a monologue: each character speaks to his or her own desire, to the desire he or she imagines in the Other.

And the same is true about the relation between us and the narrator, in an inverted way. We recognize throughout the narrator's desire, insofar as he always lets us know the desires with which he imbues his characters, until that uncanny moment at which he let us also know a surplus desire: vengeance. Who is the 'character' who desires it, and hence deserves it? It is at this moment that *we* feel discomfort, not knowing from whose gaze we are looking at the scene. Our sole other alternative is to accept this vengeance without wondering who is seeing it, and thereby to become its sole addressee, without any discomfort, but with all the pain this position invariably reserves for its holder.

But if it is the reader who desires (and deserves) revenge, then it is also the reader who at this moment is the actual narrator. The dialogue between reader and narrator reveals itself at this point as a monologue between the reader and her desire, as imagined in the Other. Following the Marxian and Freudian approach to the crisis and the symptom, respectively, this moment of exception, in which the 'normal,' 'nonpathological,' course of things (dialogue) fails, should reveal the true structure of what is actually taking place also in the 'normal' situation.[2] Consequently, the true structure of the 'normal' dialogue with the other, the neighbor, is that of a monologue, insofar as it is always a 'conversation' between the subject and the gaze imagined by it in the Other. As for the attractive or envied Ms Bürstner, she comes only after this gaze, as she is the object of/in the subject's desire (or fear), something that cannot be constituted without a prior gaze that makes her desirable (or threatening). This prior gaze appears (both in this specific scene and in the text in general) to be constituted in the relation between K. and Grubach (as the stand-in of the conventional petit-bourgeois gaze), but is actually constituted out of the self-referentiality of each character.

Indeed, it is only in literature (or films, and arguably art in general) that it would be a hyperbolic (and ridiculous) overinterpretation to say, for instance, Grubach might also, as K. does, have an ulterior motivation because of which she wants K. to believe that she desires him, and so, she fakes it. The text itself is here the limit, and since it gives us no such indication, such a reading would be absurd. But in real life there is no limit to the suspicions, the hypotheses, the oscillations in judgment we might have about the other's motivations, which is why there we are much more prone to be in dialogue with our imagined desire in the field of the Other. Literature, then, is, paradoxically, an instance of repose from our tormenting monologue, and an experience in which we are given more chances, compared to reality, to encounter *really* another gaze. After all, if we end up desiring vengeance it is because the narrator forced us into that position.

The everyday encounter with our neighbor, or the encounter with the random "neighbor," and the ubiquitous encounter with the unknown "neighbor"—all are encounters with oneself.[3] The 'normal' state of affairs is that in which the "internal opposition" between the subject and the gaze imagined by it in the Other appears as "an external opposition," as a relation between two subjects such that the one subject, *whose own* value as desirable or not is supposed to be expressed, counts directly only as an object, whereas the other subject, *in which* that value is to be expressed, counts directly only as signifier. Both use-value or the "object," the appearance of being or "the semblance of being," and exchange-value or the signifier are the effects of an empirically not given surplus, that is, in psychoanalysis, of "*objet a,* " and "*the objet a in the field of the visible is the gaze*" (Lacan 1998, 95; 1981, 105). Signifiers mean nothing unless they are interpreted, and gazes are that which interprets them. In my encounter with the other, I (i.e., it, the unconscious) provide(s) the gaze that interprets the other's signs as to his or her desire. And this desire, although it should precede the other's signs as their intention, will always already have caused their emergence only after my interpretation.

Let us take two examples less innocuous than K.'s and Grubach's infatuations. To begin with a classical and timeless example, in just about all accounts of ethics, sooner or later, the question is raised whether one should risk one's life to save another, usually, the other who is drowning. The example is invariably treated as one in which the other's desire is transparent: he desires, in fact, needs, to be saved. Even if in my rescuing attempt, the drowning other happened to have to drown me in order to save himself, he would still stand in moral impunity, as we saw Kant arguing. The motives, however, of the savior tend to be scrutinized much more thoroughly and treated with considerable suspicion. What if the drowning other happens to be Jeff Buckley, and I recognize and save him out of pure narcissistic motives (my name in the newspapers, the claim that I have saved a talented composer, poet, and singer, even the possibility of becoming friends with him, etc.)? And what if, in addition to this, he desires to be drowned, and it is only my own desire imagined in the field of the Other that to be saved is his desire? As for the possibility that the drowning other might be a psychotic killer who is faking drowning so that he drowns me, this is generally not discussed in the context of ethics, albeit a favorite subject in more thriller-oriented genres. Even if because of totally different reasons, we can again ask in this last case: What if it is my own desire imagined in the field of the Other that to be saved is his desire?

By contrast, (re)turning now to the second, modern and timely, example, if somebody who is starving or his life conditions correspond to what in our Western societies barely makes it to the level of survival conditions, and in his attempt to survive happens to drown me, then his act, far from entering the realm of moral impunity, is immediately raised to the level of radical, if not diabolical, evil, as, in fact, "terrorism" does in the mass media and, likely, in the consciousness of many people. This is to say that, unlike in the above example, here the other's motivation is unambivalently and without any oscillation interpreted as a psychotic compulsion to kill "us," whereby the thought never crosses "our" minds that, perhaps, drowning some of "us" may be the only chance they have left ("we" have left them) to save themselves from drowning. (To be sure, survival is a "pathological self-interest," itself based on some ideological will, but there is something to be said about the fact that some of us have to struggle daily for it, whereas others among us barely need to think about it.) *Who* are we when we see those strugglers as psychotic murderers? *What* and *whose gaze* is this, which desires so badly to be killed by the other?

Notes

Introduction

1. Mentioning only some of the most popular titles, representative texts of this line of production include: the two volumes of Deleuze and Guattari's *Capitalism and Schizophrenia* (see Deleuze and Guattari 1987 and 1998); Negri's *The Savage Anomaly* (see Negri); Hardt and Negri's *Empire* (see Hardt and Negri); Massumi's *A User's Guide to Capitalism and Schizophrenia* (see Massumi); some of the articles included in *A Deleuzian Century?* (see Buchanan); and a few of the articles included in *The New Spinoza* (see Warren Montag and Ted Stolze), a collection that also includes several readings of Spinoza that one could not by any standards classify under the rubric of "neo-Spinozism" in the derogatory sense I give to the term in this context. By the same token, the work of some of the above mentioned authors, such as Deleuze's, is far from monolithically "Neo-Spinozist" (see, for instance, Deleuze, 1991, 1994, 1994a, and 1995; or, for a more hybrid case, see Deleuze and Guattari 1986). Put in a rather reductionist way, in the case of both Deleuze and the other "Neo-Spinozists," the demarcating line is determined by the extent to which their understanding of Spinoza is mediated through Bergson's vitalism, rather than a signifier-orientated model and rhetoric, so that we could say that the contemporary opposition between Lacanian Spinozians and Bergsonian "Neo-Spinozists" bears many similarities to the schism between Freudian and Jungian psychoanalysis. The centrality of the opposition "vital energy—signifier" in this distinction is reconfirmed, rather than undermined, by phenomena such as Deleuze's cinema books, in which, explicitly drawing on Henri Bergson's (1859–1941) *Matter and Memory*, Deleuze produces a formalist analysis of cinema, whose main concepts, far from reeking of "Neo-Spinozism," rearticulate several central psychoanalytic concepts. Central among them is the gaze (revamped as the "out-of-field [*hors-champ*]"), which simultaneously functions, as Lacan's gaze retroactively does, as a critique of Jacques Derrida's thesis that "there is no outside-text; *il n'y a pas de hors-texte*" (Derrida 1976, 158). The particular work of Bergson on which Deleuze draws in his cinema books—as Maurice Merleau-Ponty, the primary inspiration of Lacan's theory of the

gaze, put it—is a description of "the brute being of the perceived world," revealing "a pre-Socratic and 'prehuman' sense of the world" (Bergson, back cover). Like Merleau-Ponty's "flesh of . . . Being"—whose "folds" also inspired Deleuze's conceptualization of Leibniz's philosophy and the Baroque, as well as Lacan's "seeingness [*voyure*]" and the gaze—*Matter and Memory* offers a purely materialist and non-anthropomorphic "description of perceived being" that lies far from the exaltation of an *élan vital* (Merleau-Ponty, 139, 146; Lacan 1981, 82; see also Deleuze 1993).

2. Unless otherwise indicated, brackets in citations are mine.

3. I use the term *performative* in the sense of not merely *constative*, a distinction originating in speech-act theory (see J. L. Austin). Briefly put, the signifier and representation are presumed to be constative when their function is assumed to be passive, describing or constating a reality assumed to be already given. By contrast, the signifier is conceived as having a performative function when its ability to change and produce reality as it describes it has been acknowledged. The distinction is of course purely conceptual and heuristic, since the signifier in practice always exercises both functions.

4. Although the term *hegemony* dates back to Stoicism, which was revived in early secular modernity in the Neo-Stoicism of Justius Lipsius (1547–1606) and others, I use it in the sense defined by Antonio Gramsci, in the early twentieth century, which is the sense meant by more contemporary theoreticians of hegemony, such as Ernesto Laclau and Chantal Mouffe (see Lipsius 1939 or 1965; Butler/Laclau/Žižek; and Laclau/Mouffe). For Gramsci, hegemony is the exercise of power by means of consent rather than coercion, a distinction introduced by Niccolò Machiavelli's (1469–1527) early sixteenth-century political theory (see Machiavelli). This distinction corresponds to that between "civil society"—with its consent or noncoercive coercion—and "state"—with its direct force or "coercion" (Gramsci 1985, 104–105). Critically drawing on Benedetto Croce, Gramsci specified hegemony, in part, as "moral and cultural," or, in Crocean terms, "ethico-political" "leadership" over allied and subordinate groups, thereby stressing the function of the "cultural front . . . alongside the merely economic and political ones" in hegemonic politics (106). Nevertheless, as Gramsci puts it explicitly in his 1929–1935 *Prison Writings*, "though hegemony is ethico-political, it must also be economic, must necessarily be based on the decisive function exercised by the leading group in the decisive nucleus of economic activity" (1988, 211–12). This economic base of hegemony presupposes that the allied groups consent to the economic interests of the "leading group," which is possible only if their experience of the hegemonic power is one in which "account [is] taken of the interests and tendencies of the groups over which hegemony is . . . exercised" (211). Herein lies the crucial role of culture and ideology in hegemony. Anticipating a major Spinozian thesis to which we shall turn below, we can say that in hegemony, one particular group of people can hegemonically represent "all people" and their interests, only insofar as "truth is the

standard both of itself and of the false" (Spinoza 1985, 479; *Ethics*, part. 2, prop. 43, schol.) That is, one particular group of people and their interests can represent all groups and interests only insofar as the former is the standard both of "itself" (its own particular interests) and of the "false" (a representation of power mediated by the imaginary, so that the conflicts of particular interests yield to a hegemonic, universal interest). As I argue both elsewhere and here, below, this distinction between power and its representation is also expressed in Spinoza's central distinction between *potentia* and *potestas* (see Kordela 1999, and the section "Is it Possible Not to Hate Representation? (Another Look at *Empire*)," here). The conceptual conditions, therefore, for a hegemonic politics have been available both in philosophy and political theory since early modernity, testifying to the fact that the hegemonic logic has increasingly marked secular politics since the seventeenth, if not the sixteenth, century. There is an extensive literature testifying to the similarities or continuities between early modern theories of the state and concepts used in modernism and postmodernism in order to describe the mechanisms of hegemonic politics and ideology. The literature on Thomas Hobbes's (1588–1679) influential theory of the state furnishes the basis to offer a few indicative examples. Darko Suvin, in his Bahktinian critique of Hobbes, equates the latter's atomized conception of man to Freud's "mechanism" (see Suvin). In his analysis of Hobbes through the work of Kenneth Burke, Nietzsche, and Lacan, Douglas Thomas reads Hobbes's "rhetoric of order" as equivalent of the Lacanian quilting point (*point de capiton*), the integrator of an ideological field (see Thomas). Bernard Willms correlates Hobbes's description of the "state of nature" to Jean-François Lyotard's conception of the logic of postmodernism (see Willms). Paul Dumouchel identifies in Hobbes's work several of the paradoxes that for contemporary epistemology characterize representation (see Dumouchel). Philip Nel links the relation between language and power in Hobbes to Foucault's concept of power-knowledge and to Wittgenstein's position on the relation between language and power, as described in Hanna Fenichel Pitkin's political rereading of Wittgenstein (see Nel). Drawing on speech-act theory, Martin A. Bertman focuses on the effects of Hobbes's rhetorical obfuscation of the distinction between the performative and constative functions of language (see Bertman). Michael Keevak reduces Hobbes's "state of nature" to specific politics of reading and links it to Freudian "anxiety" (see Keevak). Debra B. Bergoffen links Hobbes's theory to Lacan's mirror stage, albeit at the cost of downplaying the significance of the symbolic order (see Bergoffen). More importantly, even when Hobbes is not approached with the intention to establish analogies between his theory and specific contemporary theories, the general consensus in the contemporary scholarship on Hobbes is that, in properly hegemonic fashion, the political effect of his arguments derives from his "retro" language and mode of representation that evoke concepts and structures familiar to the reader from a long, presecular tradition. See, for instance, Tracy B. Strong's historical reading of Hobbes's *Leviathan* as an application of rhetorical strategies known from the Protestant scriptural interpretation (see Strong). Finally, scholars such as Michel de Certeau, Perry Anderson, and José Antonio Maravall, among others, have established an approach to the early modern and baroque state and culture as hegemonic (see de Certeau 1984 and 1988; Anderson; and Maravall).

5. This is certainly true of Slavoj Žižek, from whose work, although appreciatively drawn upon with regard to several other aspects of Lacanian theory, the present work takes a distance. In the section significantly entitled "Spinozism, or, the Ideology of Late Capitalism," in his *Tarrying with the Negative*, Žižek remarks that "contemporary Spinozists (Deleuze, for example)," endeavor "to unearth in Spinoza a theory of communication that breaks completely with the Cartesian problematic of contact between self-conscious monadic individuals." In the "Neo-Spinozist's" accounts, "individuals . . . form a community . . . through the intermixture of partial affects where one 'passion' echoes another and thus reinforces its intensity." Žižek then proceeds to state that this "Neo-Spinozist" movement is to be traced back to "a process labeled by Spinoza *affectum imitatio*" (1993, 218). My sharp differentiation between Spinoza (and Lacanian Spinozism) and "Neo-Spinozism" would be untenable if Spinoza's *affectum imitatio* did indeed entail the "intermixture of partial affects" and the "community" Žižek describes, but this, as we shall see in the section "From Libido to Enjoyment," is not the case. What is further interesting is that it would be no exaggeration to claim that if one replaced in Žižek's description of the "Neo-Spinozist" endeavor the words "affects" and "passion" with "signifier" or its cognates, and paraphrased only a little, one could come up with the following Lacanian statement: "[T]he subjects . . . more docile than sheep, model their being on the moment of the signifying chain which traverses them. . . . [T]he displacement of the signifier determines the subjects in their acts, in their destiny, in their refusals, in their blindness, in their end and in their fate, their innate gifts and social acquisitions notwithstanding, without regard for character or sex, and that, willingly or not, everything that might be considered the stuff of psychology, kit and caboodle, will follow the path of the signifier. . . . Falling in possession of the letter . . . its meaning possesses them" (Lacan 1988, 44). And reading this passage, one might have the same reaction Žižek has in the face of "Neo-Spinozism": "All this may appear very 'subversive,' if measured by the standards of the classical ideological notion of 'autonomous subject'—but isn't this very Spinozist [read here: Lacanian] mechanism at work in what we call the 'postindustrial society of consumption'; i.e., isn't the so-called 'postmodern subject' the passive ground traversed by partial affective links [or, the symbolic chain] reacting to images which regulate his or her 'passions' [or, "psychology" and "fate"], unable to exert control over this mechanism?" (Žižek 1993, 218). Of course, the incommensurable difference between the two passages, because of which one

actually should *not* react to both in the same way, lies in the fact that the said "Neo-Spinozism" presents this structure, clothed in a revolutionary rhetoric, as the ideal realization of the subject's full potential. By contrast, for Lacan, this state of affairs describes "ostriches," "line[d] up" in the trap of "repetition compulsion" (Lacan 1988, 43). In other words, and regardless of what is truly Spinozian and what not, Žižek is right and properly Lacanian in reacting against the "Neo-Spinozist" celebration, as presumably revolutionary, of what effectively is nothing other than the state of the "postindustrial society of consumption." It is indeed very plausible to see, as Žižek argues, the "so-called 'fundamentalism' on which today's mass media more and more confer the role of the Enemy par excellence (in the guise of self-destructive 'radical Evil': Saddam Hussein, the narco-cartels . . .)," as a reaction to this "postindustrial" state, and hence "to the ruling Spinozism, as its inherent Other"—if by "ruling Spinozism" we mean exclusively the said "Neo-Spinozism," as opposed to the Spinozian theory itself (Žižek 1993, 219). I think there is much more to be gained from recognizing and sustaining the distinction between the two. Now, this is arguably what, after Alain Badiou's *Deleuze: The Clamor of Being* (2000), Žižek also attempts to do in *Organs without Bodies* (2004), but in an almost inverted way than the one meant here. For in this more recent reexamination of Deleuze, Žižek is willing to recuperate certain aspects of Deleuze's work, insofar as they can be shown to be reducible to either the Hegelian or the Lacanian line of thought, but what remains unassimilable to this reduction is persistently attributed to Spinoza, in whom Žižek remains adamantly unwilling to see anything less evil than the superego itself. As he writes: "Spinoza's unheard-of endeavor is to think ethics itself outside the 'anthropomorphic' moral categories of intentions, commandments, and the like. What he proposes is stricto sensu an *ontological ethics*, an ethics deprived of the deontological dimension, an ethics of 'is' without 'ought.' What, then, is the price paid for this suspension of the ethical dimension of commandment, of the Master Signifier? The psychoanalytic answer is clear: superego" (2004, 41). I do not think, as we shall see, that this is the properly psychoanalytic answer to Spinoza's ethics. By the way, note that I occasionally accept certain "Neo-Lacanian" readings of Deleuze for the sake of the argument, even as I know that one could argue that this reading does not adequately represent Deleuze's work.

6. In the same context of Spinoza's reading of Adam, Žižek also writes: "Two levels are opposed here, that of imagination and opinions and that of true knowledge. The level of imagination is anthropomorphic: we are dealing with a narrative about agents giving orders that we are free to obey or disobey, and so forth. . . . The true knowledge, on the contrary, delivers the totally nonanthropomorphic causal nexus of impersonal truths. One is tempted to say that here Spinoza out-Jews Jews themselves. He extends iconoclasm to man himself—not only 'do not paint god in man's image' but also 'do not paint man himself in man's image' " (2004, 40).

Ironically, the premise that one must on a certain level not "paint man himself in man's image" is the basic methodological premise of two of the central figures in Žižek's own thought, Marx and Lacan. Read Marx's formal analysis of capital and the commodity (roughly the first one-third of *Capital*, volume 1) and tell me whether there is anything anthropomorphic in it. Even the God and the Son of Christianity reveal themselves as non-anthropomorphic in Marx, as they simply replicate the automatic movement of exchange- and surplus-value. And, as we shall see below, it is precisely anthropomorphism that Lacan criticizes Hegel for, while praising Freud's superior mechanistic model—the latter, of course, being understood as the symbolic order and not as some positivistic model from mechanics. It remains nevertheless true that there is not a single enunciation in Spinoza's discourse on absolute or true knowledge that acknowledges the real, the point at which the machine fails to produce a "nonanthropomorphic causal nexus of impersonal truths." But the moment you include the false (fiction) as one of the two standards of this absolute knowledge, the whole picture changes.

7. Note also that in his discussion of the presumed absence of the function of the death drive in Spinoza, Žižek mentions the following Hegelian example in order to exemplify the logic of what he calls *both* "death drive" and "desire at its purest": "[W]hat is missing in Spinoza is the elementary 'twist' of dialectical inversion characterizing negativity, the inversion by means of which the very renunciation of desire turns into desire of renunciation, and so on" (2004, 34). In another context, Žižek writes: "At the very moment of achieving autonomy, of suspending the hold of heteronomous, externally imposed laws, the subject is thus forced to confront a far more severe Master whose injunction decenters him from within. A homologous inversion takes place in the domain of pleasures: the very renunciation to pleasures brings about a paradoxical surplus enjoyment, an 'enjoyment in pain,' in displeasure, baptized by Lacan *jouissance*, the 'impossible'/traumatic/painful enjoyment beyond the pleasure principle. If we read these two theoretical gestures together, the conclusion which imposes itself, of course, is that Law, in its most radical dimension, is the 'superego,' i.e., an injunction to enjoyment with which it is impossible to comply" (1992, 182). In other words, as far as Žižek is concerned, "death drive," "desire at its purest," "Law," "enjoyment," and "superego" are all one and the same. There are several Lacanian terms that function as cognates, and we shall examine them below, but this is not the case of the above terms. Nevertheless, the assumption that these concepts are practically synonyms indeed underlies Žižek's thought, as is particularly evident in his (and Alenka Zupančič's) accounts of ethics, whose dimension is also reduced to the death drive (see Zupančič). By contrast, I maintain that, to use Lacan's phrase, the death drive is not to be collapsed with the ethical space "between two deaths" (1992, 270). True, Lacan makes ample reference to the death drive in the context of his discussion of ethics and Sophocles' *Antigone*. For example: "In effect,

Antigone herself has been declaring from the beginning: 'I am dead and I desire death'. . . . An illustration of the death instinct [read: drive] is what we find here" (281). But Lacan also points out a crucial difference because of which it cannot be said that all of us, in our everyday life, insofar as the death drive is also operative there, are in the same state as Antigone or as we ourselves at the moment of a truly ethical act: "[F]rom Antigone's point of view life can only be approached, can only be lived or thought about, from the place of that limit where her life is already lost, where she is already on the other side," from where "she can see it and live it in the form of something already lost" (280). To refer to a common manifestation of the death drive, namely, repetition compulsion (which, by the way, is indeed one of its true cognates), it is rather impossible to be compelled to repeat from a place in which life is lived and seen as lost. Nor is the distinction between the death drive and the ethical purely a matter of degree, so that one could say: yes, but in its radical form, the death drive becomes the "between two deaths." As we shall see in the discussion of ethics below, the difference is genuinely structural.

8. It is arguably due to the general disregard of Lacan's parallel relations to Spinoza and Kant (and the unilateral foregrounding of the latter's role) that many contemporary Lacanian theoreticians tend to allow the superegoic, sadistic act—motivated by "desire in its pure state," and, consequently, culminating "in the sacrifice . . . of everything that is the object of love"—to overlap with the ethical act itself (Lacan 1981, 275). Conducive to this tendency is itself the convergence of sadism and Kant's ethics, insofar as both seem, as Lacan argues in his "Kant with Sade [*Kant avec Sade*; 1962]," to involve the sacrifice of "the object of love" or of the "pathological self-interest." But Lacan's point in foregrounding this convergence lies in showing that a proper ethics cannot be derived from Kant's position, precisely because its logical conclusion is sadism. Nevertheless, to my knowledge, Žižek prefers to take at face value throughout his work simply the fact of this convergence. In his recent *Organs without Bodies*, for instance, he identifies a "classificatory confusion" in Kant's distinction among "ordinary," "radical," and "diabolical" evil, which he explains as follows: "[I]f [Kant] were to assert the actual possibility of 'diabolical evil,' he would be utterly unable to distinguish it from the Good," since "both acts would be nonpathologically motivated," so that "the travesty of justice would become indistinguishable from justice itself" (2004, 37–38). Therefore, to overcome Kant's "confusion," all we need to do expectably is to follow "the shift from this Kantian inconsistency to Hegel's reckless assumption of the identity of 'diabolical' evil with the Good itself" (38). Well, that's exactly what Lacan also saw: that Kant's ethics leads to the above conclusion, which is why Lacan does not want Kant's position to be the last word in ethics. By contrast, for Žižek, the Kantian/Hegelian indistinguishability of "diabolical evil" and "Good" remains his ethical motto, as his analysis of innumerable examples of 'ethical acts' throughout his work indicates. And this remains so even as he simultaneously discerns

the fundamental inconsistency at the basis of the Kantian ethical edifice. In Žižek's words: "According to Kant, if one finds oneself alone on the sea with another survivor of a sunken ship near a floating piece of wood that can keep only one person afloat, moral considerations are no longer valid. There is no moral law preventing me from fighting to death with the other survivor for the place on the raft; I can engage in it with moral impunity. . . . Does this strange exception not demonstrate that ruthless egotism, the care for personal survival and gain, is the silent 'pathological' presupposition of Kantian ethics, namely, that the Kantian edifice can maintain itself only if we silently presuppose the 'pathological' image of man as a ruthless utilitarian egotist?" (38, n. 44). If this is the case, how is it, then, possible to speak of "ethics" while our theory persists to be based on the Kantian principle of the "non-pathological," which, as Žižek argues, can provide only a theory of ruthless utilitarian egotism? Lacan's project of ethics, by contrast, is motivated by an opposition to all Western ethics, which, from Aristotle to Kant and beyond, has always been predicated on the fact that "a whole register of desire," whose constitution takes place beyond the pleasure principle, "is literally situated . . . outside of the field of morality" (Lacan 1992, 5). This exclusion of desire marks not only Kant but also sadism, as Sade's work indicates, in which, although it is presumably "a treatise truly about desire, there is little . . . even nothing" about it; instead, what there is, is desire's and pleasure's "submission . . . to the Law." And this submission is for Lacan characteristic of all Western ethics, including "Christian ethics," in which "the Sadian fantasy situates itself better . . . than elsewhere," drawing the logic of the "Christian commandment," "Love thy neighbor as thyself," to its logical consequences (Lacan 1989, 74–75). As Copjec, who sustains the distinction between Kant and Sade in order to denounce the general "conflation of . . . ethical action with perversion," puts it, "the pervert . . . surrenders his *right* to jouissance [as pure sexual enjoyment] in order to assume it as a *duty* that he has contracted to carry out" (2002, 208, and 225). Sade serves as the foil through which Lacan can show the underside of the Western conceptualizations of ethics, and functions as an intermediary stage in the development of Lacan's own ethics, as inclusive of desire—something that, to repeat, remains ostracized from all Western accounts of ethics, Kant and Sade included. Not irrelevant to the present argument is the fact that Žižek, as well as Zupančič, argue that there is a shift in Lacan's work in which his ethics of desire yielded to an ethics of the drive and the real. David Martyn has shown extensively that "there is really no textual evidence on which to distinguish, as Žižek and Zupančič do, Lacan's 'early' ethics of desire from his 'late' ethics of the Real" (240, n. 28). Lacan's ethics remains throughout his work an ethics of desire, a subject that, among the philosophers invoked in this context, figures prominently only in Spinoza.

9. In this sense, Lacan treats funeral rites in Sophocles' *Antigone* in the same way Lévi-Strauss treats the incest prohibition in *The Elementary*

Structures of Kinship, namely, as something that, in his own words, "is in origin neither purely cultural nor purely natural. . . . It is the fundamental step because of which, by which, but above all in which, the transition from nature to culture is accomplished. In one sense, it belongs to nature, for it is a general condition of culture. . . . However, in another sense, it is already culture, exercising and imposing its rule on phenomena which initially are not subject to it" (Lévi-Strauss, 24–25). Paraphrasing the issue, the Japanese philosopher and literary critic Kojin Karatani writes: "If we do not consider culture as an a priori given, it can only be deduced from nature. But culture does not emerge from nature. Lévi-Strauss solved this by turning to 'prohibition'. . . . The prohibition of incest is 'what man makes,' but it is not made by man, because it is this prohibition itself that makes man into man" (1995, 95–96). Similarly, funeral rites are "what man makes," but they are not made by man, because it is these rites themselves that make man into man, forming "a general condition of culture," yet "exercising and imposing [their] rule" on death, a phenomenon that initially is not subject to culture. In the context of Hegel's reading of *Antigone*, Žižek makes the same point about the funeral ritual, arguing that it is "the act defining the very emergence of man" (1989, 218). In Hegel's words, the "blood-relationship supplements" through the funeral ritual "the abstract natural process [death] by adding to it the movement of consciousness . . . or better . . . the blood-relation . . . takes on itself the act of destruction" (1977, 271). In Žižek's succinct paraphrase, "in the funeral rite, the subject confers the *form* of a free act on an 'irrational,' contingent natural process," or, in other words, although death is a "forced choice," through the funeral rite, "the subject assumes, repeats as his own act, what happened anyway" (1989, 219). Limit cases, such as the funeral rites and the incest prohibition, indicate to us that not only can culture not be derived from nature, but that the human being is a being for which nature is always already culture—a thesis which, as we shall see, is advanced by Spinoza. In this view, Antigone's act, her retreat into language—as a purely differential, nonevaluative formal system—posits a demand to the discourse (culture) that it recall its own self-referentiality, and hence the arbitrariness of its values. As Karatani writes, once the prohibition of incest is treated "as a logical sine qua non for the existence of a formal structure," such as a cultural system of organization and values, it reveals itself as "the prohibition of self-referentiality," what in set theory is called "formal typing." Any "formal system is always disequilibrate and excessive," being doomed to choose " '*both* this and that' "; only through this formal typing or incest prohibition (the prohibition of self-referentiality) can any system measure up to "the necessity of choosing '*either* this or that' " (1995, 93–94). Antigone's act underscores the arbitrariness of the discourse's choice between "this or that," and hence between good and evil—since this choice is based on the prohibition of its own self-referentiality—and the fact that the sole necessary thing lies in "the link between" nature and culture or being and signifier, because of which, to repeat Lacan's words, "the register of being of someone who was identified by name has to be preserved by funeral rites" (Lévi-Strauss, 25). Although the prohibition of self-referentiality (also known as castration) is necessary for any system to function in such a way so that people can choose "either this or that," its momentary disregard (as practiced by Antigone) is also necessary for any shift from a given system to a new, and hence for the ethical act as an act that ignores established norms and values. The foundation of any new system presupposes such a disregard of the prohibition (law) of the preceding system's self-referentiality, which explains Freud's persistence on the myth of the murder of the father (law) as the founding moment of society.

10. Already in his third seminar, on psychoses, Lacan had established the distinction between language, as a synchronic, purely differential system, and discourse, as a diachrony. Unlike language which is nondirectional, discourse is teleological and hence imbued with value judgments. In Lacan's words: "Firstly, there is a synchronic whole, which is language as a simultaneous system of structured groups of opposition, then there is what occurs diachronically, over time, and which is discourse. One cannot but give discourse a certain direction in time, a direction that is defined in a linear manner. . . . But it is not quite exact to say that it is a simple line, it is more probably a set of several lines, a stave. It is in this diachronism that discourse is set up" and that action, as we saw *apropos* Adam, becomes possible (1993, 54). Unlike all human action, the ethical act is executed not from the place of directional discourse but from that of the sheer differentiality of language, which is why it is an act (and not an action) that remains meaningless from the perspective of the given discourse and can become meaningful only if a new discourse emerges, which is organized in such a way so that this act retroactively obtains meaning. In "Kant with Sade," Lacan explicitly distinguished his concept of ethics, predicated on one's detachment from discourse and retreat into the field of pure language, from the Western tradition whose foil is sadism, by concluding that "it would not be possible for Sade, as is suggested by P. Klossowski even as he notes that he does not believe it, to have attained a sort of apathy which would be 'to have reentered the bosom of nature, in a waking state, in our world,' inhabited by language" (1989, 75). The distinction between discourse, as a teleological system, and language, as a purely differential system, is further reinforced through Lacan's reference to the former as a "machine" (in his second seminar) or an "automaton" (in his eleventh seminar). A "machine" or an "automaton" is by definition teleological, insofar as "implicit in the metaphor of the human body as a machine" is always the "energy myth," that is, the "energy function," on which Freud "throughout his work . . . placed the accent," and according to which living beings considered as machines have "to be fed" and "looked after . . . because they tend to wear out," and, in the last analysis, they "look after themselves all on their own, in other words, they represent

homeostats" (Lacan 1991a, 75–76). The *telos* of the human body as a machine is the conservation of energy. This is why the living being considered as "*automaton*" is "governed by the pleasure principle," "which is a principle of homeostasis" (Lacan 1981, 53–54 and 31). Thus, the "network of signifiers," considered as discourse, that is, as "automaton," aims at the homeostasis or the retention of an equilibrium of energy in the subject, and the only thing lying "beyond the *automaton*" is "the *tuché*," the "encounter with the real." The latter entails "*suffrance*," namely, "pain" (52–53, 56, and 56, n. 1). Pain is governed not by a homeostatic mechanism but by "*Zwang*, constraint, which Freud defines by *Wiederholung* [repetition]" (56). If in "modern biology," "life was going to be defined in relation to death," it is because beyond the pleasure principle lies, as its own precondition, repetition compulsion or the death drive, and hence the possibility of sacrifice (Lacan 1991a, 75). Hegel, as we shall see more extensively below, could not conceive of death or sacrifice as determinant in the subject's relation to discourse precisely because "in Freud something is talked about, which isn't talked about in Hegel, namely energy," since "between Hegel and Freud, there's the advent of the world of the machine" (1991a, 74). As long as the death drive is not taken into account, the question of ethics also cannot be addressed adequately, for there is no criterion on the basis of which to distinguish between a sacrifice of the pleasure principle motivated by the superegoic demand to sustain the discourse at all costs and a sacrifice of the discourse itself, namely, the retreat into language. Finally, note that Lacan explicitly differentiates the era of the metaphors of energy and the machine from the theocratic, feudal society in which "people . . . had slaves" and "didn't realise that one could establish equations for the price of their food and what they did in their *latifundia*," as is evident in the fact that "there are no examples of energy calculations in the use of slaves" and that "there is no hint of an equation as to their output." True, "slaves" "wear out . . . as well, but," Lacan continues, "one doesn't think about it, one thinks that it is natural for them to get old and croak" (1991a, 75). If the decisive distinction is one between slave- and remunerated labor, then the above metaphors essentially refer not so much to the literal advent of machines, but to the advent of capitalism, in which "an equation as to their output" is required for laborers to be paid. Nevertheless, even if in principle, the logic of the machine is, by this token, introduced already with the gradual shift from feudalism to capitalism in the sixteenth and seventeenth centuries, the legal abolition of slavery, as well as the domination of the world by the machine, historically indeed postdates Hegel.

11. In addition to this movement of the "forward march of the phenomenology of spirit" toward the "completed discourse" of the master qua science, Lacan makes also brief reference to another scenario, which he decides to "leave . . . to one side" (1991a, 71). In this, "completed discourse" is identified as "what we call the post-revolutionary stage," the

"moment discourse has reached its completion" so that "there won't be any further need to speak" (71). This version of the "march" of history allows us to see that, conversely, all it takes for a discourse to be experienced by its subjects as "completed," that is, without the "need to speak" further, is to represent itself as the moment at which history "has reached its completion," that is, as the "end of history." Today, this mode of self-representation can be said to be characteristic of the "post-revolutionary stages" only if by that term we mean the stages following the revolution's collapse, as is the case of the current postmodern global stage of capital. (Note that by "stage" I do not imply any conception of history based on developmental stages of capital. For a detailed elaboration of this point, see Kordela 2006.) As Žižek puts it, for the last "twenty or twenty-five years," since "the collapse of socialism," what has "disappeared" is "the belief that humanity . . . can actively intervene and somehow steer social development," so that "we are again accepting the notion of history as fate" (Žižek, in Mead, 40). Postmodernism massively disseminates the conviction that, whereas in the past the "idea was that life would somehow go on on earth, but that there are different possibilities," "now we talk all the time about the end of the world," and it is indeed "much easier for us to imagine the end of the world than a small change in the political system" (40). In Žižek's succinct capitulation, the postmodern motto is that: "Life on earth maybe will end, but somehow capitalism will go on" (40). Interestingly, like everything else Žižek ever said or did, this statement remained for the interviewer and author of the article a "bewildering" "paradox" or an "absurdity"—albeit at least "accessible"—merely testifying to the fact that Žižek is a person who presumably "contradicts himself all the time" and leaves "the audience perplexed about what exactly [he] st[ands] for." The irony is in the fact that Mead herself had earlier in the same article entirely reconfirmed Žižek's motto by stating that the U.S.A. is "a country where radical socialism is about as likely to take root as radical fruitarianism" (39–40).

12. As Bruce Fink writes in his translation of Lacan's seminar XX, the verb "*jouir*" from which the noun "*jouissance*" derives, "means 'to come' in the sexual sense: 'to reach orgasm,' " and in the syntactical pattern "*jouir de*," it also "means to enjoy, take advantage of, benefit from, get off on, and so on" (Lacan 1998, 3, n. 8).

13. Žižek offers an apt account of the sadist's status as the Other's victim in " 'In His Bold Gaze My Ruin is Writ Large' " (see Žižek 1992a, 211–72). Note that Hegel himself comes close to a model that articulates the truth of the sadist as a victim of the Other, albeit not in the context of his dialectic of the master and the slave. This occurs in the context of the "universal Idea" and the "cunning of reason." In Hegel's famous words: "It is the particular that is involved in the struggle with others, and of which one part is doomed to perish. It is not the universal Idea [Other] which involves itself in antithesis and struggle, exposing itself to danger; it remains in the background, and is preserved against attack or injury. This may be called the *Cunning of Reason*, that it allows the passions to

work for it, while what it brings into existence suffers loss and injury. This is the phenomenal world, part of which is negative [victim-slave], part positive [sadist-slave]. Compared to the universal [master], the particular is for the most part too slight in importance: individuals are surrendered and sacrificed" (1988a, 35). Here, although the Idea remains inexorably isolated in its "background," without any point of contact with the individuals' "passions," the master-slave relation between the Idea and the purely instrumental particular individuals is recognized and, in fact, elevated to the status of a universal relation. If, with Hegel, *all* individuals are in the service of the Other (Idea), "Lacan's theoretical innovation," beyond restoring the Other in its (Spinozian) aimless status, was, as Copjec puts it, "to argue that," contrary to appearances, it is only "the pervert" who is the "*servant* of the Other" (2002, 227).

14. To the consensual, evolutionist readings of Spinoza is also to be included the neuroscientific approach, of which Antonio Damasio figures as an eminent proponent, and which I address elsewhere (see Damasio 2003; and Kordela, forthcoming).

Part I. Secular Causality and Its Enjoyment

1. The following is a concise passage from Aristotle's *Metaphysics* introducing the four primary causes and advancing the thesis that knowledge consists in their knowledge: "But since it is manifest that one ought to be in possession of a science of primary causes (for then we say that we know each individual thing when we think that we are acquainted with the first cause); and since causes are denominated under four different heads, the first of which we assert to be the substance and the essence of a thing . . . and the second cause we affirm to be the matter and the subject; and the third is the source of the first principle of motion; and the fourth that cause that is in opposition to this—namely, both the final cause and the good" (1991, 17; bk. I, 983a).

2. In Thomas Aquinas's words: "But since being caused is not essential to being as such, there exists an uncaused being. . . . So the one God is the agent, prototype, and goal of all things, and the source of their matter. . . . Nothing existent can be presupposed to the issuing of everything from its first cause. . . . [C]reation . . . must proceed . . . from nothing. . . . Crafts presuppose materials provided by nature; natural causes presuppose matter which they form and transform; but if God presupposed anything in this way he would not be the universal cause of all existence; so he must bring things into existence from nothing. We think of creation as a change, even though it isn't. In a change something begins in one state and ends up in another; but in creation there is nothing to begin with. . . . [M]aking and being made are more appropriate terms than changing and being changed" (84–85; "Chapter 4: Creation," vol. 8, 44–45).

3. In his remarkable *Hegel on Spinoza*, Pierre Macherey has demonstrated that Hegel's homage to Spinoza was predicated on his necessar-

ily and profoundly anti-Spinozian reading of Spinoza, which systematically molded, in Eugene Holland's summary of Macherey's point, Spinoza's "non-finalistic, anti-subjective materialism" so as to comply with "Hegel's own teleological-subjective-idealist premises" (Holland, §7; see Macherey 1979; for an English translation of the second chapter of this book, see Macherey 1997). Hegel acknowledged Spinoza as the first properly secular philosopher, as the direct successor of Descartes, and as his own precursor only insofar as he misread him—and he did so not accidentally but necessarily and programmatically. Macherey's exposition of the difference between Spinoza and Hegel is "not an assertion that Hegel happened to get Spinoza wrong, but a demonstration that, given his premises and project, Hegel *had to* get Spinoza wrong, *in a specific way* and for specific reasons" (Holland, §7). Holland also remarks that in his book "Macherey . . . poses rather than answers the question of what Spinoza might contribute to Marxism as a replacement for Hegel" (n. 10). Beyond being an endeavor to retrieve Spinozian thought from its Hegelian, "Neo-Spinozist," and other inappropriate inflections, the present work is also an attempt to point to directions that might facilitate possible answers to Macherey's question.

4. Spinoza makes also the distinction between "*natura naturans*" and "*natura naturata*," what Seymour Feldman translates in his introduction to the *Ethics* as "nature naturing " and "nature natured," respectively (11). Although "*natura naturans*" indicates nature as active or "productive," and "*natura naturata*" designates nature as passive or "produced and referring to the modes," "both are different dimensions of one and the same substance of God" (Feldman, 11). As Spinoza writes: "[B]y *Natura naturans* we must understand what is in itself and is conceived through itself, *or* such attributes of substance as express an eternal and infinite essence, i.e. . . . God, insofar as he is considered as a free cause. But by *Natura naturata* I understand whatever follows from the necessity of God's nature, *or* from any of God's attributes, i.e., all the modes of God's attributes insofar as they are considered as things which are in God, and can neither be nor be conceived without God" (Spinoza 1985, 434; *Ethics*, part I, prop. 29 dem. and schol.). The distinction in question is not one between two differing natures since it is "God's attributes" that determine "all the modes." As Spinoza puts it: "*In nature there is nothing contingent, but all things have been determined from the necessity of the divine nature to exist and produce an effect in a certain way*" (1985, 433; *Ethics*, part I, prop. 29.). In Gilles Deleuze's (1925–1995) words, "*Natura naturans* (as substance and cause) and *Natura naturata* (as effect and mode) are interconnected through a mutual immanence," because of which there is a "univocity of attributes" or properties, "where the attributes in the same form constitute the essence of God as naturing nature and contain the essences of modes as natured nature" (1988, 92). As Yirmiyahu Yovel writes, the "distinction" between "*natura naturans*" and "*natura naturata*" "replaces the traditional dualism of the Creator and the things he creates" by introducing a monism in which the two natures are one and the same,

but seen, in the former case, as free (insofar as God is a free cause), and, in the latter, as determined (insofar as everything is determined by God's attributes) (159). See also De Dijn, particularly "Chapter 9: On God (*Ethics* I)," 195–213. Edwin Curley attempts to establish a distinction between *natura naturans* and *natura naturata* by equating the former with God and with "the eternality and immutability of the fundamental laws of nature" (43). Given, however, that everything in nature is necessary, and hence eternal and immutable, rather than contingent, everything in nature itself constitutes nature's "fundamental laws," *natura naturans.* This seems to agree with Curley's own further assertion that "[w]hat Descartes had called the secondary cause of motion, the laws of extended nature, become [in Spinoza] the primary cause of motion" (43).

5. I am equating science, that is, hard science, with positivism only for heuristic reasons. It is well known, at least since quantum physics, that physics' logic today is not positivistic. By contrast, it is rather a certain philosophical and theoretical tradition, which remains positivist and criticizes immanent causality and psychoanalysis. We shall return to the nonpositivist character of contemporary physics below.

6. Beyond Wittgenstein and Karl Kraus, other critics of psychoanalysis with regard to its model of causality and validation, and, hence, its scientific status, include Karl Popper and Adolf Grünbaum (see Wittgenstein 1958, 1976, and 1979; Kraus; for a recapitulation of Wittgenstein's and Kraus's critiques from a perspective that shares their premises, see Bouveresse; Popper 1962, 1974, and 1982; for Grünbaum's own critique, including his criticism of Popper's critique, see Grünbaum).

7. I stress that the definition of a signifying element involves its articulation with *"all"* other signifying elements to distinguish differentiality from simple relationality. Relationality pertains to several phenomena in mechanical physics. For instance, two bodies moving parallel to one another, in the same direction, and with the same speed, are immobile in relation to one another. This remains true regardless of whether, say, a third body moves parallel to them, in the same direction, with twice their speed. A signifying element by contrast, not only cannot be defined in relation to only one other signifying element, but not even merely in relation to all other actually present elements, say, all the signifiers of a book. All signifiers not included in the given book may effect the meaning of its signifiers, as is evident in the fact that different readers have different readings of one and the same book. To put it in an anthropomorphic way, we could say that, unlike relational elements, differential elements, such as signifiers, behave as if they knew that a signifier that is not actually there could potentially be there. This explains why for Spinoza, for whom God or substance is immanently or differentially caused, the potential is the actual, as follows from his assertion that *"things could have been produced by God in no other way, and in no other order than they have been produced"* (Spinoza 1985, 436; *Ethics,* part I, prop. 33).

8. For Spinoza's pantheism, see the "Introduction," here.

9. "Wovon man nicht sprechen kann, darüber muß man schweigen [whereof one cannot speak, thereon one must remain silent]" (Wittgenstein 1963, 115; 7). In his seminar XVII, Lacan credits Wittgenstein for having grasped "que le fait est un attribut de la proposition crue [that the fact is an attribute of the crude proposition]," under the precondition that by "crude proposition" is meant the locus "où l'on distingue l'énoncé de l'énonciation [where one distinguishes the statement from the enunciation]." This distinction "est une operation que . . . je n'hésite pourtant pas à declarer arbitraire [is an operation which . . . I nevertheless do not hesitate to declare arbitrary]." As a result, and "comme c'est la position de Wittgenstein [as is Wittgenstein's own position]," "il n'y a à ajouter nul signe d'affirmation à ce qui est assertion pure et simple [there is no sign of affirmation to be added to that which is assertion pure and simple]," since "l'assertion s'annonce comme vérité [the assertion announces itself as truth]." It follows, that "quels que soient les faits du monde . . . la tautologie de la totalité du discours, c'est cela qui fait le monde [whatever the facts of the world may be . . . it is the tautology of the totality of discourse that makes the world]." Hence, "ce qu'on peut dire après avoir lu Wittgenstein [what one can say after having read Wittgenstein]" is that "il n'y a de sens que du désir [there is no sense but (that) of desire]." It is because sense is for Lacan a matter of desire, that, although there is no doubt that "cette operation dite wittgensteinienne n'est-elle rien qu'une extraordinaire parade, qu'une détection de la canaillerie philosophique [this operation called Wittgensteinian is nothing other than an extraordinary display, a detection of philosophical rascality]," Lacan cannot be satisfied with the conclusion of the *Tractatus*. For if it is desire and not logical deduction that has the last word, then "toute canaillerie repose sur ceci, de vouloir être l'Autre, j'entends le grand Autre, de quelqu'un, là où se dessinent les figures où son désir sera capté [all rascality relies on the will to be the Other, I mean the big Other, of someone, where the figures, in which his desire will be captivated, take shape]" (Lacan 1991, 67–69). In short, Wittgenstein's otherwise admirable enterprise falls short of grasping knowledge's transferential relation with the Other's desire.

10. The differential constitution of particles and waves in quantum physics was first observed in the famous "double-slit experiment." This showed that electrons behave either as simple particles or as waves interfering with one another, depending not on the *actual* existence of a second emission of electrons through a second slit (which would interfere with a first emission through a first slit), but on whether a second slit is closed or open, so that a second emission of electrons *could* occur, even if it actually does not. This is why the quantum universe is not merely relational, as is the mechanical universe, but differential (see n. 7 in Part I, here). Commenting on the significance of this experiment, Žižek writes: "it is as if a single electron (a particle that, as such, must go through one

of the two slits) 'knows' whether the other slit is open and behaves accordingly; if the other slit is open, it behaves as a wave, if not, as an 'ordinary' particle." Drawing on psychoanalytic vocabulary, we could say that "a single electron seems to 'know' if it is being observed or not" by the gaze, as it were, opened up by the other slit when it is open, "since it behaves accordingly" (Žižek 1996, 276). But already Roger Joseph Boscovich's (1711–1787) atomic theory, with its substitution of quasi-material point-centers of action (*puncta*) for the rigid units of matter, and its concomitant kinematics, which uses only two dimensions (length and time)—rather than, as in Newtonian dynamics, three (mass, length, and time)—had established particles as a system of elements whose identity is constituted only through the differential relations of each particle to all others. Philosophers such as Giambattista Vico, Leibniz (whose *Monadology* and relational space had influenced Boscovich), and Kant had also produced similar atomic theories. Nevertheless, in spite of these similarities between quantum physics and any analysis of the signifier and subjectivity, it should also be pointed out that the former is an incommensurably simplified or embryonic form of the latter. This is already evident in the fact that, even though one could not have predicted how an electron will behave when the second slit is closed or open without having already seen through an experiment the empirical behavior of the said electron, once this is known, one knows and can predict how the electron will always behave when the other slit is open and when not, unlike in human behavior, where the fact that a joke might make me laugh does not entail that I will necessarily laugh every time I hear it. And, as we shall see below, even though there is a realm of quantum behavior where exact prediction is impossible, the alternatives of possible quantum behavior, in the current state of quantum physics, remain incomparably more limited than those opened up by the signifier. Which is to say, the validity of such arguments about the homology between quantum physics and the field of the signifier derives from the theoretical potential of the former, the fact that nothing prevents us from assuming that its complexity could increase to the level where the indeterminacy of prediction could be as diverse as hardly to account for an experimentally testable prediction.

11. Herein lies another of Israel's major misunderstandings of Spinoza's thought, which is expressed in the form of a blatant contradiction. To link Spinoza to the scientific project of secular modernity, Israel invokes the fact that "at the core of Spinoza's philosophy . . . stands the contention that 'nothing happens in Nature that does not follow from her laws, that her laws cover everything that is conceived even by the divine intellect, and that Nature observes a fixed and immutable order,' that is, that the same laws of motion, and laws of cause and effect, apply in all contexts and everywhere" (244; referring to Spinoza, *Tractatus Theologico-Politicus*, 126–27; and to Paty 196–97). "Certainly," Israel infers, "this is a metaphysical system which cannot be proved or disproved scientifically,"

whereby by "scientifically" Israel clearly means by way of experimental, mechanistic physics, for he continues, thereby contradicting himself: "But it [Spinoza's metaphysical system] is nevertheless also a 'scientific' theory conceivable only since the rise of the seventeenth-century 'mechanistic world-view,' claiming as it does that the laws science demonstrates through experiment and mathematical calculation are universally valid and the sole criterion of truth" (244). If for Spinoza, as Israel rightly puts it, "the same laws of motion, and laws of cause and effect, apply in all contexts and everywhere," then it is not "through experiment" but solely through theoretical contemplation of the given data that one should be able to infer these unconditionally "same laws" of nature. Israel's contradiction is due to his indiscriminate use of "experiment" and "mathematical calculation" or formalism. The statements that "Spinoza's conception of truth, and the criterion for judging what is true, is 'mathematical logic,' " and that "mathematical rationality universally applied provides, from Spinoza to Marx, the essential link between the Scientific Revolution and the tradition of radical thought," are true only insofar as by "Scientific Revolution" we mean mathematical formalism and not experimental mechanics (Israel, 244). For, like mathematics and Spinoza, Marx neither used nor could ever identify the "eternal laws of commodity-exchange" through "experiment" (Marx 1990, 301). And neither Spinozian nor Marxian thought can serve to legitimize empiricism. On the contrary, both testify to what Georg Simmel (1858–1918) has aptly argued with regard to modern secular thought, namely, that it (like the economy that accompanies it, capitalism) is formalist or purely "intellectual" and "abstract," insofar as, from the moment at which money "express[es] the value relations between other objects," ignoring the particular "identity" or qualities of these objects, "money passes from the form of directness and substantiality . . . to the ideal form; that is, it exercises its effects merely as an idea which is embodied in a representative symbol." Even the materiality of money (paper money or a coin) is a secondary effect, "a product" or "pure embodiment," "of the fundamental power or form of our mind" to be able to "balance against each other not only two" dissimilar "things, but also the relations of these two to two others, and so unite them by judging them equal or similar" in terms of their abstract value, beyond their positive characteristics (146–48). Once we differentiate between formalism and experimental mechanics, it is impossible to argue, as Israel does, that Spinoza's "philosophy was based on modern science both experimental and deductive" (244).

12. Lacan treats the signifier as a value, homologous to capital, for, as he says already in his second seminar (1954–1955): "Speech is first and foremost [an] object of exchange" (1991a, 47). In *The Order of Things* (1970; French original: *Les Mots et les choses*, 1966), Michel Foucault also presupposes this homology between capital and secular sign, as is evident in his distinction between the secular, "binary" sign, and the theocratic,

"ternary" sign. The sign of theocracy, Foucault writes, was based on "the similitudes that link the marks to the things designated by them," thus consisting of three parts: the mark, the thing, and the similitude between the two, which fixed their link as an "organic," rather than constructed and arbitrary, bond (1970, 42). The secular, "binary sign" arrives after "the destruction of the organic," the demise of which made the link between mark and thing arbitrary (42). While this transformation was happening on the level of the sign, in economy, Foucault continues, " 'money,' " ceased to " 'draw its value from the material of which it is composed,' " and began to "receive its value from its pure function as sign. . . . Things take on value, then, in relation to one another . . . but the true estimation of that value has its source in human judgment. . . . Wealth is wealth because we estimate it, just as our ideas are what they are because we represent them. Monetary or verbal signs are additional to this" (175–76; citing Scipion de Grammont, *Le Denier royal, traité curieux de l'or et de l'argent* [Paris 1620, 48]). In his *S/Z* (based on his two-year seminar at the *École pratique des Hautes Étude* in 1968–1969, and published in French in 1970), Roland Barthes also draws this homology between money and signifier (see Barthes, particularly the chapter "Index, Sign, Money," 39–41). Also in the years 1969–1970, in his seventeenth seminar, Lacan draws on this homology and on Marx's surplus-value to define the concept of "surplus-enjoyment" as the equivalent of Marx's surplus-value on the level of the secular signifier. In Lacan's words: "Quelque chose a changé dans le discours du maître à partir d'un certain moment de l'histoire. . . . [À] partir d'un certain jour, le plus-de-jouir se compte, se comptabilise, se totalise. Là commence ce que l'on appelle accumulation du capital . . . l'impuissance à faire le joint du plus-de-jouir à la vérité du maître . . . est tout d'un coup vidée. La plus-value s'adjoint au capital—pas de problème, c'est homogène, nous sommes dans les valeurs [Something changed in the discourse of the master at a certain moment in history. . . . [F]rom a certain day on, the surplus-enjoyment [*plus-de-jouir*] started to be counted, accounted, totalized. Here begins what one calls accumulation of capital . . . the impotence of adjoining the surplus-enjoyment to the truth of the master . . . is suddenly voided. The surplus-value adjoins itself to capital—no problem, they are homogenous, we are within values]" (Lacan 1991, 207; translation mine). We shall return to the surplus-enjoyment's function of "adjoining" itself "to the truth of the master" below. Of course, the homology between capital and secular sign is also central to the work of Alfred Sohn-Rethel (1899–1990), and, much earlier, to the pioneering work of Georg Simmel. But the pathbreaking moment is of course to be found in Marx's work itself, particularly his concept of commodity fetishism (see Simmel; Sohn-Rethel 1977 and 1978; and Marx 1990, particularly the chapter "The Fetishism of the Commodity and Its Secret," 163–77).

13. It is in this sense of the real as the unrealized historical cause-effect that the term *transcendence* is used throughout this work.

14. To these sciences whose object is differential substance we should of course add cybernetics, the science of information, whose "past," as Lacan pointed out in 1955, "consists in nothing more than the rationalized formation of what we will call, to contrast them to the exact sciences, the conjectural sciences" (1991a, 296). "Conjectural sciences" is Lacan's term for the "specific group of sciences which are normally designated by the term human sciences," including of course psychoanalysis, insofar as "human action is involved in any conjuncture" (296). The beginnings of conjectural sciences date back in 1654, when Pascal advanced "the probability calculus," that is, "the form of calculation, not of randomness, but of chances, of the encounter in itself." Probability calculus "enables one to determine immediately what a gambler has the right to expect at any given moment when the succession of turns which make up a game is interrupted," the "succession of turns" being "the simplest form one can give to the idea of the encounter" (299). Thus, the "science of what is found at the same place," the exact or hard science, "is substituted for by the science of the combination of places as such," so that "everything which up until then had been the science of numbers becomes a combinatory science." In this science, the "more or less confused, accidental traversal of the world of symbols is organized around the correlation of absence and presence," and "the search for the laws of presence and absence will tend towards the establishing of the binary order which leads to what we call cybernetics" (299–30). In other words, like the sciences of the signifier, the subject, and capitalist economy, cybernetics is a science that studies the *difference* between presence and absence. For "information," "as the father of cybernetics, Norbert Wiener, put it," is "nothing but *difference*," the latter being the essence of both the signifier and capital, insofar as "value productivity is not determined by what it produces, but by whether or not it produces *difference*" (i.e., surplus-value) (Karatani 2003, 267).

15. In his *Organs without Bodies* (2004), Žižek opts for another course of argument, in which anti-Platonism is not subjugated to an overarching Platonism but rather constitutes a positive alternative to it, even as Žižek's Deleuze remains in many regards similar to Badiou's. Thus, Žižek writes, for instance, that Hitchcock's *Vertigo*, "is, in a sense, the ultimate anti-Platonic film, a systematic materialist undermining of the Platonic project, akin to what Deleuze does in the appendix to *The Logic of Sense*" (2004, 157). In *Vertigo*, Žižek writes, "the murderous fury that seizes Scottie when he finally discovers that Judy, whom he tried to make into Madeleine, is (the woman he knew as) Madeleine, is the fury of the deceived Platonist when he perceives that the original he wants to remake in a perfect copy is already, in itself, a copy." Therefore, both the film and Deleuze are anti-Platonist in showing us that "(what we took to be) *the copy turns out to be the original*" (157). I venture that Badiou would not disagree with this conclusion, but would likely add that this is

the case already in Plato's work itself, and/or that whatever the hierarchy between "original" and "copy" may be, we remain within the Platonist problematic.

16. Note, however, that even as the univocity of Being is defined as a transhistorical surplus, the function of this surplus varies historically. God, as the surplus of theocratic feudalism, functioned very differently than the secular capitalist surplus, which is a lack. The difference in the function of the secular and the presecular surplus is evident in the difference between what Lacan calls the University Discourse and the Discourse of the Master, respectively (see Lacan 1991, particularly the chapter "Le maître et l'hystérique," 31–41). Put simply, in theocracy, the surplus (gaze or will) of the Other was not lacking and, hence, it did not need to be imagined by the subject in the Other. The official discourse (scriptures, theological debates, etc.) determined for the subject the surplus. It is only in secular thought that the subject must itself procure a surplus that is then adjoined to the truth of the Other, just as only in capitalism does surplus-value adjoin itself to capital, while feudalist economy was one of equilibrium.

17. In Lacanian psychoanalysis, there are many terms that can function as cognates of surplus-enjoyment (*plus-de-jouir*), such as "gaze," "*objet a*," "lack," "organ," "phallus," "nothing," and several others, including the "unconscious" itself, which is the surplus par excellence, as Lacan's equation of the unconscious with the God of secular thought indicates. (We shall return to this equation below). On a certain level, it is important to sustain the conceptual distinction between these terms, insofar as they serve different functions within different conceptual clusters, such as those pertaining to the four distinct drives (oral, anal, scopic, and invocatory). But on another level, because there is a structural homology among the drives, as well as because of the fact that "toute pulsion est virtuallement pulsion de mort [every drive is in effect death drive]," these terms are also interchangeable (Lacan 1971, 215; translation mine). A passage that highlights both levels simultaneously comes as a response to Safouan's question: "*Beyond the appearance, is there a lack, or the gaze?*" To this Lacan replies: "At the level of the scopic dimension, in so far as the drive operates there, is to be found the same function of the *objet a* as can be mapped in all the other dimensions. The *objet a* is something from which the subject, in order to constitute itself, has separated itself off as organ. This serves as a symbol of the lack, that is to say, the phallus, not as such but in so far as it is lacking. It must, therefore, be an object that is, firstly, separable and, secondly, that has some relation to the lack. . . . At the oral level, it is the nothing, in so far as that from which the subject was weaned is no longer anything for him. . . . The anal level is the locus of metaphor—one object for another, give the faeces in place of the phallus. . . . At the scopic level, we are no longer at the level of demand, but of desire, of the desire of the Other. It is the same at the level of the invocatory drive, which is the closest to the experience of the unconscious. Generally speaking, the

relation between the gaze and what one wishes to see involves the lure. The subject is presented as other than he is, and what one shows him is not what he wishes to see. It is in this way that the eye may function as *objet a*, that is to say, at the level of the lack (–Φ)" (1981, 103–104).

18. The same is true of Being in theocratic feudalism, which also needed three names for its nomination: (1) soul, as that which appears to be true and real; (2) mortal bodies, as that which appears to be an illusion; and (3) God, as that which is really true and real. This explains why Christianity necessarily required both the division between body and soul and the latter's immortality, *and* consequently a God of a double ontological status, that is, both transcendent divinity and incarnated man.

19. In Lacan's words: "Si . . . il n'avait pas comptabilisé ce plus-de-jouir, s'il n'en avait pas fait la plus-value, en d'autres termes, s'il n'avait pas fondé le capitalisme, Marx se serait aperçu que la plus-value, c'est le plus-de-jouir [If . . . [Marx] had not made surplus-enjoyment a matter of accountancy, if he had not made out of it surplus-value—in other words, if he had not laid the ground of capitalism—Marx would have realized that surplus-value is surplus-enjoyment]." Which is why, as Lacan concludes: "Ce n'est pas parce qu'on nationalise, au niveau du socialisme dans un seul pays, les moyens de production, qu'on en a fini pour autant avec la plus-value, si on ne sait pas ce que c'est [Just because, on the level of socialism in a single country, one nationalizes the means of production does not mean that one is done with surplus-value, if one does not know what it is]" (1991, 123–24; translation mine).

20. Another way of conceiving the surplus as differential (non-)substance is through what Lacan, drawing on Freud, has defined as *Vorstellungsrepräsentanz*. This, Lacan says, is a "binary signifier," insofar as it introduces "the division of the subject" in which "when the subject appears somewhere as meaning, he is manifested elsewhere as 'fading,' as disappearance" (1981, 218). In other words, the *Vorstellungsrepräsentanz* divides the subject between meaning and being, whereby the former's appearance entails the latter's disappearance. Insofar as "this signifier [*Vorstellungsrepräsentanz*] constitutes the central point of the *Urverdrängung* [primary repression]," namely, "the point of *Anziehung*, the point of attraction, through which all the other repressions will be possible, all the other similar passages in the locus of the *Unterdrückt* [repressed]," it itself precedes not only language but also the differentiation between language and being, being both signifier and (non-)being (218). *Vorstellungsrepräsentanz* is the initial moment that institutes the distinction between language and being, while it itself is an undifferentiated signifier-being. We could also say, borrowing Jacques-Alain Miller's distinction between R1 and R2, that *Vorstellungsrepräsentanz* or differential (non-)substance must be conceived as the *real* (R1) qua purely *formal* or *transcendental function*, which determines the real (R2) qua stain or gap, that which in each subsequent repression will remain unrepresented within representation.

21. My critique of Badiou in this regard concurs with Žižek's, which approaches the question from another, yet intrinsically correlative, of Badiou's three conditions of the ethical act, namely, in Badiou's words: "That truth does not have total power means, in the last analysis, that the subject-language, the production of a truth-process, does not have the power to name all the elements of the situation. At least one real element must exist, one multiple existing in the situation, which remains inaccessible to truthful nominations, and is exclusively reserved to opinion, to the language of the situation" (2001, 85). As Žižek writes: "[T]here is a Kantian problem with Badiou that is grounded in his dualism of Being and Event and that has to be surpassed. The only way out of this predicament is to assert that the unnameable Real is not an external limitation but an *absolutely inherent* limitation. Truth is a generic procedure that cannot comprise its own concept-name which would totalize it (as Lacan puts it, 'there is no meta-language,' or as Heidegger puts it, 'the name for a name is always lacking'—and this lack, far from being a limitation of language, is its positive condition, that is, it is only because [of] this lack that we have language. So, like the Lacanian Real that is not external to the Symbolic but makes it non-all from within . . . the unnameable is inherent to the domain of names" (2004, 107). As will become clear in the second part of the present work, this "unnameable Real" or "concept-name" is what Lacan calls the gaze, without which language would be impossible because it would mean nothing. This is why comprising truth's "own concept-name" within itself could either result in totalizing it or forming a "meta-language" (and, hence, politically, totalitarianism), or in making what was up to that moment seen as truth to appear suddenly as false, that is, as an ideological opinion. The latter possibility, as we preliminarily saw in the introduction, and as we shall see in more detail in the second part, is a requirement for the ethical act.

22. As we shall see in the second part, in truth, the not-All that Lacan introduces in order to extract Kant's absolute measure of the all is not the "feminine" but of another kind.

23. Note that, just as Žižek has produced a reading of Hegel that goes against the grain of the traditional understanding of Hegel, in which, through the mediation of Lacanian thought, Hegelian structures (inadvertently) end up looking more like Spinozian structures, one can easily undertake the same project with Kant and produce a nontraditional, more Spinozian/Lacanian-like reading. In fact, the following passages from Kant's *Prolegomena* lend themselves to such a reading as they explicitly argue that the thing in itself is a pure thought (noumenon) presupposed for the cognition of appearances, and emerging out of reason's "desire for completeness" (All). In Kant's words: "The sensible world is nothing but a chain of appearances connected according to universal laws; it has therefore not subsistence by itself; it is not the thing in itself, and consequently must point to that which contains the basis of this appearance, to beings which cannot be

cognized merely as appearances, but as things in themselves. In the cognition of them alone can reason hope to satisfy its desire for completeness in proceeding from the conditioned to its conditions. . . . What is the attitude of reason in this connection of what we know with what we do not, and never shall, know? This is an actual connection of a known thing with one quite unknown (and which will always remain so), and though what is unknown should not become the least more known—which we cannot even hope—yet the notion of this connection must be definite, and capable of being rendered distinct. We must therefore think an immaterial being, a world of understanding, and a Supreme Being (all mere noumena), because in them only, as things in themselves, reason finds that completion and satisfaction, which it can never hope for in the derivation of appearances from their homogeneous grounds, and because these actually have reference to something distinct from them (and totally heterogeneous), as appearances always presuppose an object in itself and therefore suggest its existence whether we can know more of it or not" (1977, 94–95; §354–55). In Kant's system, the conditioned (which is governed by "universal laws") is "totally heterogeneous" from its condition (which is free), and it is therefore a matter of pure interpretation whether one wants to assume that by "thing in itself" is meant a physical object in itself or "something distinct" from the conditioned, such as the (logical, noumenal or transcendental) conditions of the conditioned, to which the conditioned always has "reference."

24. Badiou's conception of the real as a positively given "thing" capable of bypassing representation is also disconcerting regarding the following, otherwise mellifluous, statement "that the world needs philosophy more than philosophy thinks" (2003, 56–57). Though it may generally come like a balm for the eye, this assertion takes an abrupt twist in the context of Badiou's discussion of philosophy, a twist in which the "world needs philosophy" only insofar as the latter is understood as yet another outlet for essentialism.

25. Marx elaborates extensively on the distinction between "circulation time" and production or "labour time" in *Grundrisse,* where he stresses that "the tendency of capital is *circulation without circulation time,*" that is, circulation that takes place both ceaselessly (eternally) and in no or zero linear time, "as opposed to labour time" that has a definite duration (1993, 671).

26. The following fragmentary address of the issue of ethics, both in this section and in subsequent parts of this work, is by no means comprehensive and remains to be examined in a more systematic way elsewhere. Here I only mention some of my thoughts about the ethical question that happen to relate directly to the present account of secular ontology.

27. This is a brief recapitulation of an argument presented in the introduction, here.

28. Now we can return to the reason why Spinoza's *affectum imitatio* has nothing to do with an "intermixture of partial affects" and the "com-

munity" to which, according to Žižek, "the so-called 'fundamentalism' " reacts (Žižek 1993, 219; see "Introduction," n. 5). *Affectus* itself is another word for libido, insofar as it, too, is an economic category, a purely quantitative magnitude of existence. In Spinoza's words: "An Affect [*Affectum*] that is called a Passion of the mind is a confused idea, by which the Mind affirms of its Body, or of some part of it, a *greater or lesser* [*majorem, vel minorem*] force of existing than before" (1985, 542; 1990, 430; *Ethics*, part III, "General Definitions of the Affects"; emphasis mine). For the same reason, as I indicated in the introduction, Spinoza's *affectum imitatio* corresponds to Lacan's chains of signifiers (values), and not, as Žižek claims, to "what psychoanalysis calls 'partial objects' " (2004, 35). In the next note we shall see that Spinoza's *affectus* also corresponds to the death drive.

29. The death drive is presupposed by both the pleasure principle (sex drive) and the reality principle as the instance that determines what is experienced as reality and what not. Freud's libido, therefore, is also presupposed in our experience of reality. Similarly, the Spinozian *affectus* is that which gives reality to bodies and ideas. In Spinoza's words: "when I say *a greater or lesser force of existing than before*, I do not understand that the Mind compares its Body's present constitution with a past constitution, but that the idea which constitutes the form of the affect [*affectus*] affirms of the body something which really involves more or less reality [*realitatis*] than before" (1985, 542; 1990, 430; *Ethics*, part III, "General Definitions of the Affects").

30. Note also that, by linking Freudian libido qua energy to the logic of the signifier ("puns, metaphors, metonymies"), Lacan explicitly links it to value, whose basic outline remains the same from the Stoics to Saussure, insofar as "all you have to do, as the wisdom of the Stoics had achieved so early on, is to distinguish the signifier from the signified (to translate, as did Saussure, their Latinized names), so as to witness phenomena of equivalence appearing there in such a way that one can understand how, for Freud, they could provide the figure of the machinery of an energetics" (1990, 9). Of course, the shifts from the Stoic conception of value and the Freudian conception of libido to the Marxian value and the Lacanian enjoyment presuppose the shift from "energetics" as "equivalence" to an "energetics" or economy of nonequivalence (i.e., one that involves surplus-value). The "Latinized names" referred to must, to my knowledge, be "*ratio et oratio* [reason and speech]," into which the Stoics translated Greek *logos*. The Stoics did not directly "distinguish the signifier [*oratio*, or, more specifically, in its Greek term, *phoné* (sound)] from the signified [*ratio*, or, in Greek *lekton*]," but established another distinction that entails the first distinction as its possibility. By conceiving of *lekta* (signifieds) as propositions rather than single words, and by severing both the *phoné* and the *lekton* from their referent in external reality (*ektos hypokeimenon*), the Stoics turned truth into a relational or conditional matter ('if A is true, then B is true') among *lekta*, so that the truth-value of relating *lekta*

depended solely on the truth-value of their components, rather than on the equivalence between a *lekton* and its *ektos hypokeimenon*. As a result, truth could no longer lay claims of adequacy with regard to its *ektos hypokeimenon*, a limitation that became the main reason why the Stoics were vehemently criticized by the Skeptics, who, unlike their later counterparts, at that moment had not yet abandoned a nonrepresentational conception of truth, even if eventually, it was on the basis of the Stoics' resort to probability and plausibility (the *eulogon*) as the criterion for believing in the truth of *lekta* or mind pictures with regard to their adequacy to reality, that they undermined belief in truth as representative of reality. At any rate, the distinction between *ektos hypokeimenon* and *lekton* renders truth self-referential and differential, that is, a value, which, as such, can be described through an energetic model.

31. This reference to changes, on the other hand, is not meant to relativize the rigidity of "eternal laws" and my thesis on relative transhistorical (i.e., transhistorical within secular capitalist modernity) structures, such as the Spinozian articulation of secular truth as "the standard both of itself and of the false," or the Marxian conception of surplus-value as the eternal law of capital. As Karatani writes, objecting to the general assumption that Marx's "*Capital* has been rebuked as having become obsolete in the epoch since it was written," the "novelty" of phenomena that Marx could not "have taken into account," such as "imperialism, joint stock companies . . . financial capital, and Keynesianism," is not "so fundamental" as it is often imagined (2003, 265). For, "as precisely presented in *Capital*" such phenomena "had already existed *as form*, if not substance, even before the advent of industrial capitalism" (265). This is to say, the changes in question are not "so fundamental" to effect in the slightest way capital's fundamental eternal laws. Already Marx states in *Capital*, "there are . . . particular branches of industry in which the product of the production process is not a new objective product, a commodity," such as "the communication industry, both the transport industry proper, for moving commodities and people, and the transmission of mere information" (Marx 1976, 133; as cited in Karatani 2003, 267). Capital, therefore, "does not care whether it gets surplus-value from solid objects or fluid information," so that "the nature of capital is consistent even before and after its dominant production branch shifted from heavy industry to the information industry." Transhistorically within capitalism, capital "lives on by the difference," that is, by dint of the fact that it is a system of disequilibrium, involving always a surplus. "*Capital*" and its laws, Karatani continues, are from the outset "an inquiry into the *forces* with which capitalist production qua the production of information (difference) organizes society" (267). Therefore, changes in economy, politics, and culture reveal a shift in which a structure that was already there, but only as form, is materially realized and empirically practiced in culture, economy, and politics.

32. We recall, however, that—Israel's linkage between an "orderly harmony of what exists" and "the origins of the evolutionary thesis" notwithstanding—Einstein's reference to God, as Israel writes, citing Einstein from Clark's *Einstein*, is framed by his "proposition that the modern scientist who rejects divine providence and a God that governs the destinies of man, while accepting 'the orderly harmony of what exists,' the intelligibility of an imminent [*sic*?] universe based on principles of mathematical rationality, in effect believes 'in Spinoza's God' "—a statement that arguably testifies to Einstein's atheism, in the most proper sense of the word (Israel 160; citing Clark 502–03; see also the "Introduction," here).

33. Regarding the antinomic character of pure reason, see Kant 1998, "The Transcendental Dialectic," Second Book, Second Chapter: "The Antinomy of Pure Reason," 459–550; A 406/B 433-A 567/B 595. Regarding the impossibility of speculatively proving the existence of God, see Kant 1998, "The Second Book of the Transcendental Dialectic," Chapter Three: "The Ideal of Pure Reason," 551–89; A 568/B 596–A 642/B 670. We shall examine closely the Kantian antinomies in the second part, here.

34. Regarding the relegation of the question of God to practical or moral reason, see Kant 1998, "The Transcendental Doctrine of Method," Second Chapter: "The Canon of Pure Reason," 672–90; A 795/B 823–A 831–B 859. Regarding the distinction between knowledge and faith, see Kierkegaard.

35. And in this way, it can also work as an argument for religiosity, but only within discourses unaware of the Spinozian-Lacanian specific meaning of 'God,' referred to above (see n. 32, earlier in this part).

36. Even all attempts in mathematics and logic, made by Hilbert, Gödel, and others, to shift the criterion of the validity of a system of knowledge from (representational) truth to its internal consistency fail to bypass this paradox, since any proof of consistency is forced to invoke principles more general than the ones comprising the given system, which, as such, are equally questionable as the principles of the system in question.

37. As for Plato and his concept of knowledge as awaiting in the subject to be recalled, God, or, rather, the gods play no role in grounding truth whatsoever, for in classical antiquity the first cause of truth is explicitly the truth of political power, that is, the truth of the master. The latter is known a priori by the slave, who "sait [knows]," with absolute certainty "ce que le maître veut [what the master wants]," namely, that the slave work for him (Lacan 1991, 34; translation mine). The slave may be capable of recalling, but, as Plato's dialogues amply testify to, only the master is capable of explicitly telling him what to recall, and hence of determining what can be known (see Lacan's elaboration of this point in Lacan 1991a, particularly the chapter "Knowledge, truth, opinion," 13–24).

38. This is particularly true of Freud's work on concepts that transcend the logic of mechanical physics and energetics (of equilibrium), such as the relation transference/countertransference and repetition compulsion or the death drive. Referring to Freud's *Beyond the Pleasure Principle*

(1920), the book in which Freud, motivated by the recurrence of traumatic dreams, was forced to acknowledge that the homeostatic logic of the pleasure principle does not suffice to explain human experience, Lacan comments: "It is as if each time he [Freud] goes too far in one direction, he stops to say—isn't this simply the restitutive tendency [pleasure principle]? But at each turn he remarks that that isn't enough, and that, after the restitutive tendency has manifested itself, something is left over which at the level of individual psychology appears to be gratuitous, paradoxical, enigmatic and is genuinely repetitive. . . . He constantly returns to his starting point, and completes another circle, and again rediscovers the passage, and finally ends up making a leap, and having made the leap, admits that there is something there which does indeed move completely off the edges of the blueprint" (1991a, 66–67). Yet, as Lacan also adds, "there is no less vacillating thought than his [Freud's]," as is evident in the fact that, unlike Descartes, "at the end, he himself admits the extremely speculative nature of the whole of his argumentation, or more precisely of his circular interrogation," "assert[ing] finally that if this articulation has seemed to him to be worth communicating, it is because he was of necessity brought down the path of this problematic" (66–67). Unlike the tradition of Cartesianism, so adept in bypassing its leaps, psychoanalytic thought developed by not shrinking before its own leaps, thanks to Freud's courage to follow "the most pressing demands of a reason which never abdicates, which does not say—*Here begins the opaque and the ineffable*" (69). Instead, Freud "enters, and even at the risk of appearing lost in obscurity, he continues with reason," and it is neither the case "that he ever renounces working with reason, nor that he retires to the mountains, thinking that everything is just fine as it is" (69). One can arguably detect here the largest influence of Freud on Lacan's own method and style.

39. Jeremy Bentham's *The Theory of Fictions*, with its concept of the "fictitious," according to which "every truth has the structure of fiction," had avowedly a decisive impact on Lacan's understanding of fiction and reading of Spinoza (Lacan 1992, 12; see Bentham). Lacan compares Bentham's epistemological contribution to that of Freud, insofar as both showed that pleasure lies on the side of the real, the latter being an effect of the fictitious that nevertheless transcends fiction. Due to its effect, the fictitious pertains not, as would be expected, to the imaginary but to the symbolic register. The latter is grounded as a system of truth by dint of an "as if," an a priori, logically inconsistent assumption. In Lacan's words: "Bentham's effort is located in the dialectic of the relationship of language to the real so as to situate the good—pleasure in this case, which . . . he articulates in a manner that is very different from Aristotle—on the side of the real. And it is within this opposition between fiction and reality that is to be found the rocking motion of Freudian experience. Once the separation between the fictitious and the real has been effected, things are no longer situated where one might expect. In Freud the characteristic of

pleasure, as that dimension which binds man, is to be found on the side of the fictitious. The fictitious is not, in effect, in its essence that which deceives, but is precisely what I call the symbolic" (Lacan 1992, 12; see also Lacan 1981, 163). Bentham's "fictitious" had an impact on other philosophers, notably, the neo-Kantian philosopher Hans Vaihinger, who, drawing on Bentham, developed the so-called philosophy of the "as if," and Octave Mannoni, who developed further the concept of the "as if" as the logical structure of the "*je sais bien, mais quand même* . . . [I know well, but, nevertheless . . .]" (see Vaihinger; and Mannoni, particularly the chapter "Je sais bien, mais quand même . . ."). Of course, it is Blaise Pascal (1623–1662) who first developed the idea of acting as if one believed, so that belief eventually becomes real (see Pascal, particularly "The Wager," 121–27). The Pascalian conception of the "as if" structure has become largely known by Louis Althusser's (inadequate) reelaboration of the concept as the elementary function of ideological interpellation (see Althusser, particularly "Ideology and Ideological State Apparatuses," 127–86). For a concise critique of Althusser's conception of ideological interpellation, see Žižek 1989, particularly the chapters " 'Law is Law' " and "Kafka, Critic of Althusser," 36–47.

40. See Greimas and Rastier. For the relevance of the Greimasian semantic rectangle to structuralism in general, and specifically Lévi-Strauss, see Fredric Jameson, particularly the third part of the chapter "The Structuralist Projection," 144–68. For its relevance to Lacan's L-schema, see Rosalind E. Krauss, particularly the first chapter, 1–30.

41. See, for instance, Foucault 1972 and 1990; and Ginzburg 1983 and 1989.

42. Jameson deserves distinction here, as the principle underpinning his entire analysis of culture is that mass culture is the contemporary medium of articulating and disseminating philosophical concepts and structures. Needless to say, there are many other practitioners of cultural studies to whom the present description of cultural studies does not do justice. My point is not to reduce the reality of cultural studies in the United States to a uniform image, but to draw attention to a dominant tendency that increasingly colonizes the field of cultural studies.

43. "Extimate" and "extimacy" (*extimité*) are words coined by Lacan out of the synthesis of the words *exterior* and *intimate* or *intimacy*, to "problematize[]," in Dylan Evans's words, "the opposition between inside and outside, between container and contained" (58). The real, the unconscious, the gaze, and the Other are all extimate, making not only the subject, as Evans writes, "ex-centric," but also society and political power (59).

44. The extimate character of Freud's libido is betrayed, against his own intentions, in his conceptual and rhetorical ambiguity of the function of consciousness (ego) or the unconscious as the source of libido and as container and contained, which has troubled many a Freud scholar. At times, Freud argues that the "ego is the great reservoir from which the

libido that is destined for objects flows out and into which it flows back from those objects" (Freud 1999, XII:6; "Eine Schwierigkeit der Psychoanalyse"; "A Difficulty in the Path of Psycho-Analysis" [1917; translation mine]). In these instances, the ego is likened with an amoeba or "protoplasmic animal whose viscous substance puts out pseudopodia" (XII:6). At other times, as in "an encyclopedia article [Freud] wrote in the summer of 1922," he argues that "we must recognize the id [unconscious] as the great reservoir of libido" (Freud 1989, 68; "Appendix B: The Great Reservoir of Libido"; " 'Psychoanalyse' und 'Libido Theorie,' " 1999, XIII, 211–33). This ambiguity raised the traditional debate about the primary or secondary character of narcissism—what comes first: the love for one's own self or the love for an external object?—a distinction that becomes untenable in Lacan's reconceptualization of narcissism as one's love for one's specular image in the mirror stage, since the specular image is both an external object and that which constitutes the ego in the first place (see Lacan 1977, 1–7; "The Mirror Stage as Formative of the Function of the I as Revealed in Psychoanalytic Experience").

45. See Hegel 1988, particularly the section "Selbstständigkeit und Unselbstständigkeit des Selbstbewusstseins; Herrschaft und Knechtschaft," 127–36; and for an English translation, Hegel 1977, "Independence and Dependence of Self-Consciousness: Mastery and Bondage" 111–19. There Hegel writes that both the master (Other) and the slave (subject) relate to the thing (the object of the bondsman's labor) negatively. Nevertheless, "the bondman['s] . . . negating of it . . . cannot go the length of being altogether done with it to the point of annihilation," for he "*works* on it" and, hence desires it. By contrast, "for the Lord, on the other hand, the *immediate* relation becomes through its mediation [via the bondsman] the sheer negation of the thing, or the enjoyment [*Genuß*] of it. What [the bondsman's] desire [*Begierde*] failed to achieve, he succeeds in doing, viz. to have done with the thing altogether, and to achieve satisfaction in the enjoyment [*Genuß*] of it. Desire [*Begierde*] failed to do this because of the thing's independence; but the lord, who has interposed the bondsman between it and himself, takes to himself only the dependent aspect of the thing and has the pure enjoyment of it [*genießt es rein*]. The aspect of its independence he leaves to the bondsman, who works on it" (Hegel 1977, 116; 1988, 133). And by working on it, as Marx added later, he also produces surplus-value, as well as, with Lacan, surplus-enjoyment (*plus-de-jouir*). This is the semantic profit produced by the bondsman's labor on the signifier, which is enjoyed not by him but by the lord/Other, insofar as this semantic labor renders the latter consistent (see Lacan 1991, particularly the chapter "L'Impuissance de la Vérité," 191–208). Note that it is not the "dialectic," that is, the presumed convertibility of roles, in the relation between master and slave, on which Lacan draws for his concept of enjoyment, but the earlier part that offers Hegel's exposition of the difference between master and slave. For, to repeat, Lacan prefers to trust not what

"Hegel *dixit*," namely, that "l'esclave avec le temps lui démontrera sa vérité [in time, the slave will show him (the master) his truth]," but rather what "Marx *dixit*," namely, that "il se sera occupé tout ce temps à fomenter son plus-de-jouir [he (the slave) will be occupied all this time with fomenting his surplus-enjoyment,]" since for Lacan, Marx's "plus-value . . . est le plus-de-jouir [surplus-value . . . is surplus-enjoyment]" (Lacan 1991, 123; translation mine).

46. See Kojève, particularly "Chapter 2: Summary of the First Six Chapters of the Phenomenology of Spirit: Complete Text of the First Three Lectures of the Academic Year 1937–1938," 31–70.

47. See, again Kojève, and Sartre, particularly "Part 3: Being-For-Others," 301–558. For Lacan's critique of Sartre's "look" and the dialectic of the "free" and the "objectified" subjects, see Lacan 1981, particularly "Chapter 7: Anamorphosis," 79–90, and "Chapter 14: The Partial Drive and Its Circuit," 174–86.

48. For the function of the other in the constitution of the subject, see Hegel 1977, particularly Part B: "Self-Consciousness," Chapter IV: "The Truth of Self-Certainty," 104–11 [1988, Part IV: "Die Wahrheit der Gewißheit seiner selbst," 120–27]; and Lacan 1977, particularly Chapter 1: "The Mirror Stage as Formative of the Function of the I," 1–7, and "Aggressivity in Psychoanalysis," 8–29.

49. Therefore, the "*'pure,' radical negativity*" of the "*Thing-in-itself*" or the "*Idea*," which for Hegel is also the Spirit of History (the mission of the Other), even if *in itself* is a "pure negativity," *for others*, that is, in its effects, it is that which guarantees that one always "forbid[s] oneself from enjoying" the goods of which one simultaneously "deprive[s] [the] others." Which is why these goods are left to be enjoyed by a third party, beyond "the phenomenal world, part of which is negative, part positive," and in which "individuals," that is, masters and slaves, "are surrendered and sacrificed." Their goods can be enjoyed only by the "universal . . . Idea," which "pays the ransom of existence and transience—not out of its own pocket, but with the passions," that is, not only the goods but also the 'good' "of individuals" (Hegel 1988a, 35). Hegel's equation of the Thing-in-itself or the sublime with the Universal Idea or the Spirit of History means nothing other than, as Lacan puts it, that "the entire forward march of the phenomenology of spirit is all of you—that's what you are here for. That's what you are doing means, even when you don't think about it. Always the puppet strings" (1991a, 70). As far as Lacan is concerned, enjoyment and its pure negativity reveal the true function of the so-called dialectic between master and slave, which lies in sustaining the sole master beyond the "phenomenal world," the Idea, that is, the Other imagined by me in the field of the Other.

50. It does no harm to repeat that the father's sacrifice by way of assuming the guilt for the death of his son, far from constituting an ethical act, which, as such, would demand the 'death' of the existing symbolic

order, is a sadistic, superegoic act, which, as such, we recall, turns him into the "instrument of *jouissance*," of the Other's enjoyment, thereby sustaining it (Lacan 1989, 63; see the "Introduction," here).

51. Karatani invokes this passage in order to argue that "even if it is true that Marx appropriated Feuerbachian criticism of religion to the criticism of the secular capitalist economy, his theory of money would be better understood if it were approached via Kant's theory of the sublime." For the latter, far from "appl[ying]," as in the case of Feuerbach, "to the criticism of religion," "already assumes the negation of religion," so that the experience of the Kantian sublime can "be found only when humans are fully enlightened and become secular beings" (2003, 214). The overarching assumption underlying Karatani's argument, however, is that for Marx, the secular subject partaking in capitalist economy is—or at least should be and can become—such a "fully enlightened and . . . secular being[]," for only in this way shall it recognize the religious character of capitalism and thus reject it. Thus, for Karatani, "Marx's critique of political economy was an extension of his critique of religion," so that, in "this respect, there is no 'epistemological break' as such" (212). By the same token, for Karatani, an "elucidation of capitalism is thereby [not only] an ethical task par excellence," but also an enlightening project, meant to complete the process of secularization impeded by capitalism's religious character (217). In other words, when Karatani writes that "it was in the monetary economy that Marx saw 'secular religion,' as it were," effectively he means that Marx saw in monetary economy the residues of a religion that can be rendered obsolete through appropriate enlightenment. The present argument, by contrast, implies that Marx saw in monetary economy the reasons because of which this economy succeeds in interpellating subjects that observe a "secular religion," that is, one whose metaphysical needs can no longer be negotiated directly within an explicitly religious context (in a dialogue with God, etc.) but can instead be negotiated only indirectly, through monetary economy, as well as the economy of the signifier (212). Karatani's reliance on the possibility of producing "fully enlightened and . . . secular beings" is all the more startling as he simultaneously and recurrently makes reference to Marx's "critique of religion" as one that, as we shall see below, dismisses theoretical analysis and criticism as effective means of abolishing religion.

Part II. Kant with Marx: Surplus, Or, Gaze

1. Half a year after SECT (see the "Acknowledgments," here), Žižek published an article in which he actually argued against the contemporary popular equation of Stalinism and Nazism. Nazism, Žižek argues there, "wurde von einer Gruppe von Leuten betrieben, die sehr böse Dinge machen wollten und dies auch taten [was carried out by a group of people who wanted to do very mean things and that's what they did]." Stalinism, by

contrast, "war das Resultat eines radikal emanzipatorischen Projekts [was the result of a radically emancipatory project]," which, unlike Nazism, "den letzten Faden, der ihn mit der Zivilisation verband, nicht durchtrennt [hat] [did not cut the last thread that connected itself with civilization]" (2005, 119 and 116; translation mine). Stalinism remained part of the Western civilization, "und aus diesem Grund kämpften im . . . Zweiten Weltkrieg, stalinistische Kommunisten und kapitalistische Demokratien gemeinsam gegen den Faschismus [and for this reason Stalinist communists and capitalist democracies fought together in World War II against fascism]" (116). Although Stalinism was a "Versuch, der Logik des Kapitals zu entfliehen [attempt to escape from the logic of capital]," it "verstand sich selbst immer noch als Teil der Tradition der Aufklärung, laut welcher die Wahrheit jedem rationalen Menschen zugänglich ist, weshalb er auch subjektiv die Verantwortung für seine Vergehen trägt—im Unterschied zu den Nazis, für welche die Schuld der Juden direkt aus ihrer biologischen Konstitution rührte [still understood itself as part of the tradition of the Enlightenment, according to which truth is accessible to every rational human being, who therefore bears the subjective responsibility for his or her offences—unlike the Nazis, for whom the guilt of the Jews derived directly from their biological constitution]" (116; translation mine). While, however, Žižek's emphasis in this article lies, for understandable reasons (i.e., critiquing the liberal tendency to collapse Nazism and Stalinism), on the structural, albeit not historical, superiority of Stalinism because of its ideals, I place emphasis on the fact that, whatever ideals a political system may foster, it is doomed to replicate the Kantian division between critical thought and political practice as long as it is structured according to the dynamic antinomy. Stalinism is the tragico-comic culmination of the Enlightenment insofar as critical thought is allowed to be expressed only from the position of being already condemned for this thought, so that its consequence bears only on the subject of thought and not on the political system. For, as Žižek writes, only "in den Schauprozessen [in the show trials]," was one allowed to enunciate criticism against the system, when "der Angeklagte öffentlich seine Vergehen gestehen und erklären [musste], wie es dazu kam [the accused had to confess publicly his offence and explain how he was led to it]" (116).

2. As argued in the first part, the totality must be formed not as a closed set but as a not-All, yet this must occur not through an infinite regression but in another way, which we shall see shortly.

3. Indicative of the way psychoanalysis conceives of the Nothing as a positive function is Lacan's statement: "[I]n anorexia nervosa, what the child eats is the nothing" (1981, 104).

4. In the following, I use "analytic" and "synthetic judgments" in the Kantian sense. In an "analytic judgment," such as "all bodies are extended," the "predicate is already thought in the concept of the subject," which is why "all analytic judgments are *a priori* even when the concepts

are empirical, as for example, 'Gold is a yellow metal,' for to know this requires no experience beyond my concept of gold, which contains the thought that this body is yellow and metal" (Kant 1977, 12; §2). In synthetic judgments, by contrast, the predicate adds a new information that is not included in the concept of the subject. Synthetic judgments can be either a priori or, if they are "of empirical origin," a posteriori (13: §2). While the statement 'this car is blue' is an a posteriori synthetic judgment, all mathematical propositions are a priori synthetic judgments. For instance, "the proposition 7 + 5 = 12" is synthetic because "the concept of twelve is by no means thought by merely thinking of the combination of seven and five," and while we may analyze the concepts "seven" and "five" as much as we want, "we shall not discover twelve in the concept" (14; §2). To arrive at "twelve" we must add the concept of addition, which is a mathematical "construction of a concept" other than simply the concepts of the numbers "seven" and "five" (15; §2). But once I know all three concepts, "seven," "five," and "addition," then "5 + 7 = 12" in all possible worlds, which is why there is no need for recourse to experience to know the outcome, and our synthetic judgment is a priori.

5. Here I am paraphrasing Kant's example of the body that instead of having either a bad or a good smell, might be odor-free (see Kant 1998, 517; A503/B531). Copjec also invokes this example to explain the failure of reason in the female mode of the mathematic antinomy (see Copjec 1994).

6. I think that the same logic is at work in Copjec's suggestion that we must accomplish the inclusion of the suppliance, the supernumerary jouissance, the *Vorlust* that is a judgment prior to any aesthetic judgment, in the universality of judgment.

7. I am not going to address here Hardt's claim that this methodology is to be found in Spinoza's *Political Treatise* itself, because I will end up repeating my criticism of the naïve acceptance of statements in a body of work, in spite of the fact that they contradict one another.

8. See Gramsci 1971, particularly 52–120 and 128–30; for the Italian original, see Gramsci 1975, notebook 8, paragraph 36, 962–63.

Conclusion: Raising a Question

1. In this context, Corngold adheres to Walter Sokel's suggestion that the narrative mode of *The Trial* is to be described by the term "*Zweisinnigkeit* (divided perspective)," expressing the coexistence of two "narrative tracks," in which "the narrator [who] wants [K.] to confess his guilt" is the "counterpoint to Joseph K.'s strategies of affirming his innocence" (224; referring to Sokel, 110). Since the narrator "too is unable to identify the offence of which K. is guilty . . . the only possibility of enriching his perspective is . . . to read it 'allegorically' (*andeutungsweise*), as pointing beyond the contrary assertion of guilt by a guilty narration to an act of verbal composition," so that what the narrator "refers us to [is] a

being who, unlike Joseph K., writes" (224). But my analysis of the above passage suggests that, beyond the "act" of writing itself, the ultimate referent of the narrator's allegorically indexical function is the presupposed *gaze* to which the narrated events *seem* as described by the specific "verbal composition." It is this gaze that bestows on the narration's pointing to the "act of verbal composition" its "guilty" character. And by revealing the gaze (as the precondition and effect of writing) negatively, that is, by rhetorically indicating its space, while leaving its specific place indeterminate, the Kafkaesque further reveals the arbitrariness or ungroundedness of this gaze.

2. Žižek exemplifies the commonality of Marx's and Freud's methodology with regard to the crisis and the symptom in the first part of the chapter "How Did Marx Invent the Symptom?," in Žižek 1989, 11–53.

3. The present argument is not meant as a solipsistic conception of the encounter. The said gaze or desire is imagined by *me* in the Other, but the entire *symbolic order,* including its failures and its self-referentiality, determine what I can and cannot imagine, even if not in a predictable way, precisely because of their failures and self-referentiality. To say that the encounter with the other is in truth an encounter with the desire the subject imagines in the Other amounts to no less than saying that the encounter with the other is the encounter with the Other (the symbolic order), taken both as an empirically given experience and as a totality. In its former aspect, it is the Other that determines the gaze I imagine in It; in its latter aspect, however, my gaze is free, insofar as the totality of the Other fails to constitute itself.

Works Cited

Althusser, Louis. 1971. *Lenin and philosophy and other essays.* Trans. Ben Brewster. New York: Monthly Review Press.

Althusser, Louis, and Étienne Balibar. 1970. *Reading Capital.* Trans. Ben Brewster. London: NLB.

Anderson, Perry. 1979. *Lineages of the absolutist state.* London: Verso.

Aquinas, Thomas St. 1991. *Summa Theologiæ: A concise translation.* Ed. Timothy McDermott. Allen: Christian Classics.

Aristotle. 1970. *Physics: Books I and II.* Trans. William Charlton. Oxford: Clarendon Press.

———. 1991. *The metaphysics.* Trans. John H. McMahon. Amherst: Prometheus Books.

Austin, J. L. 1975. *How to do things with words.* Ed. J. O. Urmson and Marina Sbisà. Cambridge: Harvard University Press.

Badiou, Alain. 1996. What is love? *Umbr(a)* 1: 7–21.

———. 2000. *Deleuze: The clamor of being.* Trans. Louise Burchill. Minneapolis: University of Minnesota Press.

———. 2000a. Frege and On a contemporary usage of Frege. Trans. Sam Gillespie and Justin Clemens [from Le Nombre et les nombres]. *Umbr(a)* 1: 95–115.

———. 2001. *Ethics: An essay on the understanding of evil.* Trans. Peter Hallward. London: Verso.

———. 2003. *Infinite thought: Truth and the return to philosophy.* Trans. and ed. Oliver Feltham and Justin Clemens. New York: Continuum.

———. ®2004. *Logics of worlds.* Trans. Alberto Toscano (unpublished manuscript).

Barthes, Roland. 1993. *S/Z.* Trans. Richard Miller. New York: Hill and Wang.

Benjamin, Walter. 1969. "Theses on the philosophy of history." In *Illuminations,* ed. Hannah Arendt. Trans. Harry Zohn. New York: Schocken, 253–64.

Bentham, Jeremy. 1932. *Theory of fictions.* Ed. C. K. Ogden. London: Kegan Paul, Trench, Trubner and Co.

Bergoffen, Debra B. 1990. The body politic: Democratic metaphors, totalitarian practices, erotic rebellions. *Philosophy & Social Criticism,* 109–26.

Bergson, Henri. 1991. *Matter and memory*. Trans. N. M. Paul and W. S. Palmer. Urzone, 1988. New York: Zone Books.

Bertman, Martin A. 1979. Hobbes: Language and the is-ought problem. *Philosophical Studies* 26: 146–58.

Bouveresse, Jacques. 1995. *Wittgenstein reads Freud: The myth of the unconscious*. Trans. Carol Cosman. Princeton: Princeton University Press.

Buchanan, Ian, ed. 1999. *A Deleuzian century*. Durham: Duke University Press.

Burke, Kenneth. 1970. *The rhetoric of religion: Studies in logology*. Berkeley: University of California Press.

Butler, Judith, Ernesto Laclau, and Slavoj Žižek. 2000. *Contingency, hegemony, universality: Contemporary dialogues on the Left*. New York: Verso.

Clark, Ronald W. 1994. *Einstein: The life and times*. New York: Avon.

Colombat, André Pierre. 1999. "Deleuze and the three powers of literature and philosophy: To demystify, to experiment, to create," in *A Deleuzian Century?* Ed. Jan Buchanan. Durham: Duke University Press, 199–217.

Copjec, Joan. 1994. *Read my desire: Lacan against the historicists*. Cambridge: MIT Press.

———. 2002. *Imagine there's no woman: Ethics and sublimation*. Cambridge: MIT Press.

Corngold, Stanley. 1988. *Franz Kafka: The necessity of form*. Ithaca: Cornell University Press.

Curley, Edwin. 1988. *Behind the geometrical method: A reading of Spinoza's ethics*. Princeton: Princeton University Press.

Damasio, Antonio. 2003. *Looking for Spinoza: Joy, sorrow, and the feeling brain*. Orlando: Harcourt, Inc.

De Certeau, Michel. 1984. *The practise of everyday life*. Trans. Steven Rendall. Berkeley: University of California Press.

———. 1988. *The writing of history*. Trans. Tom Conley. New York: Columbia University Press.

De Dijn, Herman. 1996. *Spinoza: The way to wisdom*. West Lafayette, IN: Purdue University Press.

Deleuze, Gilles. 1988. *Spinoza: Practical philosophy*. Trans. Robert Hurley. San Francisco: City Lights Books.

———. 1990. *The logic of sense*. Trans. Mark Lester with Charles Stivale. New York: Columbia University Press.

———. 1991. *Cinema 1: The movement—image*. Trans. Hugh Tomlinson and Barbara Habberjam. Minneapolis: University of Minnesota Press.

———. 1993. *The fold: Leibniz and the baroque*. Trans. Tom Conley. Minneapolis: University of Minnesota Press.

———. 1994. *Masochism: Coldness and cruelty*. Urzone, 1989. New York: Zone Books.

———. 1994a. *Difference and repetition.* Trans. Paul Patton. New York: Columbia University Press.

———. 1995. *Cinema 2: The time—image.* Trans. Hugh Tomlinson and Robert Galeta. Minneapolis: University of Minnesota Press.

———. 1995a. *Negotiations: 1972–1990.* Trans. Martin Joughin. New York: Columbia University Press.

Deleuze, Gilles, and Félix Guattari. 1986. *Kafka: Toward a minor literature.* Trans. Dana Polan. Minneapolis: University of Minnesota Press.

———. 1987. *A thousand plateaus: Capitalism and schizophrenia.* Trans. Brian Massumi. 4th edition. Minneapolis: University of Minnesota Press.

———. 1998. *Anti-Oedipus: Capitalism and schizophrenia.* Trans. Robert Hurley. Minneapolis: University of Minnesota Press.

Derrida, Jacques. 1976. *Of grammatology.* Trans. Gayatri Chakravotry Spivak. Baltimore: The Johns Hopkins University Press.

———. 1995. *The gift of death.* Trans. David Wills. Chicago: The University of Chicago Press.

Dumouchel, Paul. 1996. Persona: Reason and representation in Hobbes's political philosophy. *Sub-stance* 80, 25: 68–80.

Evans, Dylan. 1996. *An introductory dictionary of Lacanian psychoanalysis.* London: Routledge.

Feldman. Seymour. 1999. Introduction. In Baruch Spinoza. *Ethics; Treatise on the emendation of the intellect; Selected letters,* ed. Seymour Feldman, trans. Samuel Shirley. 2nd Ed. Indianapolis: Hackett, 1–20.

Foucault, Michel. 1970. *The order of things: An archaeology of the human sciences.* Trans. anon. New York: Vintage.

———. 1972. *The archaeology of knowledge, and, The discourse on language.* Trans. A. M. Sheridan Smith. New York: Pantheon Books.

———. 1990. *The history of sexuality.* 3 vols. Trans. Robert Hurley. New York: Vintage Books.

———. 1997. *The politics of truth.* Ed. Sylvère Lotringer and Lysa Hochroth. New York: Semiotext(e).

Freud, Sigmund. 1959. *Group psychology and the analysis of the ego.* Trans. and ed. James Strachey. New York: W. W. Norton.

———. 1961. *Beyond the pleasure principle.* Trans. and ed. James Strachey. Intro. Gregory Zilboorg and Peter Gay. New York: W. W. Norton.

———. 1963. Negation. In *General psychological theory.* New York: Collier.

———. 1989. *The ego and the id.* Trans. John Riviere. Rev. and ed. James Strachey. Intro. Peter Gay. New York: W. W. Norton.

———. 1998. *The interpretation of dreams.* Trans. James Strachey. New York: Avon Books.

———. 1999. *Gesammelte Werke.* Ed. Anna Freud. London: Imago, 1952; Frankfurt/M: Fischer.

Ginzburg, Carlo. 1983. *The night battles: Witchcraft and agrarian cults in the sixteenth and seventeenth centuries.* Baltimore: The Johns Hopkins University Press.

———. 1989. *Clues, myths, and the historical method.* Trans. John and Anne C. Tedeschi. Baltimore: The Johns Hopkins University Press.

Gramsci, Antonio. 1971. *Selections from prison notebooks.* Ed. and trans. Quintin Hoare and Geoffrey Nowell-Smith. Cambridge: Harvard University Press.

———. 1975. *Quaderni del carcere.* Ed. Valentino Gerratana. 4 Vols. Turin.

———. 1985. *Selections from cultural writings.* Ed. David Forgacs and Geoffrey Nowell-Smith. Trans. William Boelhower. Cambridge: Harvard University Press.

———. 1988. *An Antonio Gramsci reader: Selected writings, 1916–1935.* Ed. David Forgacs. New York: Schocken Books.

Greimas, A. J., and F. Rastier. 1968. The interaction of semiotic constrains. *Yale French Studies* 41: 86–105.

Gribbon, John. 1991. *In search of Schroedinger's cat.* London: Avon.

Grünbaum, Adolf. 1984. *The foundations of psychoanalysis: A philosophical critique.* Berkeley: University of California Press.

Hacker, P. M. S. 1987. "Languages, Minds and Brains." In *Mindwaves: thoughts on intelligence, identity, and consciousness,* ed. Colin Blakemore and Susan Greenfield. Oxford: Blackwell.

Hardt, Michael. 1991. Translator's foreword: The anatomy of power. In Antonio Negri. *The savage anomaly: The power of Spinoza's metaphysics and politics.* Trans. Michael Hardt. Minneapolis: University of Minnesota Press, xi–xvi.

Hardt, Michael, and Antonio Negri. 2000. *Empire.* Cambridge: Harvard University Press.

Hegel, G. W. F. 1956. *The philosophy of history.* Trans. J. Sibree. New York: Dover.

———. 1974. *Lectures on the history of philosophy.* 3rd Vol. Trans. E. S. Haldane. Reprint edition. Prometheus Books.

———. 1977. *Phenomenology of spirit.* Trans. A. V. Miller. Oxford: Oxford University Press.

———. 1988. *Phänomenologie des Geistes.* Ed. Hans-Friedrich Wessels and Heinrich Clairmont. Hamburg: Felix Meiner.

———. 1988a. *Introduction to the philosophy of history.* Trans. Leo Rauch. Indianapolis: Hackett Publishing Company.

Heidegger, Martin. 1962. *Kant and the problem of metaphysics.* Trans. J. S. Curchill. Bloomington: University of Indiana Press.

Heisenberg, Werner. 1957. Quantum theory of fields and elementary particles. *Review of Modern Physics* 29: 269–78.

———. 1963. Die Entwicklung der einheitlichen Feldtheorie der Elementarteilchen. *Naturwissenschaften* 50: 3–7.

Holland, Eugene. 1998. Spinoza and Marx. *Cultural Logic* 2:1 (Fall).

Israel, Jonathan I. 2001. *Radical enlightenment: Philosophy and the making of modernity 1650–1750.* Oxford: Oxford University Press.

Jameson, Fredric. 1972. *The prison house of language: A critical account of structuralism and Russian formalism.* Princeton: Princeton University Press.

Kafka, Franz. 1992. *The trial.* Trans. Willa and Edwin Muir. New York: Schocken Books.

———. 1998. *Der Prozess.* Ed. Joseph Kiermeier-Debre. Munich: Deutscher Taschenbuch Verlag.

Kant, Immanuel. 1959. What is enlightenment? In *Foundations of the metaphysics of morals and "What is enlightenment?"* Trans. Lewis White Beck. Indianapolis: The Liberal Arts Press, 85–92.

———. 1977. *Prolegomena to any future metaphysics.* Trans. Paul Carus and James W. Ellington. Indianapolis: Hackett.

———. 1998. *Critique of pure reason.* Trans. Paul Guyer and Allen W. Wood. New York: Cambridge University Press.

———. 2000. *The critique of judgment.* Trans. J. H. Bernard. Amherst: Prometheus Books.

Karatani, Kojin. 1995. *Architecture as metaphor: Language, number, money.* Ed. Michael Speaks. Trans. Sabu Kohso. Cambridge: MIT Press.

———. 2003. *Transcritique: On Kant and Marx.* Trans. Sabu Kohso. Cambridge: MIT Press.

Keevak, Michael. 1998. Fear of fear in Hobbes's *Leviathan. Studies in Language and Literature* 8 (December): 45–63.

Kelsen, Hans. 1929. *Vom Wesen und Wert der Demokratie.* Tübingen: J. C. B. Mohr.

Kierkegaard, Søren. 1985. *Philosophical fragments/Johannes Climacus.* Ed. and trans. Howard V. Hong and Edna H. Hong. Princeton: Princeton University Press.

Kojève, Alexandre. 1980. *Introduction to the reading of Hegel: Lectures on the Phenomenology of Spirit.* Assembl. Raymond Queneau. Ed. Allan Bloom. Trans. James H. Nichols Jr. Ithaca: Cornell University Press.

Kordela, Kiarina A. 1999. Political metaphysics: God in global capitalism (the slave, the masters, Lacan, and the surplus). *Political Theory* 27, no. 6 (December): 789–839.

———. 2006. Capital: At least it kills time (Spinoza, Marx, Lacan, and temporality). In *Rethinking Marxism* 18, no. 4 (October): 539–63.

———. forthcoming. Still looking for Spinoza (Pantheism, Truth, Death, and Affect). In *Spinoza Now,* Ed. Dimitris Vardoubakis. Stanford: Stanford University Press.

Kraus, Karl. 1974. Unbefugte Psychologie. In *Werkausgabe.* Vol. 4. Munich: Kösel Verlag.

Krauss, Rosalind E. 1994. *The optical unconscious.* Cambridge: MIT Press.

Lacan, Jacques. 1971. *Écrits II.* Paris: Seuil.

———. 1977. *Écrits: A selection.* Trans. Alan Sheridan. New York: W. W. Norton.

———. 1981. *The four fundamental concepts of psychoanalysis.* Trans. Alan Sheridan. Ed. Jacques-Alain Miller. New York: W. W. Norton.

———. 1988. Seminar on "The Purloined Letter." Trans. Jeffrey Mehlman. In *The purloined Poe: Lacan, Derrida, and psychoanalytic reading,* ed. John P. Muller and William J. Richardson. Baltimore: The Johns Hopkins University Press, 28–54.

———. 1988a. *Book I: Freud's papers on technique 1953–1954.* Ed. Jacques-Alain Miller. Trans. John Forrester. New York: W. W. Norton.

———. 1989. Kant with Sade. *October* 51 (Winter): 55–104.

———. 1990. *Television: A challenge to the psychoanalytic establishment.* Ed. Joan Copjec. Trans. Denis Hollier, Rosalind Krauss et al. New York: W. W. Norton.

———. 1991. *Le séminaire. Livre XVII: L'envers de la psychanalyse, 1969–1970.* Ed. Jacques-Alain Miller. Paris: Seuil.

———. 1991a. *Book II: The ego in Freud's theory and in the technique of psychoanalysis 1954–1955.* Ed. Jacques-Alain Miller. Trans. Sylvana Tomaselli. New York: W. W. Norton.

———. 1992. *Book VII: The ethics of psychoanalysis 1959–1960.* Ed. Jacques-Alain Miller. Trans. Dennis Porter. New York: W. W. Norton.

———. 1993. *Book III: The psychoses, 1955–56.* Ed. Jacques-Alain Miller. Trans. Russell Grigg. New York: W. W. Norton.

———. 1994. *Livre IV: La relation d'objet.* Ed. Jacques-Alain Miller. Paris: Seuil.

———. 1998. *Book XX. Encore, 1972–1973: On feminine sexuality; The limits of love and knowledge.* Ed. Jacques-Alain Miller. Trans. Bruce Fink. New York: W. W. Norton.

Laclau, Ernesto, and Chantal Mouffe. 1985. *Hegemony and socialist strategy.* Trans. Winston Moore and Paul Cammack. London: Verso.

Leibniz, Gottfried Wilhelm von. 1965. *Monadology and other philosophical essays.* Trans. Paul Schrecker and Anne Martin Schrecker. New York: Macmillan.

———. 1966. *Opuscules et fragments inédits.* Ed. L. Couturat. Hildesheim: Georg Olms.

———. 1992. *Discourse on metaphysics and the monadology.* Trans. George R. Montgomery. Buffalo: Prometheus Books.

———. 1996. *New essays on human understanding.* Ed. and trans. Peter Remnant and Jonathan Bennett. Cambridge: Cambridge University Press.

Lévi-Strauss, Claude. 1969. *The elementary structures of kinship.* Ed. Rodney Needham. Trans. James Harle Bell and John Richard Von Sturmer. Boston: Beacon Press.

Lipsius, Justus. 1939. *Two books of constancie.* Ed. Rudolf Kirk. Trans. John Stradling. New Jersey: Rutgers University Press.

———. 1965. *Von der Bestendikeit [De constantia].* Ed. Leonard Forster. Stuttgart: J. B. Metzlersche Verlagsbuchhandlung.

Lotringer, Sylvère. 2004. Forword: We, the multitude. In Paolo Virno, *A grammar of the multitude.* Trans. Isabella Bertoletti et al. Los Angeles: Semiotext(e).

Macherey, Pierre. 1979. *Hegel on Spinoza.* Paris: François Maspero.

———. 1997. The problem of the attributes. Trans. Ted Stolze. In *The New Spinoza,* ed. Warren Montag and Ted Stolze. Minneapolis: University of Minnesota Press, 64–94.

Machiavelli, Niccolò. 1977. *The prince: A new translation, backgrounds, interpretations, peripherica.* Trans. and ed. Robert M. Adams. New York: W. W. Norton.

Mannoni, Octave. 1969. *Clefs pour l'imaginaire ou l'autre scène.* Paris: Seuil.

Maravall, José Antonio. 1986. *Culture of the baroque: Analysis of a historical structure.* Trans. Terry Cochran. Minneapolis: University of Minnesota Press.

Martyn, David. 2003. *Sublime failures: The ethics of Kant and Sade.* Detroit: Wayne State University Press.

Marx, Karl. 1975. A contribution to the critique of Hegel's philosophy of right. In *Early writings.* Trans. Rodney Livingstone and Gregor Benton. New York: Vintage.

———. 1976. *Capital: A critique of political economy.* Vol. 2. Trans. Ben Fowkes. Harmondsworth: Penguin Books.

———. 1990. *Capital: A critique of political economy.* Vol. 1. Trans. Ben Fowkes. London: Penguin Books.

———. 1993. *Grundrisse: Foundations of the critique of political economy (rough draft).* Trans. Martin Nicolaus. London: Penguin Books in association with New Left Review.

Marx, Karl, and Friedrich Engels. 1998. *The German ideology (including* Theses on Feuerbach *and* Introduction to the critique of political economy). Amherst: Prometheus Books.

Massumi, Brian. 1992. *A user's guide to capitalism and schizophrenia: Deviations from Deleuze and Guattari.* Cambridge: MIT Press.

Mead, Rebecca. 2003. Life and letters: The Marx brother (how a philosopher from Slovenia became an international star). *The New Yorker* (May 5): 38–47.

Merleau-Ponty, Maurice. 1968. *The visible and the invisible.* Ed. Claude Lefort. Trans. Alphonso Lingis. Evanston: Northwestern University Press.

Miller, Jacques-Alain. 2001. *Clear like day letter for the twenty years since the death of Jacques Lacan written by Jacques-Alain Miller to an enlightened public.* Trans. Barbara P. Fulks. New York, The Wooster Press.

Montag, Warren, and Ted Stolze. 1997. *The new Spinoza.* Minneapolis: University of Minnesota Press.

Negri, Antonio. 1991. *The savage anomaly: The power of Spinoza's metaphysics and politics.* Trans. Michael Hardt. Minneapolis: University of Minnesota Press.

Nel, Philip. 1993. Political relations and the analogy with language. *Theoria* (October): 47–59.

Pascal, Blaise. 1995. *Pensées.* Trans. A. J. Krailsheimer. London: Penguin.

Paty, M. 1988. Einstein et Spinoza. In *Spinoza, science et religion,* ed. Renée Bouveresse. Actes du Colloque du Centre Culturel International de Cerisy-la-Salle. Paris: Vrin.

Pfaller, Robert. 1998. Negation and its reliabilities: An empty subject for ideology? In *Cogito and the unconscious,* ed. Slavoj Žižek. Durham: Duke University Press, 225–246.

Pilger, John. 2002. *The new rulers of the world.* London: Verso.

Popper, Karl R. 1962. *Conjectures and refutations.* New York: Basic Books.

———. 1974. Replies to my critics. In *The philosophy of Karl Popper,* vol. 2, ed. P. A. Schilpp. LaSalle, IL: Open Court.

———. 1982. *The open universe: An argument for indeterminism.* London: Routledge and Hutchinson.

Russell, Bertrand. *History of Western Philosophy.* Cited in Alan Woods, The History of Philosophy. http://easyweb.easynet.co.uk/~socappeal/philosophy/chapter5.html.

Sartre, Jean-Paul. 1992. *Being and nothingness: A phenomenological essay on ontology.* Trans. Hazel E. Barnes. New York: Washington Square Press.

Saussure, Ferdinand de. 1966. *Course in general linguistics.* Ed. Charles Bally et al. Trans. Roy Harris. London: Duckworth.

Schmitt, Carl. 1985. *Political theology: Four chapters on the concept of sovereignty.* Trans. George Schwab. Cambridge: MIT Press.

Simmel, Georg. 1990. *The philosophy of money.* 2nd edition. Ed. David Frisby. Trans. Tom Bottomore and David Frisby from a first draft by Kaethe Mengelberg. London: Routledge.

Sohn-Rethel, Alfred. 1977. *Warenform und Denkform; Mit zwei Anhängen.* Frankfurt am Main: Suhrkamp.

———. 1978. *Intellectual and manual labor.* Trans. Martin Sohn-Rethel. London: Macmillan.

Sokel, Walter. 1983. The trial. In *Deutsche Romane des 20. Jahrhunderts: Neue Interpretationen,* ed. Michael Lützeler. Königstein: Athenäum.

Spinoza, Baruch (Benedict de). 1951. *A theologico-political treatise and a political treatise.* Trans. and intro. R. H. M. Elwes. New York: Dover.

———. 1985. *The collected works of Spinoza.* Vol. I. Ed. and Trans. Edwin Curley. Princeton: Princeton University Press.

———. 1990. *Die Ethik (Lateinisch und Deutsch).* Trans. Jakob Stern. Stuttgart: Reclam.

Stone, Norman. 1984. *Europe transformed 1878–1919.* Cambridge: Harvard University Press.

Strong, Tracy B. 1993. How to write scripture: Words, authority, and politics in Thomas Hobbes. *Critical Inquiry* 1, no. 20 (Autumn): 128–59.

Suvin, Darko. 1989. The subject as a limit-zone of collective bodies (Bahktin, Hobbes, Freud, Foucault, and counting: An approach). *Discours social / Social Discourse: The International Working Paper Series in Comparative Literature* 1–2, no. 2 (Spring–Summer): 187–200.

Thomas, Douglas. 1993. Burke, Nietzsche, Lacan: Three perspectives on the rhetoric of order. *The Quarterly Journal of Speech* 79, no. 3 (August): 336–55.

Vaihinger, Hans. 1924. *The philosophy of "as-if."* Trans. C. K. Ogden. 2d ed. New York: Harper and Row.

Waite, Geoff. 1996. *Nietzsche's corps/e: Aesthetics, politics, prophecy, or, the spectacular technoculture of everyday life*. Durham: Duke University Press.

Willms, Bernard. 1972. *Die politischen Ideen von Hobbes bis Ho Tschi Minh*. 2. ed. Stuttgart: W. Kohlhammer.

Wittgenstein, Ludwig. 1958. *The blue and brown books*. Oxford: Blackwell.

———. 1963. *Tractatus logico-philosophicus / Logisch-philosophische Abhandlung*. Frankfurt am Main: Suhrkamp.

———. 1976. Ursache und Wirkung: Intuitives Erfassen. *Philosophia* (Philosophical Quarterly of Israel) 6.

———. 1979. *Wittgenstein's lectures, Cambridge 1932–1935: From the notes of Alice Ambrose and Margaret MacDonald*. Ed. Alice Ambrose. Oxford: Blackwell.

Woods, Alan. *The History of Philosophy*. 1998. http://easyweb.easynet.co.uk/~socappeal/philosophy/chapter 5.html

Yovel, Yirmiyahu. 1989. *Spinoza and other heretics*. 2 Vols. Vol. 1: *The Marrano of reason*. Princeton: Princeton University Press.

Žižek, Slavoj. 1989. *The sublime object of ideology*. London: Verso.

———. 1992. *Enjoy your symptom! Jacques Lacan in Hollywood and out*. New York: Routledge.

———. ed. 1992a. *Everything you always wanted to know about Lacan (but were afraid to ask Hitchcock)*. London: Verso.

———. 1993. *Tarrying with the negative: Kant, Hegel, and the critique of ideology*. Durham: Duke University Press.

———. 1996. Lacan with Quantum Physics. In *FutureNatural: Nature, science, culture*, ed. George Robertson, Melinda Mash et al. New York: Routledge, 270–89.

———. 2002. *Welcome to the desert of the real: Five essays on September 11 and other related dates*. London: Verso.

———. 2004. *Organs without bodies: On Deleuze and consequences*. New York: Routledge.

———. 2005. Moralische Krise? Aber sicher! Trans. Isolde Charim. *Profil* 9 (February): 116–19.

Zupančič, Alenka. 2000. *Ethics of the real: Kant, Lacan*. London: Verso.

Index